GUIDE TO TEACHING BRASS

(E)
7, 6, 5, 4, 3, 2, 1
7, 6, 5, 4, 3, 2, 1
5, 4, 3, 2, 1
4, 3, 2, 1
3, 2, 1
(F)
(E)
123, 13, 23, 12, 2, 1, 0
123, 13, 23, 12, 2, 1, 0
23, 12, 2, 1, 0
12, 2, 1, 0
2, 1, 0
(F)
23 (F#)

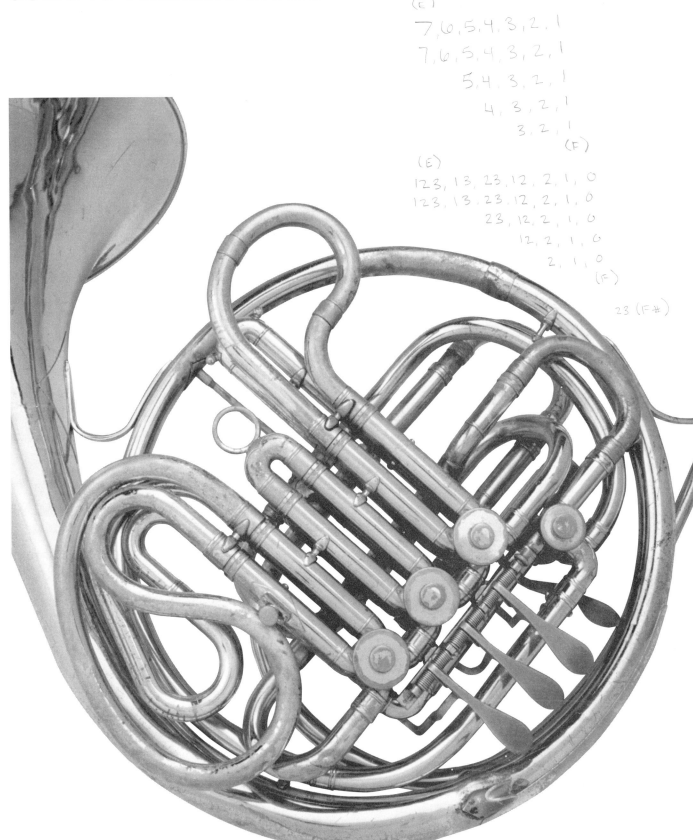

GUIDE TO TEACHING BRASS

SIXTH EDITION

Dan Bachelder
Professor of Music
Brigham Young University

Norman Hunt
Late of
California State University
Sacramento

McGraw
Hill

Boston   Burr Ridge, IL   Dubuque, IA   Madison, WI   New York   San Francisco   St. Louis
Bangkok   Bogotá   Caracas   Kuala Lumpur   Lisbon   London   Madrid   Mexico City
Milan   Montreal   New Delhi   Santiago   Seoul   Singapore   Sydney   Taipei   Toronto

McGraw-Hill Higher Education ⚛

A Division of The **McGraw-Hill** *Companies*

GUIDE TO TEACHING BRASS, Sixth Edition

Published by McGraw-Hill, an imprint of The McGraw-Hill Companies, Inc., 1221 Avenue of the Americas, New York, NY 10020. Copyright © 2002, 1994, 1991, 1984, 1978, 1968, by The McGraw-Hill Companies, Inc. All rights reserved. No part of this publication may be reproduced or distributed in any form or by any means, or stored in a database or retrieval system, without the prior written consent of The McGraw-Hill Companies, Inc., including, but not limited to, in any network or other electronic storage or transmission, or broadcast for distance learning. Some ancillaries, including electronic and print components, may not be available to customers outside the United States.

This book is printed on acid-free paper.

6 7 8 9 0 QPD/QPD 0 9 8 7 6

ISBN-13: 978-0-07-241423-3
ISBN-10: 0-07-241423-5

Publisher: *Phillip A. Butcher*
Executive sponsoring editor: *Christopher Freitag*
Editorial coordinator: *Sarah Dermody*
Senior marketing manager: *David S. Patterson*
Senior project manager: *Christine A. Vaughan*
Production supervisor: *Rose Hepburn*
Freelance design coordinator: *Mary Kazak*
Cover designer: *Sarah Studnicki*
Cover and interior image: *Copyright © Photodisc, Inc. All rights reserved.*
Photo research coordinator: *David A. Tietz*
Photo researcher: *Amy Bethea*
Compositor: *A-R Editions, Inc.*
Typeface: *10/12 Palatino*
Printer: *Quebecor World Dubuque Inc.*

Library of Congress Cataloging-in-Publication Data

Bachelder, Daniel F. (Daniel Fred), 1939–
    Guide to teaching brass / Dan Bachelder, Norman Hunt.—6th ed.
      p. cm.
    Includes bibliographical references (p.), discographies, and index.
    ISBN 0-07-241423-5 (acid-free paper)
    1. Brass instruments—Instruction and study. I. Hunt, Norman J. II. Title.
MT418 .H9 2002
788.9'193'071—dc21   2001030066

www.mhhe.com

CONTENTS

PREFACE

The *Guide to Teaching Brass* was conceived and written by Norman Hunt, late of California State University, Sacramento. Subsequently, Mr. Hunt wrote two additional editions before I was approached by Brown and Benchmark to write the fourth and fifth editions. Since much of the book's premise has been kept intact, it would be remiss of me not to include Norman Hunt's expression of gratitude to those who helped make the book a success:

> The author would like to express his gratitude to Frederick W. Westphal, Ph.D., his colleague at California State University and consulting music editor for Brown and Benchmark Publishers, for his help in the organization and the preparation of this volume. A special thanks to Len Cramer for his excellent photographic work.
>
> To the following teachers, without whom the basic concepts contained in this book would not have been possible, I acknowledge a debt of gratitude: Mr. Lorn Steinberger, formerly principal trombonist, Los Angeles Symphony Orchestra and Utah Symphony Orchestra; Mr. Robert Marstellar, formerly principal trombonist, Los Angeles Symphony Orchestra and brass instructor, University of Southern California; Professor Emory Remington, Eastman School of Music; and Professor André LaFosse, Paris Conservatoire National de Musique.
>
> —Norman Hunt

The *Guide* is a pedagogical reference designed to be an aid to the teacher, performer, and/or composer who is seeking further information on the intricacies of the brass instruments. It is organized into twelve chapters: the first part dealing with basic pedagogical information pertaining to all of these instruments, the second part dealing with information that is unique to each instrument. Common information in part 1 includes intonation, care of instruments, breath support, embouchure, articulation, mouthpieces, and vibrato. Part 2 includes a history of each instrument, chromatic fingering, charts, foreign language identification, general range, transpositions, mutes, daily warmup, selected literature and recordings.

In this, the sixth edition, I have revised and enlarged the previous editions to include new exercises, expanded pedagogical procedures, additional information, and pictures, specifically:

1. Updated historical information, with new photographs illustrating the brass instruments.
2. Additional solo repertoire and recordings.
3. Updated bibliography of recent books and periodicals on related subjects.
4. Additional exercises for combined brasses (appendix I).

I wish to express my sincere appreciation to the faculty members in the School of Music at Brigham Young University for their contribution to the *Guide:* Glenn Williams, Gaylen Hatton, Newell Dayley, David Blackinton, David Brown, Steve Call, Neal Woolworth, Duane Dudley, Irvin Bassett, with special thanks to Steve Call and David Brown for their time, extra help, and expertise. I want to thank Steve Call and David Brown in particular for the use of their many instruments in the photographs, and acknowledge also Llewellyn B. Humphreys, orchestral personnel manager of the Utah Symphony, for allowing pictures of his natural horn with crooks. I am grateful to a number of students who posed for pictures: Alisha and Matt Croft, Paul Evans, Claire Edwards Grover, Elena Hansen, Joseph Jensen, Jessica Lynes, Alina Gardner Meyer, Shirley Pryor and Emily Zappe. Glenn Williams and Mark Philbrick provided the expert photographic work, and David Brown, Ryan Williams, and Claire Edwards Grover contributed invaluable repertoire lists from their individual areas of expertise.

I also wish to thank the following companies for recent pictures and permission to use them in the *Guide:* DEG Music Products, Inc.; Selmer-Bach Corp.; Conn Product Division of United Musical Instrument, USA, Inc.; Edwards Company; Universal Music Corp.; and Harold Hansen.

I must acknowledge John Almeida, University of Central Florida; Bryan W. DePoy, Southeastern Louisiana University; Stephen P. Kerr, Liberty University; James Ode, Meadows School of Arts, Southern Methodist University; and Dr. Darryl White, University of Nebraska, for reviewing and critiquing the fifth edition of this book. Their keen perceptions assisted me in the refining of this new edition.

And finally, my sincere appreciation to my wife, Lila, not only for her writing and editing skills, but for her unflagging love and belief in me.

Daniel Bachelder, Ph.D.
2002

PART 1

CHARACTERISTICS COMMON TO ALL BRASS INSTRUMENTS

CHAPTER 1

GENERAL, ACOUSTICAL, AND INTONATION CONSIDERATIONS

Brass instruments, which are used in symphony orchestras, bands, brass ensembles, jazz ensembles, and numerous instrumental combinations, have two distinct characteristics in common. First, they are constructed of brass, which can be plated with silver or gold lacquer. Second, the sound is produced by the vibration of the player's lips. Both conditions must be met for an instrument to qualify as a member of the brass family.

The brasses are divided into two classifications: conical (cone-shaped) and cylindrical (cylinder-shaped) instruments. Since all brass instruments are a combination of conical and cylindrical tubing, they are classified according to whether they have a greater proportion of conical or cylindrical tubing. The tuba, euphonium, baritone, cornet, and horn are conical instruments; the trumpet and trombone are cylindrical.

In brass instruments, the length of tubing determines the pitch, while the proportions of conical and cylindrical tubing, the thickness of brass, the lacquer or silver plating, the mouthpiece dimensions, and the ability of the performer determine the tone quality.

BRASS SOUND

Lip Vibration

The brass instrument player must have the ability to achieve a lip vibration. Air from the lungs passes between the lips and causes them to open and close rapidly. The opening produced by the air separating the lips is called the *lip aperture*. One opening and closing of the lips by the air is a four-phase cycle:

1. Air from the lungs produces pressure behind the lips.
2. At maximum pressure, the lips separate; air pressure and velocity are high because of the small opening.
3. The lips continue to separate to maximum opening, the size of the opening depending on lip tension and the amount of air. The velocity and air pressure drop as the opening in the lips becomes larger.
4. With decreased velocity and air pressure, the lips come back together because of the tension of the lips. When the lips touch they produce a sound.

A performer's lip vibration completes 440 of these cycles each second to sound the tuning note A (Figure 1.1). The quality of lip vibration is a result of the amount of air from the lungs, position of tongue, size of mouth cavity, lip configuration (embouchure), and muscular tension. A performer must produce a pitch that can be resonated by the brass instrument.

FIGURE 1.1
A 440

Brass Resonator

Resonance is the transmission of a vibration from one body to another, which can take place only when the two bodies are capable of vibrating at the same frequency. The column of air within the brass instrument and the mouth acts as a resonator for the vibrating lips. Because of the volume of air within the instrument, resonance can occur only at specific pitches or frequencies. For example, trombone in first position can play only those notes indicated in the example on the following page. Resonance begins with lip vibrations emitted through the mouthpiece into the instrument. When these vibrations reach the bell, they are reflected back against the continuing lip vibrations. If the reflected vibrations match the continuing lip vibrations, resonance is produced. The matching vibrations produce an amplification or a resonating frequency of the brass instrument.

Mouth Cavity, Tongue, and Throat

Many performers mistakenly believe that the quality, strength, and volume of a brass tone are related to the amount of air blown through the instrument. In reality, the tone depends on the quality and amplitude of the lip vibrations, as well as on the size of the mouth cavity. The throat cavity, mouth cavity, mouthpiece, and the brass instrument are the resonating chambers.

Harmonics

A sound with a single vibration is a pure sound, which is rare. Virtually no vibrating body can produce a pure sound. All musical instruments produce composite sounds that consist of a main (or fundamental) sound plus additional pure sounds called *overtones*. The terms *partials* and *harmonics* describe the composite sound, which is the fundamental with its additional pure overtones. The term *overtone* does not include the fundamental.

The harmonics or partials of the composite sound closely match the possible notes that the brass instrument will resonate. For example, a trombonist playing the lowest first position B-flat, a composite sound of harmonics, will be able to perform those notes in first position that match the harmonics of the composite sound. Because of this fact, the term *harmonic series* designates those notes that can be performed by a brass instrument in a given slide or valve setting. See the following example.

Tone Color

Tone color represents the basic characteristics of sound that distinguish one instrument from other instruments. The number of harmonics sounded and their strengths determine the tone color of the brass instrument. Spectrum analysis of a trombone tone is illustrated using pitch "A" (220 Hz) at 97 db with the bell 28 inches from the microphone.

Each brass instrument has a different spectrum of harmonics on a given pitch. The spectra of a trombone, trumpet, tuba, and F horn are compared using pitch "A" (440 Hz) performed at a mezzo forte volume (Figure 1.2).

PROBLEMS OF INTONATION

Intonation problems are due to instrument construction, instrument temperature, tendency of partials, melodic and harmonic tuning, and, obviously, the player.

Instrument Construction

A brass instrument should be constructed so that its harmonic series are in tune; the instrument must be

HARMONIC SERIES FOR THE TROMBONE AND BARITONE

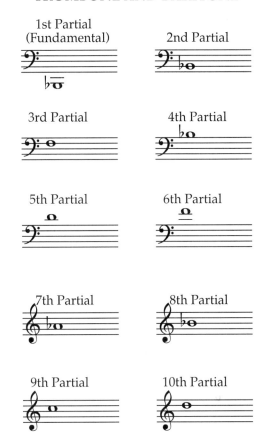

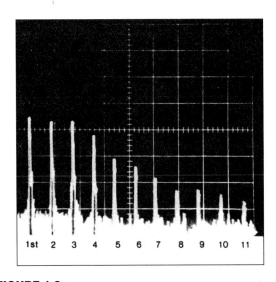

FIGURE 1.2a
The trumpet A 440 has a strong fundamental with its second through eleventh partials being progressively weaker.

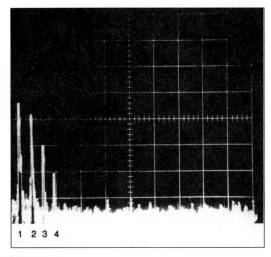

FIGURE 1.2b
A 440 is an extremely high note for the tuba and produces the fundamental with its second, third, and fourth partials being progressively weaker.

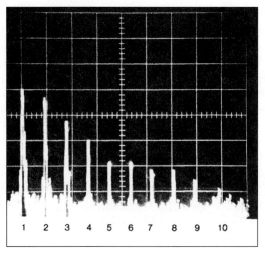

FIGURE 1.2d
The trombone A 440 is characterized by a strong fundamental with its second through tenth partials progressively weaker.

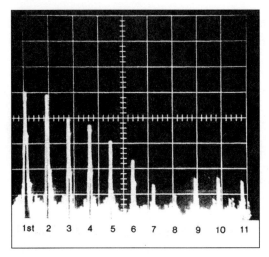

FIGURE 1.2c
The horn has a strong fundamental with an equivalent second partial. Eleven partials are present, the eighth being very weak.

able to achieve semitones (chromatic steps) between the harmonic series partials. The trombone, constructed with a slide, can illustrate the problem a valved instrument has in achieving seven descending semitones. A trombonist requires approximately 110 inches of tubing to play the B-flat harmonic series. In order for the performer to play the A harmonic series (the next lower semitone), the tubing needs to be lengthened by 5.95 percent; thus, 116¹⁰⁄₁₆ inches of tubing are needed. For each succeeding semitone, the percentage of increase stays the same, and as a result, there is a progressive increase between the slide positions needed to play all seven semitones.

As illustrated in Figure 1.3, if a valved instrument were manufactured so that the first, second, and third valves produced three successive semitones, then when these valves were combined to produce the next semitones in the series, these tones

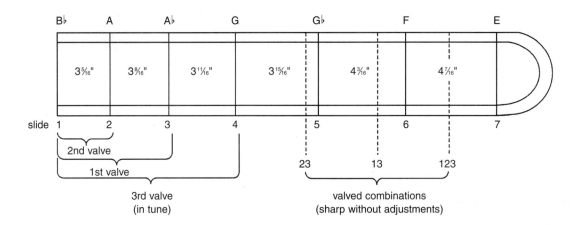

FIGURE 1.3
Valve Lengths and Combinations as Compared to the Trombone.

would be progressively sharper. In order to solve this problem, the valves are manufactured to produce a flatter pitch when pressed—the second valve is five cents flat; the first valve, five cents flat; the third valve, twenty-one cents flat—so that the combinations will not be as sharp.

In equal temperament, there are 1200 cents in an octave and 100 cents between each semitone or half-step.

COMPARISON OF INTONATION WITH AND WITHOUT ADJUSTMENTS OF TUNING SLIDES*

With Adjustments Using a B-flat instrument				Without Adjustments			
0	B-flat	=	in tune	0	B-flat	=	in tune
2	A	=	5 cents flat	2	A	=	in tune
1	A-flat	=	5 cents flat	1	A-flat	=	in tune
3	G	=	21 cents flat	3	G	=	in tune
1–2	G	=	1 cent sharp	1–2	G	=	11 cents sharp
2–3	G-flat	=	8 cents flat	2–3	G-flat	=	18 cents sharp
1–3	F	=	7 cents sharp	1–3	F	=	23 cents sharp
1–2–3	E	=	28 cents sharp	1–2–3	E	=	59 cents sharp

* The chart is courtesy of Conn Product Division of United Musical Instruments, USA, Inc. from a pamphlet entitled *The Inside Story of Brass.*

Even with the valves adjusted, there are still sizeable intonation problems in the last three semitones, especially the 1–2–3 combination, which is twenty-eight cents sharp.

Specific intonation problems and solutions for each brass instrument are discussed in the instrument chapters. Some of these solutions include the following: four-valve, compensating and noncompensating systems for euphonium and tuba; first and third valve slides for trumpet and tuba; main tuning slide for tuba and euphonium; and hand-in-bell adjustment for the horn.

Temperature

Another problem contributing to intonation is temperature change. As a brass instrument becomes warmer, its pitch becomes progressively sharper. The larger the instrument, the greater the pitch variation. As the air inside the instrument becomes warmer, the molecules become more active; this causes the frequency of the pitch to rise. Most tubas will vary from ten to thirteen cents for every 10 degrees change of temperature; euphonium, eight to nine cents; F horn, seven to eight cents; and trumpet, four to five cents. Performers need to make allowances for the increased temperature of their instruments as they play.

Partials

The partials in a harmonic series also have intonation problems. As stated, partials are notes that can be played with the same fingering or slide position. In the B-flat harmonic series (first position on the trombone or open position on other brass instruments), the third partial and its octaves are usually sharp; the fifth partial and its octaves are usually flat. Trombone partials are illustrated below. A similar chart can be constructed for each descending harmonic series or slide position. With a valve instrument, the adjustment will vary because of the problems in tubing length.

The tuning problems of partials are calibrated with equal temperament. Since brass ensembles, orchestras, choral ensembles, and bands do not usually use equal temperament, a combination of tuning possibilities is needed to eliminate intonation problems within a chord and to temper individual notes of the scale. Since harmonic and melodic tuning is subject to debate even among professionals, it is important to remember that intonation is constantly being adjusted to meet aural requirements.

TROMBONE PARTIALS

CHAPTER 2

CARE OF INSTRUMENTS

Brass instruments, because of their sturdy construction and few moving parts, require less care, upkeep, and repair than do any other group of musical instruments. However, brass instruments will not remain in the best playing condition if neglected. Musicians should give continual attention to three areas of instrument care: (1) damage prevention, (2) cleaning procedures, and (3) maintenance and repair.

DAMAGE PREVENTION

Removing Instrument from Case

The case should be placed on the floor so that the lid latches are vertical to the floor before the case is unlatched and opened. If the case is placed in an upright position and allowed to fall open, items held by the lid could fall onto the horn.

Of all the brass instruments, only the trombone requires that the slide and bell sections be assembled. Proper procedure for trombone assembly is to hold the bell downward by the cross bar with the left hand and point the slide downward with the right hand. Then attach and tighten the parts by turning the threaded coupling. Never attach the slide with the bell pointed upward, since the inner slide may come loose and hit the bell.

When removing other instruments from the case, use two hands: one at the bell section and the other at the lead pipe. Picking the instrument up by the valves, valve slides, or tuning slides can damage the instrument.

After the instrument is removed from the case, remove the mouthpiece from the case and carefully insert it into the lead pipe receptacle. Gently tighten the mouthpiece in the receptacle by giving it a quarter turn. Do not hit or "pop" the mouthpiece with the hand, because this may cause it to become stuck.

Protection of Valves and Slides

Brass instruments should not be carried or set down in a way that places pressure on the valve slides or valve casings. This pressure can alter the delicate alignment within the valve slides or valves.

The slide of the trombone and the tuning slides of other instruments, such as the first and third valves of a trumpet, should never be moved when dry. If the slide is moved without grease or oil, small particles between the inner and outer slides can cause scratches.

If a slide or valve becomes stuck, apply penetrating oil on the stuck portion overnight or until it loosens sufficiently. Do not try to free a stuck valve or slide with pliers or a wrench, and do not use force. If the penetrating oil does not work, take the instrument to a competent repairman.

Rest Periods in Practice or during Rehearsals

Instruments should be placed in the case during rest periods of a rehearsal. Any time an instrument is left on a chair or on the floor, it is susceptible to damage. The tuba should not be left standing on its bell, and trombones should not be placed vertically with the bell resting in the seat of a chair and the end of the slide touching the floor.

Procedure after Rehearsal, Performance, or Practice

After a rehearsal or performance, the mouthpiece should be placed in its protective bag and secured in the case. If a protective bag is not available, make sure that the mouthpiece is *secured in the case*. A loose mouthpiece in the case will dent the instrument.

Drain moisture from all slides before putting the instrument in its case. The acids from the mouth can gradually erode the inside of the instrument. Often small rust spots on the outside of the lead pipe are actually acid spots eating their way from the inside to the outside of the pipe.

The instrument should be strapped securely in the case, with the lid completely latched. All the latches and the handle of the case need to be strong enough to hold the instrument securely.

All other items in the case, such as a music lyre, should be firmly anchored. Any loose object in the case can dent the instrument, especially the bell or valve casings. Items such as music, lunch, books, or gym clothes should never be carried in the case with the instrument.

Oral Hygiene

It is advisable for musicians to brush their teeth and rinse their mouths prior to playing a brass instrument. Candy or soft drinks are especially harmful, since the sugar, combined with the moisture from the mouth, produces a mixture of highly concentrated, sticky acid.

Protection of the Instrument in the Case

The case should never be used as a chair, step stool, or suitcase; it cannot withstand excessive weight. When a case is mistreated in this way, damage such as dents, sprung slides, and misshapen valve casings can occur. Placing items in the case and forcing the lid shut may also cause similar damage.

Soft Cases

Because soft cases do not offer the protection of hard cases, extra care must be taken when carrying an instrument in a soft case. The benefits of a soft case are its lightness and its ability to be stored in the luggage racks of most airplanes.

CLEANING PROCEDURES

It is important to keep the inside tubing of a brass instrument immaculately clean. Unless the instrument is cleaned regularly, dirt can cause sluggish valves and slides, as well as permanent damage to the inside and outside of the instrument.

Materials

The following materials are needed for cleaning and lubricating the brass instrument:

1. cleaning rod
2. flexible brush
3. strong cord weighted at one end
4. several strips of cheesecloth
5. slide cream
6. valve oil

Procedure

A basic cleaning routine applicable to all brass instruments is as follows:

1. Remove all slides, valves (if piston type), and valve springs. Make sure that the valves are placed in order with corresponding felts and springs on a table covered with a soft cloth.
2. Immerse the instrument in a bathtub or large sink of lukewarm water (a hose is often used for a tuba or sousaphone). Add a mild soap (not detergent) to the lukewarm water, since detergent or hot water may cause the lacquer to peel. Let the instrument soak for a few minutes to loosen all dirt. Slides and valves should be soaked separately to avoid denting the instrument.
3. After soaking, use a flexible brush to clean the lead pipe and all cylindrical tubing, including the valve slides. Take special care to avoid scratching the interior of the slides.
4. Next, clean the valve casings and valves.
   - Wrap a cleaning rod spirally with cheesecloth (make sure entire rod is covered).
   - Run the wrapped rod through the casing several times while rotating the rod (be sure the rod goes through the casing without effort).
   - Clean the valves completely. (See Figures 2.1, 2.2, and 2.3.)
5. Drain soapy water and rinse the entire instrument several times with lukewarm water. Rinse all slides, valve casings, and valves.
6. Dry all working parts with a soft, lint-free cloth (such as cheesecloth).

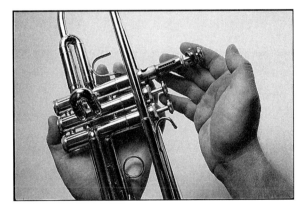

FIGURE 2.1
Removing piston valve (© Spencer Grant/Photo Edit)

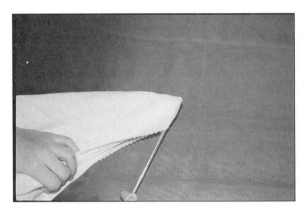

FIGURE 2.2
Cleaning rod prepared for insertion (© Robert Folz/Visuals Unlimited)

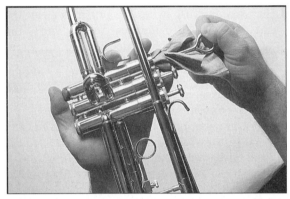

FIGURE 2.3
Cleaning rod inserted in valve casing (© Spencer Grant/Photo Edit)

7. Replace all slides, after lubricating them with slide grease, petroleum jelly, or slide cream. Replace corks and felts to the appropriate valve, and oil the valves with valve oil. Return valve casing caps and springs to their original locations, and insert valves into their correct valve casings. Make sure the valve parts align with the valve slides when depressed.

8. Clean the mouthpiece with a mouthpiece brush. (See figure 2.4.)

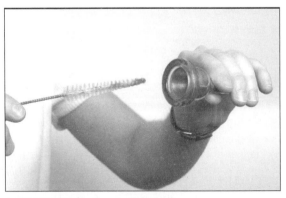

FIGURE 2.4
Clean the mouthpiece daily. Use a mouthpiece brush to clean the throat and backbore of the mouthpiece.

Rotary Valves

Rotary valves are rarely disassembled for cleaning purposes. Trombones, horns, and tubas that have rotary valves can be cleaned by running lukewarm water through the valve section and then lubricating the valves by placing a few drops of oil in each valve crook and allowing the oil to run into the valve. Next, remove the valve caps and place a few drops of oil on each shaft. Since the rotary valve is *rarely* disassembled, this procedure is discussed under maintenance and repair. (See Figures 2.5 and 2.6.)

FIGURE 2.5
Oiling rotor (© Spencer Grant/Photo Edit)

FIGURE 2.6
Oiling shaft (© Spencer Grant/Photo Edit)

Cleaning the Trombone Slide

The slide, the most delicate part of the trombone, must be handled at all times with care. The slightest dent, bend, or bow will impair proper slide action. Because there is very little clearance between the inner slide and the outer slide, these parts must be absolutely clean in order to work with greatest efficiency. During the cleaning process, the slide must be held carefully to prevent twisting or bowing.

Begin cleaning by removing the outer slide from the inner slide and placing them both on a table covered with a cloth. Wrap a trombone slide cleaning rod with a strip of cheesecloth (6 to 8 inches wide and 5 or 6 feet long). Thread the cheesecloth through the eye of the rod and wrap the entire rod spirally until it is thoroughly covered. (See Figures 2.7 and 2.8.) Grasp the outer slide and hold only the side that is to be cleaned. Do not hold the slide by the brace while cleaning; this may cause the slide to be sprung. (See Figures 2.9 and 2.10.)

FIGURE 2.9
Holding slide, wrong

FIGURE 2.7
Cleaning rod, spiral wrap

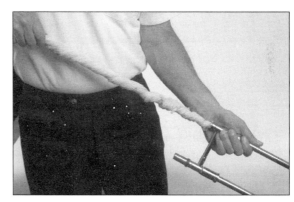

FIGURE 2.10
Holding slide, right

FIGURE 2.8
Cleaning rod, wrapped

Run the cleaning rod several times through the tube being held while rotating the rod. Make sure that the cleaning rod is not forced while going into the outer slide and that the cleaning rod does not hid the *end of the slide*. Carefully measure the distance the rod needs to cover before you insert it into the outside tubes. Many trombonists prefer the flexible rod with brushes for the outer slide because it can clean the curved end without damaging it (see Figures 2.11 and 2.12). Another way to clean the curved section is to tie one end of a weighted cord, longer than the entire outer slide length, to a small piece of cheesecloth. The weighted end is carefully threaded through the outer slide and then pulled through with the cheesecloth attached. One must be extremely careful to tie only an amount of cloth to the cord that will easily go through the curved section. If the cord breaks or if the cloth becomes caught in the curve, the task of removal is difficult. The only way to remove the stuck cloth is to insert a wire with a hook on its end and snag the material. A common error is to attempt to push the material through the slide using a wire. This only causes the cheesecloth to become more tightly wedged against the sides of the tube.

The inner slide is also cleaned with cheesecloth wrapped around the cleaning rod. The procedure is to wrap the rod, using the same method as previously discussed, with a clean strip of cheesecloth.

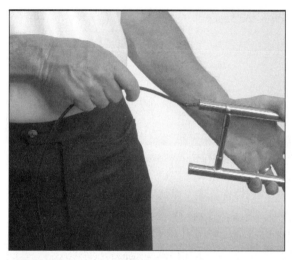

FIGURE 2.11
Flexible brush used incorrectly in cleaning outer slide

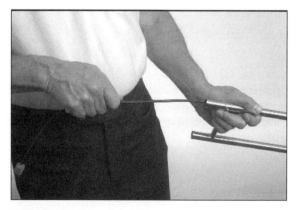

FIGURE 2.12
Flexible brush used correctly in cleaning outer slide

Since the inner slide has a lead pipe on one side, the thickness of cloth for this side must be considerably smaller to accommodate the smaller lead pipe circumference. The rod should always be inserted at

the lead pipe entrance, which is the receptacle for the mouthpiece. Were it inserted from the opposite direction (from the stocking toward the lead pipe), there would be a danger of catching the edge of the lead pipe and causing damage.

After the inner and outer slides have been thoroughly cleaned and rinsed, lubricate the stockings of the inner slide sparingly with trombone slide cream. It is not necessary to lubricate the entire inner slide, since the stockings make contact with the outer slide. After lubrication, spray the stockings with water. Many brands of slide cream are on the market. The author prefers "Slide-O-Mix," marketed by United Musical Instruments USA, Inc., or "Superslick" with a drop of Conn Formula 3M silicone on the cream.

MAINTENANCE AND REPAIR

A few situations require a brass instrument teacher or performer to make minor repairs without the benefit of a trained repairman. A broken valve string (Figures 2.13–2.18), a dented mouthpiece stem, or a stuck mouthpiece are some of the common repairs that can be easily accomplished without sophisticated repair equipment.

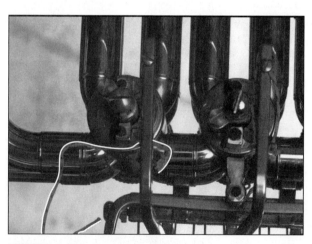

FIGURE 2.13
Tie a small knot in the end of the cord and thread the cord through the hole found midway in the extension rod.

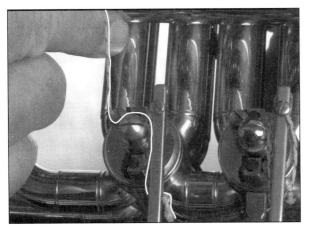

FIGURE 2.14
Pull firmly on the cord to set the knot, then wind it clockwise around the stop arm set screw.

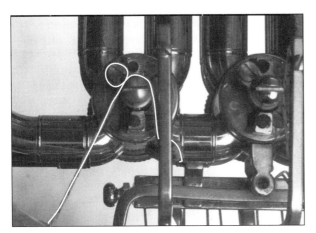

FIGURE 2.15
Continue wrapping the cord clockwise around the stop arm set screw. Hold the string firmly with the stop arm held against the post that leaves the valve in open position; then tighten the stop arm set screw, making sure that the key (the valve key that will eventually power the rotary valve) is in the proper alignment.

FIGURE 2.16
Next, wrap the cord around the hub counterclockwise.

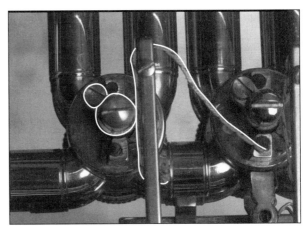

FIGURE 2.17
Run the cord through the hole near the end of the extension lever.

FIGURE 2.18
Form a small loop in the cord with the loose end underneath; place the loose end over the set screw of the extension lever and tighten the screw.

Align the horn keys by taking the horn down so that the keys are touching a flat surface, thereby making them level. Tighten the set screws so that the keys are held in this position, then cut the excess cord.

Another tool used to adjust the horn strings is a horn level string jig. It holds all three levers in perfect alignment and allows both hands to be free.

Disassembly Procedure for Rotary Valves

Remember that disassembling and cleaning a rotary valve (Figure 2.19) is rarely done and should only be performed when necessary, and not by beginning students. Many professionals and advanced performers prefer that a competent repairman disassemble the rotary valve. The following steps are recommended:

1. Remove the string after carefully studying how it is installed.

2. Unscrew the stop arm screw a few turns (the screw located exactly in the center of the valve).
3. Remove the valve cap in the back of the valve.
4. Tap lightly on the loosened stop arm screw with a wood handle of a screwdriver or rubber hammer until the valve covering on the back of the valve comes out.
5. Remove the stop arm screw completely and slide the valve out the back of the casing.
6. Use a brush or cloth to thoroughly clean the valve and valve casing. Do not use abrasives that may damage the plating.
7. Oil the shafts; then place the valve in the casing.
8. Place the stop arm screw on the shaft after inserting it in the casing. Be sure to place the screw so that the stop arm rests between the corks.
9. Replace the back valve covering and the back valve cap.
10. Replace the string.

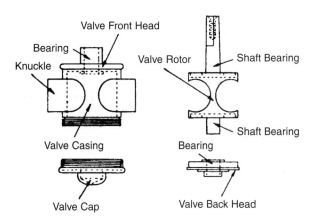

FIGURE 2.19
Rotary valve (Courtesy—Conn Product Division of United Musical Instruments, USA, Inc.)

Removing a Stuck Mouthpiece

A mouthpiece can become stuck if the instrument is dropped and lands on the mouthpiece, if the mouthpiece is tapped too hard after being placed into the instrument, if it is twisted too tightly into the instrument, or if it has dirt along the stem. If this happens, a mouthpiece puller must be used to remove the mouthpiece. Never use pliers, a wrench, or "strong-arm" tactics.

The mouthpiece puller fits all brass instruments and comes in a single piece so that individual parts cannot be lost. The arms of the unit are placed in alignment with the lead pipe, while the middle section, with screw and screw handle, fits around the mouthpiece. Turn the handle clockwise until the mouthpiece comes free (Figure 2.20).

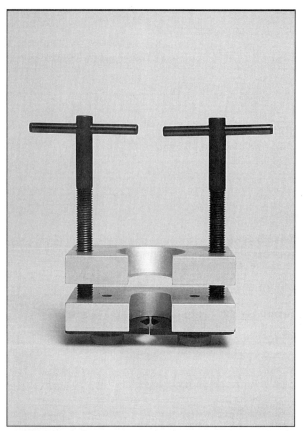

FIGURE 2.20
Mouthpiece puller (© Spencer Grant/Photo Edit)

Adjusting Rotary Valve Alignment

Remove the valve cap on the back of the valve and check to see if the guide marks on the back of the valve are aligned perfectly. These marks determine where the rotor meets the knuckle in the casing. When the rotor is not in alignment, the horn or trombone has a tendency to sound stuffy because a portion of the valve slide tube is closed. Usually, poor alignment is caused by worn corks. An experienced performer can place blocks of cork or rubber in the cork stop plate and then shave them down until the guide marks are aligned. Rubber guides can also be purchased to fit a particular horn, trombone, or tuba.

Adjusting Springs

The baritone, tuba, and euphonium have a separate spring that is placed at the bottom of the valve casing with the valve resting on top. If the valve action is too stiff or too loose, use the following procedure to adjust the spring tension. Hold the base of the spring and turn it clockwise to loosen the tension, and counterclockwise to tighten the tension. A spring should never be *stretched;* this causes the coils to be unequal and produces an uneven response. All the springs should resist the valves with equivalent pressure.

Piston Valve Alignment with Valve Port and Valve Tube

One reason an instrument may sound stuffy is that the valve ports do not align with the valve tubes. If the felt in the valve cap is too thick or too thin, or if the valve corks are not the proper thickness, the valve ports will not align properly with the valve tubes.

One way to check the alignment is to remove the valve tube slide and depress the valve. Look into the open valve tube and observe if the valve ports align properly. A lighted valve mirror can help determine if a correction needs to be made. If the valve port does not align properly, adjustment of the felts and valve stem corks is necessary.

Removing Dents in Mouthpiece Stem

The dropping of a mouthpiece may dent the stem. Since such a dent is in a very crucial place—close to the lip vibration—the mouthpiece should be repaired immediately. A mouthpiece trueing tool can reshape the stem (Figure 2.21). Insert the tool into the mouthpiece stem and twist until the stem has returned to its original shape. Needle-nose pliers are also effective in removing dents in the mouthpiece stem.

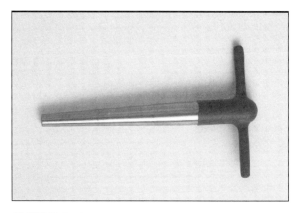

FIGURE 2.21
Mouthpiece trueing tool. The mouthpiece trueing tool is used when the stem of a mouthpiece is dented. By inserting the mouthpiece trueing tool into the damaged shank of the mouthpiece (this includes any brass mouthpiece) and twisting, the shank is repaired.

Eliminating Valve Noise

Most noisy valves are a result of worn valve cap felts, valve stem corks, or felts. These should be replaced on a regular basis; the amount of felt and corks should be aligned, as mentioned above. Valve noise can also be caused by worn valve guides that slide in the groove inside the valve casing. These should be replaced by a competent repairman. The quietest valve guides are made of teflon instead of metal.

CHAPTER 3

BREATHING AND BREATH SUPPORT

To produce a good tone and sustain a phrase, a player must have a good embouchure and supply adequate breath support. Breathing, an important pedagogical concern, must be worked on constantly during performance. Elements of breathing and breath support include posture, inhalation, exhalation, open throat, and breath exercises.

POSTURE

A person's breathing mechanism does not work to full capacity without a good posture (Figure 3.1). To demonstrate this, take a full breath while slouching, and then inhale with a good posture—chest high, shoulders back but not raised, abdominal muscles relaxed. Notice how much more air can fill the lungs.

To inhale properly, a player must observe the following points on posture:

1. Back is straight, but not rigid.
2. Head is erect, as though its crown were being lifted.
3. Abdominal muscles are relaxed.
4. Throat and neck are relaxed and free.

Figure 3.2 is an example of poor breathing posture when standing. The sitting position should feel like the standing position (Figure 3.3). Unnecessary muscle tension must be avoided. Figure 3.4 is an example of poor breathing posture when sitting.

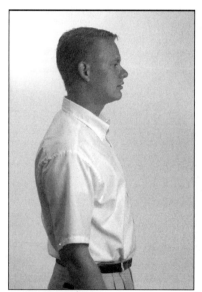

FIGURE 3.2
Poor breathing posture (standing)

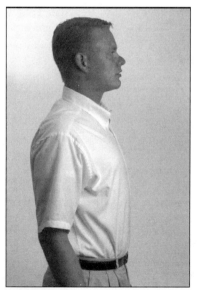

FIGURE 3.1
Correct breathing posture (standing)

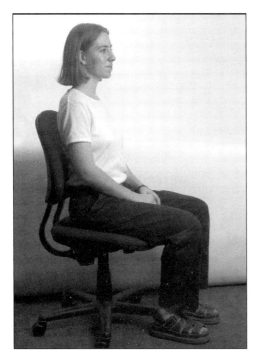

FIGURE 3.3
Correct breathing posture (sitting)

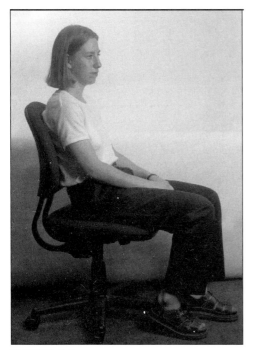

FIGURE 3.4
Poor breathing posture (sitting)

INHALATION

The diaphragm and external intercostal muscles control inhalation (Figure 3.5). The diaphragm, a large muscular membrane that forms the floor of the chest cavity, is in the shape of a dome in its relaxed state. On contraction, the diaphragm forces

the internal organs down and out against the relaxed abdominal muscles that encircle the body at the waist. A full inhalation is not possible if the abdominal area is not relaxed because the tension of the abdominal muscles will prevent the diaphragm from contracting completely.

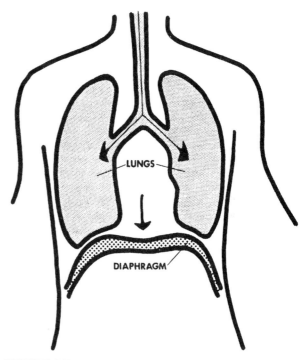

FIGURE 3.5
Lungs and diaphragm, inhalation

As the diaphragm moves down and out, the exterior intercostal muscles lift the rib cage. This is possible because the ribs slope downward from the chest bone. Attached by cartilage, each rib can move when these muscles that interlace the interior and exterior of the rib cage contract. When the exterior intercostal muscles lift the rib cage, the chest cavity expands (Figure 3.6).

Sometimes the external intercostal muscles contract so much that the clavicle bones of the upper chest lift. This extra muscular effort to expand the high chest usually promotes tension in the throat, neck, and shoulders, which is counterproductive. Inhalation, briefly outlined, involves the following actions:

1. Diaphragm contracts downward.
2. Abdominal muscles are relaxed.
3. Exterior intercostal muscles contract, lifting the rib cage and expanding the chest cavity.
4. Posture is with back straight, chest high, and shoulders relaxed.
5. Throat remains open and relaxed

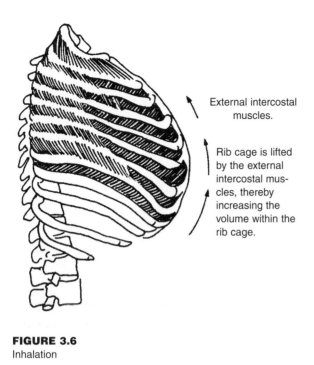

FIGURE 3.6
Inhalation

External intercostal muscles.

Rib cage is lifted by the external intercostal muscles, thereby increasing the volume within the rib cage.

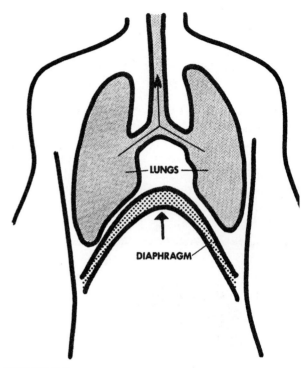

FIGURE 3.7
Lungs and diaphragm, exhalation

EXHALATION

During normal breathing, exhalation is the process of relaxation (Figure 3.7). The diaphragm returns naturally to its dome shape, and air is automatically expelled from the lungs. However, during physical exertion or performance on a wind instrument, the abdominal and internal intercostal muscles are essential in exhalation—the abdominal muscles contract inward, putting pressure on the internal organs, pressure that in turn puts pressure on the relaxed diaphragm and expels air from the lungs. The duration of the exhalation depends on the embouchure resistance, the range, the dynamics, and the amount of air in the lungs. A loud, low passage consumes air more quickly than a high, soft passage. A tubist uses more air than a horn player.

The diaphragm muscles act along with the internal intercostal muscles, which interlace the inside of the rib cage, to reduce the size of the chest cavity (Figure 3.8). An outline of the exhalation process is as follows:

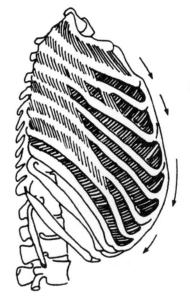

Internal intercostal muscles.

They contract to bring the rib cage down, thereby decreasing the volume within the rib cage.

FIGURE 3.8
Exhalation

1. Back remains straight (not rigid).
2. Chest is in a high, relaxed position.
3. Inner abdominal muscles contract steadily, promoting a firm and *continuous* support to the resistance at the embouchure.
4. The throat (glottis) remains open and relaxed, with minimum resistance by the throat.
5. Internal intercostal muscles contract, reducing the circumference of the rib cage.

OPEN THROAT

The brass player must learn to keep the throat in a modified yawn position, which opens the passageway (Figure 3.9). In this position, the throat relaxes as if a hot piece of food were on the back of the tongue. Most teachers prefer that their students' inner, abdominal muscles contract inward and are resisted antagonistically by the diaphragm, which does not totally relax. This technique of soft playing will allow the throat to stay open and still produce a soft sound. The throat should never restrict or hold the air before exhalation. Conceiving inhalation as a continuous flow of air produces the best results.

FIGURE 3.9
Yawn breath

BREATHING EXERCISES

Mouthpiece

Hold the stem of the mouthpiece so that there is resistance during exhalation of the air from the lungs.

1. Maintain posture and an open throat (modified yawn).
2. Tighten the hand to increase resistance.
3. Exhale as much air through the mouthpiece as possible, while gradually increasing the resistance.
4. Repeat several times.

Inhale, Hold, Exhale, Rest

1. Inhale for six counts with proper posture and the epiglottis open, using a modified yawn (Figure 3.9).
2. Hold the air for six counts by keeping the diaphragm contracted, not by locking the air behind the epiglottis.
3. Exhale completely in six counts and maintain posture.
4. Rest for six counts.
5. Progressively increase tempo and decrease the number of counts until all steps—inhale, hold, exhale, and rest—take one count.

Instrument Resistance

1. After a full inhalation, exhale air through instrument with as much air velocity and speed as possible. Maintain a good posture and an open throat.
2. Do the same exercise with the valves depressed; this adds resistance. (Trombonists can extend slide.)
3. Increase resistance by depressing valves part way (half valve) and repeat exercises. (Trombonists can do this if they have the F valve.)

Calisthenic Exercise I

1. Stand with the body erect and feet together.
2. Extend the arm outward in a horizontal position level with the shoulders, as if trying to touch the opposite walls (Figure 3.10).
3. Inhale with the throat (epiglottis) in a modified yawn and the abdominal muscles relaxed.
4. Exhale the air from the lungs with the mouth in position of the word "who." When the air is nearly depleted, try to increase the exhalation with a crescendo of air.
5. Repeat several times.

FIGURE 3.10
Breathing development exercises, arms horizontal

Calisthenic Exercise II

This exercise is designed to place the body in a position that will allow maximum efficiency of the breathing mechanism.

1. Stand erect, chest high and abdominal muscles relaxed.
2. Bend the arms at the elbows and take hold of the tops of the ears. Concentrate on the sensation of raising the body toward the ceiling, yet keeping the heels on the floor.
3. While in this position, inhale with the epiglottis fold open by using a modified yawn.
4. Inhale as much air as possible, causing complete expansion of the rib cage by the intercostal and diaphragm muscles.
5. Exhale, keeping the throat in the modified yawn and maintaining the sensation of the body being stretched toward the ceiling with the heels on the floor.

Breathing Tube (Breath Builder)

A breathing tube called the "Breath Builder" can be purchased at Breath Builder Inc., 3111 So. Valley View Blvd., Suite E-129, Las Vegas, NV 89102, c/o Harold Hansen, Ph. 702-221-9008. The purpose of the breathing tube is to give variable resistance during the inhalation and exhalation process. When used in a daily routine, the inhalation and exhalation muscles can be developed to give better breath support and air capacity.

With metronome set at 104:

1. Exhale six counts to position ball at the top of the tube
2. Inhale six counts maintaining the ball at the top of the tube
3. With your free hand, begin to cover the holes at the top of the tube, starting with the smaller hole and working to the larger hole. This will increase the resistance. (See Figure 3.11.)

Breath Bag Exercise

The purpose of the breath bag is to measure the air capacity of the brass player's lungs. After expelling carbon dioxide, the by-product of exhalation, into the bag, the player can inhale this gas from the bag without the effect of lightheadedness that comes from taking too much oxygen from the air. Therefore the process of exhalation and inhalation can be repeated as many times as desired without any ill effects.

You will need:

1. a large bread bag
2. ½ inch plastic tube 3 inches long
3. twist tie or rubber band

With metronome set at 104:

1. inhale in six counts
2. exhale in six counts
3. repeat six times

See Figure 3.12.

Breathing should be natural and relaxed during all these exercises. Since playing a brass instrument requires a greater amount of air than normal breathing, these processes of inhalation and exhalation must be developed. The continuous abdominal and intercostal support of the air exhaled is required to play a brass instrument adequately.

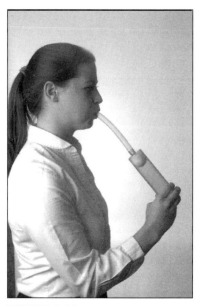

FIGURE 3.11
"Breath Builder" developed by Harold Hanson and pictured with his permission

FIGURE 3.12
Breathing development exercises

Breath for the Phrase or Passage

A sufficient breath means having enough air to play the phrase using only the top two-thirds of the usable lung capacity; the last one-third is held in reserve (the portion not exhaled from the lungs during normal breathing). Exhaling the last one-third requires the contraction of the abdominal and internal intercostal muscles. These muscles, when used on fully expanded lungs, produce the greatest potential for brass air support.

Consideration of factors such as instrument size, lung capacity, number of notes in the phrase, and perceived volume are necessary in determining the "size" of the breath.

Sing and "Mouthpiece Buzz"

Vocalization of the potential phrase helps to solidify interpretation, accuracy, intonation, and breath support. The voice, our most accessible musical instrument used as a model for brass performance, helps realize the intended ideal.

CHAPTER 4

EMBOUCHURE

REQUIREMENTS TO PLAY A BRASS INSTRUMENT

Before pursuing the performance of a brass instrument or selecting appropriate candidates for an instrument, consider certain requirements: (1) proper lower and upper jaw alignment, (2) straight teeth, (3) lip formation conducive to vibration, and (4) adequate muscular development of the lips. If any one of these four requirements is not met, performance on a brass instrument will be difficult, if not impossible.

Lower and Upper Jaw Alignment

The lower jaw should rest directly below the upper jaw and be the same size to assure alignment. If the difference in jaw size is too great, adaption to embouchure requirements is impaired. Ten to 15 percent of the population have a small lower jaw that is set behind the upper jaw. This is called *disto-clusion* by orthodontists. Protrusion, where the lower jaw is larger and is set in front of the upper jaw, occurs in five percent of the population. In either case, a shift of the jaw is often necessary to produce an embouchure that produces adequate lip vibration. Such a shift of the jaw can cause strain and facial muscle fatigue. Modern dental surgery can change the position and size of the jaw; however, the operation is usually not done until the jaw has stopped growing, in the late teens.

Teeth

Normally the teeth are aligned with the outlines of the jawbones, the lower teeth resting against the upper with their grinding surfaces striking one another. In this position the upper front teeth slightly overlap the lower teeth. Irregularities of the teeth that produce problems for brass performers include (1) crowding of the teeth in the upper arch or both arches, (2) sharply rotated teeth that could dig into the lips, (3) extreme overlap, (4) teeth that erupt far out of their normal position, (5) teeth that incline inward or outward, and (6) teeth that fail to come together completely. Dental work can alleviate some of these problems, but the time and expense required may not be a practical solution for brass performers. Even with dental problems, a student can still play an instrument that does not require lip vibration.

Lip Construction

A significant number of people have a lip construction that forms a hard point in the center of the upper lip, sometimes called a "cupid's tip." Often people with this lip construction cannot produce a lip vibration; if they can, it is with a split airstream and double pitch vibration. One solution to this problem is to move the mouthpiece off center so that only one portion of the lip will vibrate. The muscles of the mouth then must adapt to this new embouchure formation.

Another variable of lip construction is lip thickness. Even though there are no absolute rules, it is more common for players with thick lips to perform trombones, euphoniums, or tubas, since the larger cup diameter is well suited to thicker lips. A performer with thick lips usually has more difficulty with the trumpet and horn, especially if the edges of both lips fall outside the rim of the mouthpiece.

Sometimes a scar in the area of the lip vibration will prevent the lips from buzzing. In such a case, performance on a brass instrument is virtually impossible.

Facial Muscles Used to Form the Embouchure

Voluntary muscles of the face produce facial motion and constitute the principal part of the face's flesh.

Like any other muscle of the body, facial muscles, when stimulated, pull against opposing groups of muscles; no muscle has the ability to push, only to contract.

Certain muscles of the face form the brass embouchure. These series of muscles are arranged in a symmetrical pattern attached to the oval muscle, which surrounds the mouth. In this arrangement, facial muscles are the only muscles that fasten to each other rather than to bone.

The embouchure is a controlled tension of opposing sets of facial muscles. It places the mouth, lip, chin, and cheek muscles in the position to produce a tone when air is blown through the lips. Muscles of the face should gently "hug" the bony structure of the face, and the lips should be positioned so that a maximum volume of sound is achieved with a minimum amount of effort (Figure 4.1).

In scientific terms, a correct embouchure is the controlled contraction of the buccinator, the orbicularis oris, and the platysma. Contraction of the zygomaticus major and minor and the risorius should be avoided, since those muscles render an inferior embouchure setting.

TEACHING AND FORMING THE EMBOUCHURE

The formation of the embouchure should be as natural as possible. If the basic physical requirements are met, it is not necessary to contort the facial muscles to form an embouchure. The steps for forming an embouchure are as follows:

1. Place the lips in an "M" position, with the jaw in its naturally relaxed position.
2. Hold the "M" position and direct an airstream at a dot on a piece of paper held below the chin in front of the lips.
3. Press the lips together slightly as in pronouncing an "M" or "P" until a lip vibration is made.
4. Expel sufficient air to produce a vibration.

The facial muscles should hug the bone structure, with chin muscles contracted and flat. The lip corners should form an "M" position as a result of antagonistic reaction to the circular muscles around the lips, while the orbicularis oris contracts to pronounce the "P." (Another way to explain this antagonistic muscular action is to think of puckering

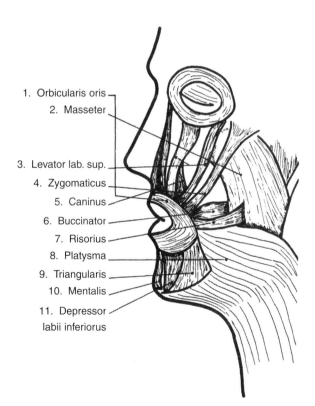

1. Orbicularis oris
2. Masseter
3. Levator lab. sup.
4. Zygomaticus
5. Caninus
6. Buccinator
7. Risorius
8. Platysma
9. Triangularis
10. Mentalis
11. Depressor labii inferiorus

Orbicularis oris closes the lips and has the ability to contract, forming a pucker. It has an action much like that of a drawstring.

Masseter is a very strong muscle that closes the jaw. When contracted, the masseter pulls at the corners of the mouth in an attempt to smile.

Levator labii superioris raises the upper lip at an angle and thus is not used extensively in the embouchure formation.

Zygomaticus muscles (major and minor) draw the lip backward and upward.

Caninus (lebator anguli) raises the upper lip in an exaggerated smile.

Buccinator (trumpeter muscle) is extremely important in the formation of a correct embouchure. It pulls back the corners of the mouth, flattens and holds in the cheeks, and helps to control the flow of air through the lips.

Risorius (platysma strand) draws the corners of the mouth backward as in a smile.

Platysma pulls back and holds down the corners of the mouth.

Triangularis (depressor anguli) pulls the corners of the mouth downward.

Mentalis raises the fleshy part of the chin and protrudes the lower lip.

Depressor labii inferioris pulls the lower lip downward and works as an antagonist to the mentalis.

FIGURE 4.1
Muscles of the face

while at the same time trying to bring the corners of the mouth back and down.)

The vibration produced should *not* require a lot of effort yet still produce a full sound. Scientifically, a maximum resonance is defined as a maximum amplitude with a minimum amount of effort.

Straw Through Mouthpiece

Another approach for teaching the formation of the embouchure is to place a small stirring straw through the throat of the mouthpiece (Figure 4.2). The embouchure is formed when the lips make contact with the straw and the mouthpiece. The performer then pretends to draw fluid through the straw. This action places the embouchure in the correct position and forces the chin to be in a flat position.

FIGURE 4.2
Straw through mouthpiece

Jaw Alignment and Airstream Direction

The direction of the airstream as it passes between the lips is governed by the alignment of the upper and lower jaws and the vibrating surface of the lips. Even if the teeth are perfectly aligned between the upper and lower jaw, the airstream tends to be directed downward to some degree, depending on the register being played. Most brass players direct the airstream toward the throat of the mouthpiece in the lower register and progressively increase the angle of the airstream downward as they go higher (Figure 4.3).

The change in airstream direction is due to the need to increase the upper lip's vibration to produce sounds in the upper register. When a musician plays in the lowest register, the upper and lower lips vibrate equally, while when one plays in the upper register the upper lip does most of the vibrating over the lower lip. There are exceptions to this rule—individuals who reverse the function of the upper and lower lips. In their case, the airstream is progressively directed upward to perform the upper register. Even though the technique is not as common, many successful professional musicians use this type of embouchure (Figure 4.4). Because upstream players often produce a strident tone, this approach is used less frequently.

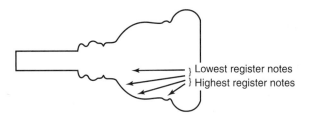

FIGURE 4.3
Downstream players

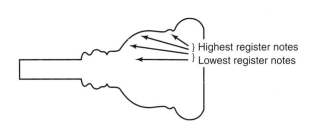

FIGURE 4.4
Upstream players

Tongue Position

The opening between the upper and lower teeth, along with the tongue position, has a tremendous influence on the tone quality, volume, and register. The placement of the tongue depends on the register and volume being played. During the lowest, loudest note, the tongue is in the position of "ah," with the lower jaw in a position to direct the airstream at the throat of the mouthpiece. This produces the maximum opening of the lips. Conversely, during the highest, softest tones, the tongue arches, which places the tongue in an "ee" position and produces the minimum opening of the lips. A high, loud note may require a flatter tongue position than that for an extremely soft note in the lower register. If the volume stays the same, the tongue changes with the register, as indicated.

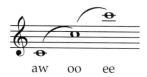

aw   oo   ee

EMBOUCHURE PROBLEMS AND SOLUTIONS

The correct embouchure results in a well-balanced muscular position that avoids the extreme pucker or excessive smile. The chin remains flat and does not bunch (Figure 4.5).

Bunched Chin

Because the chin has the antagonistic control of the lower lip, a bunched chin can be a problem (Figure 4.6). It causes upper-register notes to be thin and uncontrollable and also affects the ability to move from one note to another. Many teachers feel that a student will never reach full potential if the bunched chin is not corrected. The following procedure for students will help solve this problem:

1. Become aware that chin muscles can be voluntarily controlled, and learn to control them consciously.
2. Buzz the lips without the mouthpiece, because this is extremely difficult with a bunched chin.
3. While buzzing the lips without the mouthpiece, add the mouthpiece. The tendency will be to return to the bunched chin; however, concentrate on how the chin felt before the mouthpiece was introduced.
4. Repeat this process in all registers and volumes until the chin is controlled.

Smile Embouchure

A smile embouchure produces a thin, above-center sound because of the elongated shape of the lip aperture and the tendency to close the jaw too much (Figure 4.7). This embouchure also places the chin muscles in a more relaxed state, thus reducing control and flexibility. The steps necessary to solve the problem are as follows:
1. Set the corners of the mouth in the position of "M" and "P."
2. Concentrate on the contraction of the chin and frowning muscles, while the orbicularis oris contracts to form a modified pitch.

3. Find a comfortable balance between antagonistic feeling of the orbicularis oris and frowning muscles.
4. Focus the orbicularis oris muscles when playing higher-register notes, yet still balance this effort with the corners and chin muscles. The corners should not predominate.

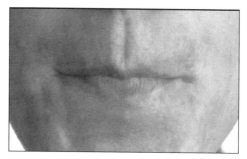

FIGURE 4.5
Correct embouchure

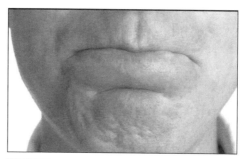

FIGURE 4.6
Chin thrust upward (wrong)

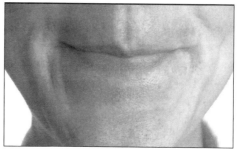

FIGURE 4.7
Smile embouchure (wrong)

MOUTHPIECE PLACEMENT

Mouthpiece placement depends on anatomical size and position of the teeth, jaw, and lips, as well as an individual's register of concentration. The placement that produces the best results is correct; however, the following general guidelines for mouthpiece placement are suggested.

Trumpet and Cornet

When playing a trumpet or a cornet, the musician usually has slightly more lower lip than upper lip inside the mouthpiece (Figure 4.8). This will vary slightly with each player, since lip thickness, teeth variables, and tone preference all affect the placement of the mouthpiece. If a darker, more resonant tone is desired, more upper lip is required.

Horn

Horn mouthpiece placement is the exact opposite of the trumpet: two-thirds upper lip and one-third lower lip (Figure 4.9). Again, variations of this placement are possible. The horn embouchure usually has less corner strength and more pucker than that of the trumpet. This causes the upper partials to have less strength and therefore produces a darker and more mellow tone.

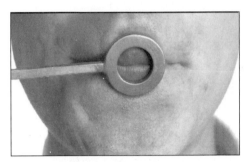

FIGURE 4.8a

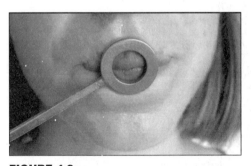

FIGURE 4.9a

FIGURE 4.8b
Mouthpiece placement for trumpet or cornet

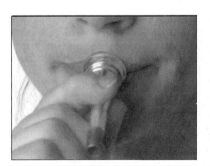

FIGURE 4.9b
Mouthpiece placement for horn

Trombone and Euphonium

The trombone and euphonium are almost always played with more upper lip than lower (Figure 4.10). Many orchestral players prefer two-thirds upper lip and one-third lower; however, this varies with each performer's concept, range, and physical requirements. Trombone players use round, supple embouchures with firm corners; these produce a resonant, focused sound. The euphonium, like the trombone, has a round supple embouchure and does not require as much corner strength. In this respect, the euphonium embouchure is more like the horn embouchure.

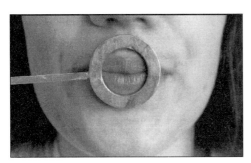

FIGURE 4.10a

FIGURE 4.10b
Mouthpiece placement for trombone and euphonium

Tuba

The tubist usually places the mouthpiece as high on the upper lip as possible (Figure 4.11). This will vary according to size of mouthpiece and the amount of upper lip. Mouthpiece placement is not as critical for the tuba as it is for the horn or trumpet.

FIGURE 4.11a

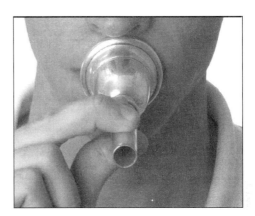

4.11b
Mouthpiece placement for tuba

WARMUP PROCEDURES

All brass players should go through a series of daily exercises to strengthen the embouchure, improve accuracy, increase range, and sharpen technical facility. A good warmup procedure should have long tones, tonguing, lip slurs, lip flexibility exercises, intervals, scales, arpeggios, and range exercises. Warmup procedure is written to be played together by all the brass instruments (Appendix 1).

CHAPTER 5

ARTICULATION

Articulation can be described as the tongue's manipulation of an airstream to create a particular emphasis of sounds. To initiate a tone, a player uses the tongue to allow air to pass from the lungs; this in turn initiates the lip vibrations. The tongue and air, coordinated with the embouchure, influence the articulation and the quality of sound. The tongue should never be isolated as a separate pedagogical entity. Rather, the tongue must always be viewed in relationship with proper embouchure, breath support, and tonal control. Since the tongue helps form the shape of the mouth cavity, its placement greatly influences the sound, register, amplitude, and attack.

THE TONGUE

The air is the primary source in the production of a brass tone; however, the tongue has a dominant influence on air and lip vibration. "Overuse" of the tongue is often one of the greatest enemies of tone production. Correct use of the tongue in brass articulation is similar to articulation in speech. To use any greater emphasis of the tongue during brass performance than that used while talking is unnecessary. As in speech, the tongue clarifies the musical line. For example, an accented note is comparable to saying "toe" loudly, with the emphasis on the "oe," not the "t."

TONE

The mouth cavity must complement the resonating frequency and volume of the tone performed. A thin, pinched sound results from the tongue being held too high in the mouth, as in pronouncing the syllable "ee," particularly in an attempt to produce a middle- or low-register note. One reason for this problem is that students are often told to start every

attack using "T" (Figure 5.1), which implies a mouth configuration of "ee" (Figure 5.2). To improve the sound, the tongue position can be changed to either "oo" or "aw" (Figure 5.3). The sound can also be improved by adjusting the space between the upper and lower jaws or by thrusting the jaw forward slightly. A fuzzy, airy sound will result if the mouth cavity is too large for the pitch and volume intended.

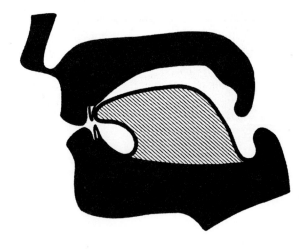

FIGURE 5.1
Tongue in "T" position

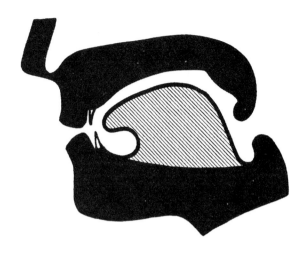

FIGURE 5.2
Tongue in "ee" position

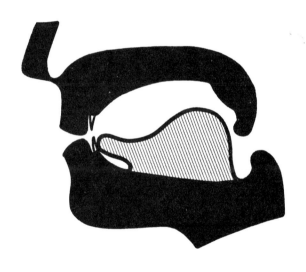

FIGURE 5.3
Tongue in "aw" position

REGISTER

To produce a full sound from the bottom register to the top, a player must change the shape of the mouth cavity, but this does not mean radically changing the space between the upper and lower jaws. Rather, the change is a change of tongue position. While playing in the lower register on all brass instruments, most performers prefer to push the jaw out slightly to help align the lips and to keep the tongue flat. One way to do this is to imagine a hot piece of pizza on the back of the tongue but not

allowed to touch the throat. However, if the tongue is too flat in the upper register, the note cannot be produced. When the jaw is too closed and the tongue is too near the roof of the mouth, the player usually overshoots the note and produces a pinched sound, as previously described.

AMPLITUDE (VOLUME)

Amplitude is controlled by the size of the mouth cavity and by air velocity. The tongue shape and the space between the upper and lower jaws determine the size of the mouth cavity. An extremely loud, high-register note requires a larger mouth cavity than does a soft, lower-register note. In a long tone starting from pianissimo to fortissimo and back to pianissimo, the mouth cavity changes from small to large to small. Many response problems result from setting the mouth cavity for a mezzo forte and then attempting to play mezzo piano or softer. In all cases, the mouth cavity must match the volume of the tone to be played.

ATTACK (AIR RELEASE)

Whether playing a single note or repeated notes, the player should use the tip of the tongue. The initial tongue placement is behind the upper teeth, where one would begin to pronounce the letters "T" or "D." The tongue moves down to a naturally relaxed position in the mouth. The tongue releases air through the lips, producing lip vibration.

Never should a student be told to pull the tongue back. Such an action tends to tighten the back of the tongue, which then affects the throat. The middle and back of the tongue must remain relaxed in all passages, regardless of the difficulty. In fact, articulated passages require even greater effort to maintain a relaxed middle and back of the tongue.

Each attack is influenced by the type of consonant used. A strong, brilliant, hard attack will be achieved by "T," "tu," "too," and "tee." A softer attack, matching the sound that follows, is accomplished with "D" or "N." Legato passages, using a legato tongue, usually are introduced by "lu," "la," "du," or "da."

Bubble Attack

A frequent problem of brass performance is the tendency to overarticulate; the result is a "bubble" at the beginning of every tone. This unclean beginning is caused by two problems: 1) allowing the air to "build up" behind the tongue before releasing it, and 2) the tongue touching the lips producing a beginning that, for a fraction of a second, does not have any partials. Most teachers advise their students never to allow the tongue to come between the lips (the only exception may be the pedal register of the trombone). To correct the tendency to put the tongue between the lips, the student can first start several notes in all registers by use of just air. Next, the student can practice starting the air with the tongue beginning its motion in the correct spot behind the teeth. Finally, the student should combine the two—the tongue starting the air and the air starting the lip vibration—practicing slowly in all registers until the problem is solved.

Chewing

Another reason for an unclear attack comes from "chewing," moving the jaw during every attack. Chewing results from not having the mouth cavity formed with the proper opening prior to the attack; the jaw then drops to create the proper opening to resonate the note. To solve this problem, the student should sustain a note and release it, not changing the jaw and embouchure position. The student should play the note again and again, using "N" or "D" to attack and making sure not to close the jaw. In order not to chew on short, lower-register notes, the student needs a more legato approach to the tongue. The student should practice this procedure in every register.

AIR AND ARTICULATION

It is important to maintain the flow of air during articulation. A device that helps to visualize and correct the use of the tongue is a breath tube. The tongue and air, used properly, keep the Ping Pong ball at the top of the tube (Figure 5.4).

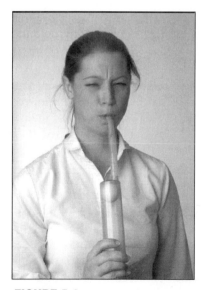

FIGURE 5.4
"Breath Builder" developed by Harold Hanson, and pictured with his permission. See page 18 for the address of the "Breath Builder."

TYPES OF TONGUING

Common Attack

Most young brass players tend to "overarticulate." In many cases the tongue is their worst enemy. In order to match attack and sound, a softer approach, "D" or "N," can replace a more brilliant attack, "T."

Staccato Articulation

Staccato, written ♩ ♩ ♩ ♩ and played ♪ ᵧ ♪ ᵧ ♪ ᵧ ♪ ᵧ, is approached by use of either a short, common attack "N" or "D" or short, brilliant attack using "T," depending on the music style. Staccato does not indicate "overarticulation" or "hammering" with the tongue. The tongue must remain relaxed with continuous air support, even though there is space between the notes. The release of a staccato note is open ended ⊏⎯⎯⊐ ; the tongue is not allowed to produce the release ⊏⎯⎯⎯⟍ .

Piccato Articulation

Written ♩ ♩ ♩ ♩ , the piccato articulation is usually played in a short fortissimo character. The tongue is in a sharp "tee," "taw," or "toe," depending on the register, and moves quickly. The breath controls the duration of the note.

Sforzando Articulation

Written *sfz* ♩, the sforzando articulation is crisper and more explosive than piccatto. To accomplish this the brass player needs to build air pressure behind the tongue before its release.

Portato Articulation

Written ¯♩ ¯♩ ¯♩ ¯♩, the portato articulation is performed with a slight separation. Usually the portato is played with a soft attack, using either "D" or "N."

Legato Articulation

Written ⌢♩ ♩ ♩ ♩, legato is performed with continuous air and uses the tongue only on the initial attack and repeated notes. Players who use legato tonguing on repeated notes should concentrate on keeping a continuous flow of air and denting the airstream with the tongue.

The use of air and tongue is graphically illustrated in the following examples.

Airstream → ⊏⎯⊐ ⊏⎯⊐ ⊏⎯⊐ ⊏⎯⊐ common attack
♩ ♩ ♩ ♩

Airstream → ⊏ ⊏ ⊏ ⊏ staccato
♪ ᵧ ♪ ᵧ ♪ ᵧ ♪ ᵧ

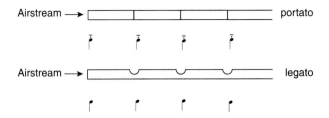

Trombone Legato

Of all the brass instruments, the trombone has the most difficulty with legato playing because of the slide. In order to approximate the legato style of other brass instruments, the trombonist must take advantage of (1) natural slurs, (2) a slide action that approximates the speed of a valve, (3) moving the slide in the opposite direction of the melodic intervals, and (4) fast slide action and legato tonguing.

Natural Slur   If the notes belong to the same harmonic series,

as in the B-flat harmonic series, no movement of the slide is necessary, and the tongue is used only for the initial attack. A passage may have just a few notes together that can be performed with a natural slur; this would not require any tonguing.

Slide Motion Opposite of Line   If a melodic line is ascending and the slide motion extending, no tonguing is needed, except if a note is repeated.

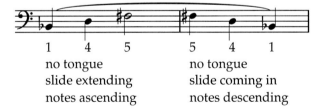

Trombonists often have the option to select slide positions to achieve the best legato playing.

In the example below the trombonist could play B-natural in fourth position and C-sharp in second position. This would result in glissando if no tongue were used. The other tongue approach would be to use fifth position for C-sharp, which would allow a smooth passage without using the tongue.

The trombonist would play D in fourth position to execute a legato phrase.

Fast Slide Action and Legato Tongue   Regardless of the positions used to eliminate the tongue, the player should move the slide quickly. Any time the slide moves in a legato passage, *it must approximate the time required to move a valve or valves.* Beginning students often surge the air when trying to move the slide quickly, but the air must remain smooth and constant.

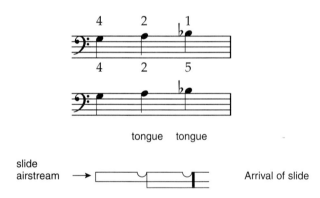

This passage has two problems. First, the step from G to A requires a fast-slide technique and a legato tongue. The A to the B-flat could be played in fifth position, but that is three positions away. It would be easier to play B-flat in first position. A legato tongue and fast-slide would then be required for the B-flat. In order to make this passage smooth, the air must be kept constant, and the tongue and slide movement must be simultaneous, the slide reaching its designated spot at the same time that the tongue initiates the tone. This requires much practice. The following passage can be used to teach and facilitate a legato style.

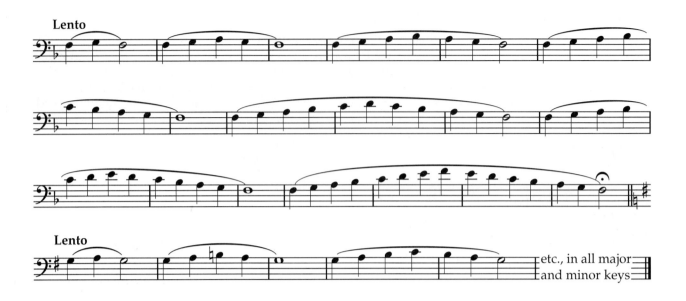

For the development of a fast, even slide arm, coordinated with a light legato articulation, scale studies of the following nature have proven very satisfactory.

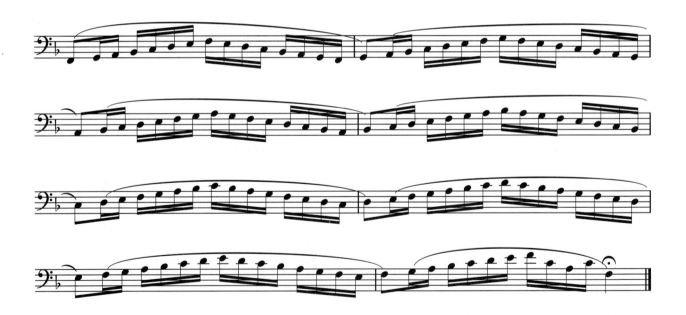

Double and Triple Tonguing

A brass player will eventually reach a technical passage that cannot be executed with a single tonguing. The musician can then use either double tonguing for notes grouped in 2, 4, 8, and so on, or triple tonguing for notes grouped in 3, 6, 9, and 12. Double tonguing produces duplets; triple tonguing produces triplets. Most teachers advise their students to use double and triple tonguing only when single tonguing is not technically possible. It is also wise to learn double and triple tonguing speeds that overlap with single tonguing speed, eliminating any gap between the two. The tongue action of double or triple tonguing is a rocking action.

Double Tonguing:
    Explosive syllables
    T-K T-K T-K T-K T-K
    Tu-Ku Tu-Ku Tu-Ku Tu-Ku Tu-Ku

Triple Tonguing:
    Explosive syllables
    T-T-K T-T-K T-T-K T-T-K
    tu-tu-ku tu-tu-ku tu-tu-ku tu-tu-ku

Double Tonguing:
    Softer syllables
    tih-kih tih-kih tih-kih
    dih-gih dih-gih dih-gih
    dih-ga dih-ga dih-ga

Triple Tonguing:
    Softer syllables
    tih-tih-kih tih-tih-kih tih-tih-kih
    dih-dih-gih dih-dih-gih dih-dih-gih
    daw-daw-gaw daw-daw-gaw daw-daw-gaw

Triple tonguing can be accomplished using the "tu tu ku" tonguing approach.

An approach to teaching double and triple tonguing is to have the student exaggerate the passage slowly, using the strongest syllables. Overemphasis on the "K" or "ku" is advised, since at faster tempos these syllables are often too soft. As the tongue becomes conditioned to the rocking action, the student can begin to increase the speed. Away from the brass instrument, players can practice the tongue action by singing technical exercises. The "Breath Builder" (Figure 5.4) is a valuable tool in teaching double and triple tonguing. It is important to use the "k" syllable with sufficient air to keep the Ping Pong ball at the top of the tube.

Another system of triple tonguing which is not used as consistently as the others is:

Triple tonguing, "tu ku tu, ku tu ku," is favored by many professional players. It is double tonguing except for a shift in syllabic emphasis; hence it can be faster as the same consonant is never repeated consecutively:

Flutter Tonguing

Flutter tonguing is used in contemporary solos and for special effects in show music, operas, musicals, and so on. Flutter tonguing is accomplished by placing the tongue in the position of "D" while passing air across the tip of the tongue, causing it to flutter. The tongue's speed is dictated by the amount of air used. Occasionally, a student cannot make the tongue flutter. In such a case, vibration of the soft palate at the back of the throat can substitute. Also, louder passages make more convincing use of the flutter tongue.

CHAPTER 6

MOUTHPIECES

MOUTHPIECES

Historically, the mouthpiece developed from an undetachable cup-shaped section, to the wooden mouthpiece of the Baroque period, to the current design of mouthpieces of today. Each mouthpiece has a characteristically designed contour that affects timbre, flexibility, range, volume, resistance, and accuracy (Figure 6.1). Brass players need to select a mouthpiece that suits their performance needs. Many players use more than one mouthpiece to adjust timbre or range, depending on the type of performance: band, orchestra, jazz, or chamber music.

SELECTING A MOUTHPIECE

A brass student's teacher needs to consider the following physical and performance requirements before selecting a mouthpiece:

Physical	*Performance*
—teeth	—desired tone quality
—lip strength	—ease of upper and lower register
—size of lips	
—jaw (position)	—endurance
	—intonation
	—flexibility
	—type of playing
	—volume of sound

Since every player has individual physical differences, there is no single standard mouthpiece. Every type of mouthpiece has advantages and disadvantages; in the selection of the proper mouthpiece, seven areas of the mouthpiece must be considered: 1) rim, 2) bite, 3) cup diameter, 4) cup depth, 5) throat shoulder, 6) throat, and 7) back bore (Figure 6.2).

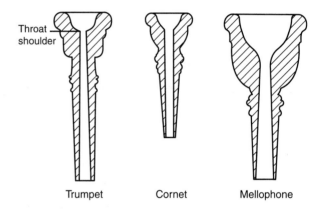

FIGURE 6.1
Mouthpiece configurations

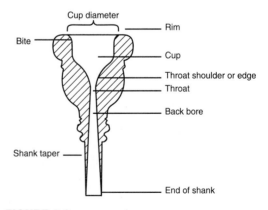

FIGURE 6.2
Mouthpiece characteristics

Mouthpiece Characteristics and Effects on Playing

The rim is extremely important because it is the area of the mouthpiece that influences endurance, sensitivity, flexibility, and vibration of the lips.

1. *Rim:* Narrow rim—greater flexibility, less endurance
Wide rim—greater endurance, less flexibility. Players with soft, fleshy lips find this useful.
Flat rim—comfortable, but holds the lips, keeping them immobile
Medium-wide—greatest compromise between flexibility and endurance

2. *Bite:* Sharp bite—greater accuracy, less flexibility, less endurance
Round bite—greater flexibility, greater endurance, less accuracy

3. *Cup Diameter:* Wide cup—lower register easier, upper register more difficult
Narrow cup—upper register easier, lower register more difficult

4. *Cup Depth:* Deep cup—darker sound, lower register more responsive, upper register flatter and more difficult
Shallow cup—brighter sound, upper register more responsive, lower register less responsive

Other Factors—Other factors to consider in selecting a mouthpiece cup are directly related to the type of music played. A symphony player usually prefers a larger, deeper cup and open back bore. A jazz player will usually select a smaller cup and back bore. If a performer obtains equally good results with a large cup as with a medium-sized cup, the larger size cup is recommended.

5. *Throat Shoulder or Edge:* Sharp throat shoulder—brighter sound helps attack (more upper partials are present), sometimes harsh and strident
Round throat shoulder—mellow, darker sounds
No throat shoulder—lack of presence and substance

Many of the timbre or tonal characteristics of each instrument are a result of different mouthpiece designs. The funnel-shaped horn mouthpiece is constructed without an edge or throat shoulder. The combination of the deep cup and no throat shoulder produces the dark, mellow quality characteristic of the horn tone color.

6. *Throat:* Large throat—greater volume, not enough resistance, control more difficult
Small throat—softer sound, easier to control, insufficient volume

The throat controls resistance. If too small, the lower and upper registers are restricted. If too large, the performer works excessively to achieve satisfactory results.

7. *Back Bore:* Back bore opens quickly—greater volume, darker sound
Back bore opens gradually—better controlled tone, more centered, less volume, brighter sound

Vincent Bach is often used as a standard mouthpiece because of its longevity as a company, affordability, and availability. Note that numerous mouthpiece manufacturers make quality mouthpieces: Yamaha, Giardinelli, Schilke, Denis Wick, Holton, Doug Elliot, and many others (see Table 6.1). Many professional players will customize their mouthpieces to the specifications they seek.

TABLE 6.1

RECOMMENDED MOUTHPIECES

Baritone
Vincent Bach, 12 C (small)—7 C (medium), beginning–intermediate
Vincent Bach, 6½ AL (large), advanced
Euphonium
Vincent Bach, 6½ AL, intermediate
Vincent Bach, 5–3 G, advanced
Schilke, 51 D, advanced
Trombone (small to large)
Vincent Bach, 12 C (small), beginning
Vincent Bach, 7 C (medium), intermediate
Vincent Bach, 6½ A Symphony tenor, advanced
Vincent Bach, 5 GS Symphony tenor, advanced
Schilke, 50, advanced
Vincent Bach, 5 G Symphony tenor, advanced
Schilke, 51, advanced
Vincent Bach, 3 G small bass, advanced
Vincent Bach, 2 G medium bass, advanced
Vincent Bach, 1 G large bass, advanced
Horn
Vincent Bach, 7 (medium), beginning–intermediate
Vincent Bach, 3 (large), advanced
Holton, MDC (medium), beginning–advanced
Holton, DC (large), advanced
Trumpet
Vincent Bach, 7 C (medium), beginning–intermediate
Vincent Bach, 5–1 (large), advanced
Tuba
Vincent Bach, 25 (small), beginning
Vincent Bach, 18 (medium–large), intermediate
Conn Helberg, (standard or 7B), advanced

CHAPTER 7

VIBRATO

Vibrato is a regular pulsating change in pitch, intensity, or both. Vibrato used before the time of Bach, vocally and instrumentally, was abolished in the nineteenth century as not matching the conservatism of the time. Vibrato for brass is still a relatively new phenomenon recognized as a serious enhancement of tone only in the last half of the twentieth century.

As brass solo performances developed and matured in the twentieth century, vibrato became an integral part of their musical enhancement. Most professional brass soloists feel that vibrato provides added tonal energy and vitality, improves intonation, has a warming effect on the tone, and lends to the expressiveness of a musical phrase.

Rules for the use of vibrato are as follows:

1. A vibrato should never be used to cover intonation problems.
2. Vibrato is commonly used on all brass instruments except for horn, where only a small percentage of players use it.
3. In orchestral playing, vibrato is not used during brass sectional playing, nor in most solos. There are some exceptions, depending on the piece.
4. Six oscillations per second produce the desired vibrato for all brass instruments.
5. Too fast a vibrato (a "nanny goat") should be avoided.
6. Some jazz groups use vibrato in sectional playing; however, this is considered passé in most contemporary jazz groups.
7. Vibrato should be controlled and not excessive.
8. A long tone can begin with no vibrato and then have vibrato added to increase the tension or direction of a musical line. A change of vibrato speed from faster to slower can result in a release of tension within a musical line.

9. All lyric solo work should use vibrato to enhance the phrasing and feeling of the piece. The horn may be the exception to this rule.

TYPES OF VIBRATO

Three types of vibrato can be produced: 1) lip (jaw), 2) hand, and 3) abdominal.

Lip (Jaw) Vibrato

Professional brass players and teachers prefer a lip vibrato, for the following reasons:

1. It is a safeguard against pressure.
2. It is not as visual as a hand vibrato.
3. It is easier to control.
4. It becomes an actual part of the tone and is not a mechanical, physical action imposed on the tone.

Vibrato Practice Routine

1. Lip vibrato is more accurately described as jaw vibrato, since it is the action of the jaw that produces the change in pitch. To learn lip vibrato, the student first pronounces "yaw, yaw, yaw, yaw" in a quarter-note pattern with the metronome set at sixty. This extremely exaggerated motion teaches the jaw to move freely. Next, the student should double the speed of the jaw to an eighth-note pattern. The motion of the jaw should still be exaggerated. The student can then double the speed again by using a sixteenth-note pattern. Again, the movement of the jaw is exaggerated. The last part of the exercise is to refine the jaw movement into a *real vibrato.*
2. This pattern should be practiced on every note of a major scale.

yaw   yaw   yaw   yaw

yaw yaw yaw yaw yaw yaw yaw yaw

ya ya ya ya ya ya ya ya ya ya ya ya ya ya ya ya

ya ya ya ya refined

3. Daily practice of vibrato in all registers with varying dynamics is recommended. Using varied speeds of vibrato will help ensure the performer's control of this valuable embellishment.

Hand (Slide) Vibrato

Trumpet players produce vibrato by changing the pressure of the mouthpiece on the lips. The right hand, with the thumb between the first and second valve casings, moves at the wrist at the desired vibrato pulsation. Hand vibrato is practiced using the same procedure as in learning lip vibrato. Very few "classical" trumpet players use this method, while jazz trumpet players often use it.

Trombone players use slide movement, a wrist-and-finger motion, at the desired vibrato oscillation. Again, this is used by few performers of classical music but by numerous jazz players. The problem many trombonists have with using slide vibrato in classical music is controlling the size of the pitch variation. When the trombone slide—a double tube—is adjusted only one-half inch, the actual instrument length adjustment increases one inch. Therefore, it is difficult to maintain a *refined* vibrato. Also, the slide must work with great freedom to allow for rapid oscillating movements.

Abdominal Vibrato

Even though diaphragm vibrato is not as popular as the lip vibrato, many brass players consider it superior, because the jaw and embouchure are not compromised by motion. Instead of adjusting the pitch with the embouchure or jaw, the air flow intensity is pulsated by the abdominal muscles. This method of vibrato is taught by having the student pulsate the intensity of the air flow by the abdomen, using "ooo, ooo, ooo, ooo." The same quarter-note, eighth-note, and sixteenth-note pattern exercises can be used, as discussed under lip vibrato. It is important that the student's concentration remain on the abdominal area and not transfer to the throat, producing glottis pulsations.

It is more difficult to relax the abdominal muscles during inhalation while focusing on abdominal muscular fluctuation; however, this can be learned. Many brass players concerned about the effects of diaphragm vibrato on the breath choose other methods of vibrato.

USE OF VIBRATO

Vibrato is rarely used by brass players orchestrally. The exceptions are solos, in which the vibrato fits the style and interpretation of the piece—for example, the trombone solo in *Bolero* by Ravel.

Vibrato provides direction, tension, and release of a sustained tone by varying its pulse and width. Tactfully applied, it provides additional enhancement, energy, and vitality to the tone.

PART 2

INDIVIDUAL INSTRUMENTS

CHAPTER 8

THE TRUMPET

HISTORY OF THE TRUMPET

Since instruments played by lip vibration existed during primitive times, the date of origin of such instruments is impossible to establish. Using lip vibration as a criterion for determining a brass instrument ancestor, the criterion for distinguishing between the primitive horn and trumpet is the difference in shape. Primitive trumpets were straight and cylindrical; horns were generally more curved and conical.

The first so-called trumpets were probably nothing more than hollowed branches, canes, or shells used to frighten away evil spirits. Any tone produced on these primitive instruments would hardly be called music today. At best, primitive trumpets could be expected to produce only one or two different tones. These early instruments, found on every continent, were either "end blown" or "side blown" (Figure 8.1).

Often referred to as "magic instruments," trumpets were mainly used at funerals, puberty rites, and sunset rituals. In fact, certain modern European cultures still use trumpets for those purposes. For example, wooden trumpets are blown at Romanian funerals.

Other primitive trumpets include the salpinx (a straight trumpet used by the Assyrians, Egyptians, and Jews), the Roman tuba, and the lituus (used by the Roman army) (see Figures 8.2–8.4).

The trumpet during the Middle Ages through the Baroque period was associated with pomp and pageantry more than any other instrument. The trumpet was known as the "nobleman" among musical instruments during this time for two reasons: 1) trumpet performers stood at the king's right hand, and 2) trumpeters held the rank of officer and were allowed to wear the feather of nobility in their caps. The trumpet was used explicitly for the nobility's purposes.

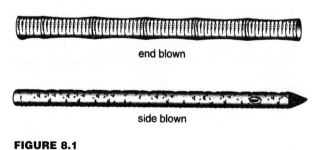

end blown

side blown

FIGURE 8.1
Primitive trumpets

FIGURE 8.2
Salpinx

FIGURE 8.3
Roman tuba (buccina), 11 feet long. The wood rod attached diagonally across the coil gave the player a shoulder support.

FIGURE 8.4
Lituus, ancient Rome

In English manuscripts of the thirteenth century, the trumpet appears as a straight, cylindrical tube made of metal with a flaring bell at one end. This instrument, known as the "buzine" or "bocine," was probably a corruption of the Roman tuba, even though it did not resemble that instrument. Because of the length of the buzine (Figure 8.5), which stood as high as a man, and its normal tendency to bend, the instrument was eventually folded into a wide flattened "S" (Figure 8.6). Eventually, through further flattening of the "S," bringing the tubes within an inch of each other, the instrument assumed a shape resembling that of trumpets today.

By the beginning of the sixteenth century, the trumpet had evolved into the form it would have for a long time. As the result of changes that took place during the sixteenth century, the trumpet's three straight lengths of tubing lay parallel to each other and were united by pieces of U-shaped tubing called bows (Figure 8.7). Trumpet playing, as well as trumpet making, progressed considerably during this century.

Monteverdi was the first significant composer to write seriously for the trumpet. Monteverdi in his opera *Orfeo* wrote for five trumpets, showing that in fact composers were beginning to write specifically for the trumpet.

During the sixteenth and seventeenth centuries, the most widely used wind instrument in Europe was the cornett, which has no connection to today's cornet. Although the cornett is associated with the development of brass instruments and was used primarily as the soprano voice with trombones, it is not a brass instrument. Known also as "cornet a bouquin," "cornetto," and "zink," the cornett was originally made of animal horn, bone, or wood. The cornett had six finger holes and a thumb hole, similar to those of the recorder. The cornett contained a detachable, cup-shaped mouthpiece and was classified by shapes and colors. There were two types. The first was a curved instrument constructed by carving out two sections and joining them together with black leather, hence the "black" instrument (Figure 8.8). The second was a straight instrument, undoubtedly the "white" instrument (Figure 8.9).

The trumpet of the seventeenth century was known as the natural trumpet, and the art of playing the natural trumpet as "clarino" playing. The instrument had no valves, slides, or pistons; its fundamental varied according to the tubing length. The two lowest partials were seldom used, the third partial being the most practical low note (Figure 8.10).

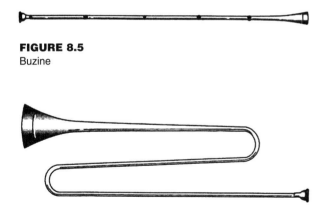

FIGURE 8.5
Buzine

FIGURE 8.6
S trumpet

FIGURE 8.8
Cornett (zink), curved black

FIGURE 8.9
Cornett (zink), white

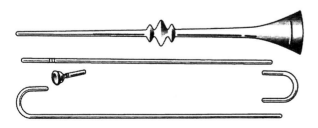

FIGURE 8.7
Disassembled natural trumpet

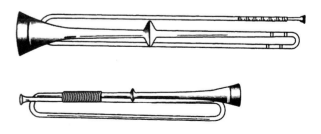

FIGURE 8.10
Natural trumpet

Early in the seventeenth century, a professional trumpeter's union (guild) known as the "Trompeter-kameradschaft" was formed. The "Kameraden" were members in the court orchestra and in concert ensembles. Their union, or guild, was an elite organization formed to keep town musicians separate from court musicians. Fines were levied against any town musician caught playing the music or even the high register of the court "Kameraden." The town musicians attended and performed at all municipal functions, including festivals and processions.

J. S. Bach used the clarino trumpet in many of his works, including the *Brandenburgh Concerto No. 2.* The art of clarino playing reached its peak in the works of J. S. Bach, Hans Richter, Michael Haydn, J. W. Hertel, J. F. Fasch, and J. M. Molter. Other important clarino composers were Karl Phillip Emanuel Bach, who in his *Magnificat* used three trumpets with kettledrums in the same brilliant manner as his father, and Leopold Mozart, father of Wolfgang, who wrote a concerto for trumpet in D.

By the late eighteenth century and nineteenth century, there was a decline of clarino playing that can be attributed to the following causes:

1. The courts of the nobility disappeared after the French Revolution, thereby eliminating the need for the court musician.
2. The increased size of the eighteenth-century orchestra caused the clarino trumpet players to "overblow" the instrument in order to be heard, producing an uncharacteristic and undesirable harsh tone.
3. The constant changing of crooks to play in different keys made the clarino cumbersome and difficult to use (discussed below).
4. The decree that released the trumpeters and kettledrummers from the "Kameradschaft" (guild) allowed untrained musicians to "misuse" the "art."

During the eighteenth century, however, much progress was made in improving brass instruments. In 1753, A. J. Hampel of the Royal Orchestra in Dresden popularized the use of crooks and tuning slides. These crooks consisted of coiled brass tubes that could be inserted into the main tube to increase its length. Since no two crooks were the same size and each represented a different key, the trumpet player had to have a crook of a different length for each key. When writing for the trumpet, the composer would specify the desired key, and the player would use the appropriate crook (Figure 8.11).

Around 1760, Koelbel, a Bohemian musician, succeeded in changing the pitch of his instrument one half-tone by placing a key on the bell of the trumpet. In 1801, Weidinger of Vienna improved on

this by placing five keys on his bugle, enabling him to play the chromatic scale. The keyed bugle was used in eighteenth- and early-nineteenth-century music (Figure 8.12). Haydn wrote his famous trumpet concerto for this instrument. Because of its limited range, it was restricted orchestrally to the performance of tutti passages.

In 1788, Charles Clogget invented the first valve. Pictured in Figure 8.13 is an example of one of the earliest valve systems. Frederick Bluehmel added three valves to brass instruments, and in 1815, Stolzel, a German, added improvements to that. Perinet of Paris and Antoine (Adolph) Sax introduced numerous mechanical improvements. The development of the valve made possible the modern-day trumpet, which is capable of performing all of the pitches in the chromatic scale with an even sound.

FIGURE 8.11
Natural trumpet with extra crook

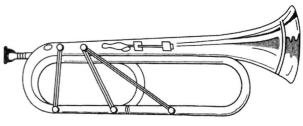

FIGURE 8.12
Keyed bugle

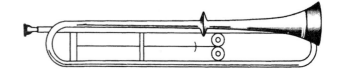

FIGURE 8.13
Valve used to change key

THE MODERN TRUMPET

Today's trumpet uses a series of tube lengths controlled by three valves. See Figure 8.14 for nomenclature of the trumpet.

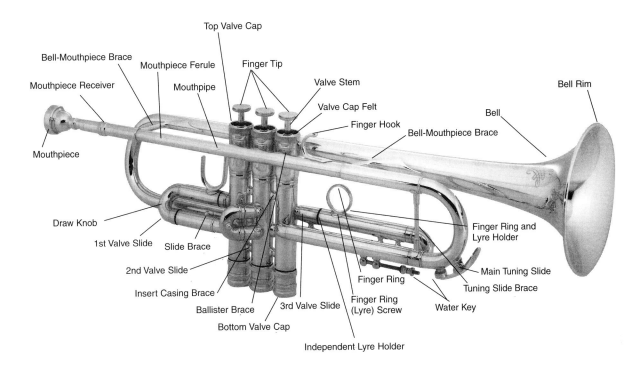

FIGURE 8.14
Nomenclature of the trumpet. (Courtesy of C. G. Conn Division of United Musical Instruments, USA, Inc., www.unitedmusical.com)

The various tube lengths may be used independently or in combination. For example, when no valves are depressed, air passes directly through the fundamental length of the trumpet. When a valve is depressed, the air is forced through a longer length of tubing. There are seven different combinations, each of which results in a tube of a different length. The sequence, which lowers the pitch by one half-step each time, is as follows: open (no valves depressed); second valve; first valve; first and second valves; second and third valves; first and third valves; and finally, first, second, and third valves. Each of these seven different tube lengths results in an overtone series, as shown in the following harmonic fingering chart, and gives the resultant pitches for a B-flat trumpet.

The first partial or fundamental is not shown in the example because it is not possible to play the fundamental with the characteristic trumpet tone quality; the bore of the tubing is too small. The seventh partial is notated with a black note to indicate that the partial is better played with another finger-

ing. The harmonic fingering chart applies to trumpet, cornet, flügelhorn, alto horn, mellophone, and baritone horn in treble clef.

The seven different overtone series result in a complete chromatic scale that covers the entire register of the instrument. Since many notes appear in more than one overtone series, they may be played with more than one valve combination. The chromatic fingering chart gives all possible fingerings with the alternate fingerings bracketed. Alternate fingerings usually change the intonation and must be used with care.

The Trumpet Family

While the B-flat trumpet is the most common in today's bands and orchestras, other trumpets are rapidly gaining popularity, especially the slightly shorter trumpet in C. In France, the C trumpet has almost replaced the B-flat trumpet in symphony orchestras, relegating the B-flat trumpet strictly to jazz performance. The modern B-flat trumpet has a 9-inch conical mouthpipe, followed by a 17-inch

HARMONIC FINGERING CHART
B♭ Trumpet, Cornet, Flügelhorn, Baritone 𝄞, Alto Horn, Mellophone

*flat partial
rarely used

CHROMATIC FINGERING CHART
B♭ Trumpet, Cornet, Flügelhorn, Baritone 𝄞, Alto Horn, Mellophone

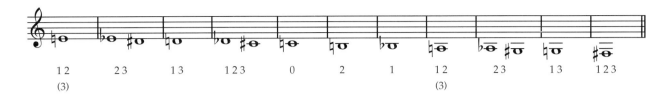

1 2	2 3	1 3	1 2 3	0	2	1	1 2	2 3	1 3	1 2 3
(3)								(3)		

cylindrical bore tuning slide. Its bell is conical, and the instrument is usually built in three bore sizes: small, medium, and large.

Figure 8.15 shows the more common trumpets pitched above and below the B-flat instrument.

All trumpets are transposing instruments except those pitched in C. Table 8.1 shows the wide variety of trumpets available, as well as their pitch, transposition, and written range.

Many smaller trumpets have extra slides or lead pipes that enable the performer to change the pitch of the instrument a half-step up or down. A common misconception is that a performer can play higher on a smaller trumpet, but the lips produce the vibration for any note, not the instrument. Because the smaller instruments require less breath support, they help the performer in the upper register; however, they do not automatically give any performer a higher range. The main advantage of the smaller trumpets is their lighter and brighter tone quality. The choice of a smaller trumpet for any

given piece of music depends on which gives the best intonation and which allows the easiest fingering patterns, trills, and transpositions.

Because many scores using members of the trumpet family are published in languages other than English, Table 8.1 may help identify the specific trumpet called for.

TRANSPOSITION OF NATURAL TRUMPET PARTS

Transposition by Clefs

Transposing trumpet parts is accomplished in two different ways, usually determined by the theoretical background of the student. The first way, transposition by clef (accepted in most of the European conservatories), is to substitute a particular clef for a particular key. The names and middle-C pitches are as follows:

FIGURE 8.15
The trumpet family (B♭ cornet, flügelhorn, B♭ or A piccolo, bell tuned E♭ trumpet, D trumpet, C trumpet, B♭ trumpet) (Courtesy—David Brown)

TABLE 8.1

FOREIGN LANGUAGE IDENTIFICATION

English	French	Italian	German
B♭ Piccolo Trumpet	Petite Trompette en Si♭	Ottavino Tromba in Si♭	Kleine Trompete in B
A Piccolo Trumpet	Petite Trompette en La	Ottavino Tromba in La	Kleine Trompete in A
E♭ Trumpet Soprano	Trompette en Mi♭	Tromba in Mi♭	Trompete in Es
D Trumpet	Trompette en Re	Tromba in Re	Trompete in D
C Trumpet	Trompette en Ut	Tromba in Do	Trompete in C
B♭ Trumpet	Trompette en Si♭	Tromba in Si♭	Trompete in B
A Trumpet	Trompette en La	Tromba in La	Trompete in A
B♭ Flügelhorn	Bugle en Si♭	Flicorno in Si♭	Flügelhorn in B
F Trumpet Alto	Bugle Alto en Fa	Flicorno Alto in Fa	Althorn
	or	or	or
	Trompette en Fa	Tromba in Fa	Altkornett in F
			or
			Trompete in F

RANGE

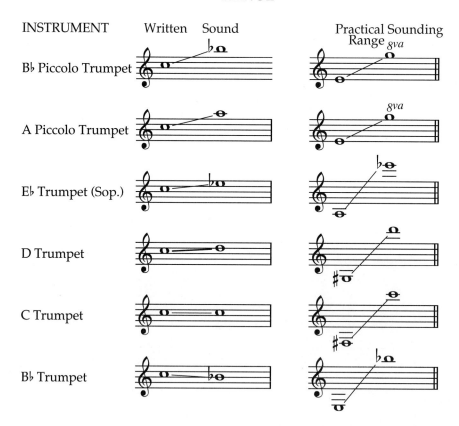

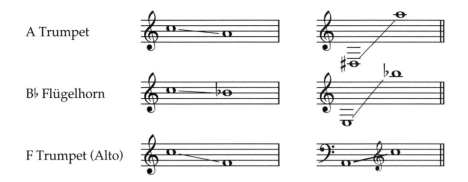

A Trumpet

B♭ Flügelhorn

F Trumpet (Alto)

TRANSPOSITION BY CLEFS

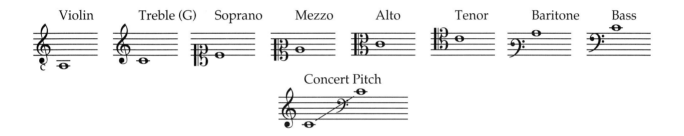

Violin   Treble (G)   Soprano   Mezzo   Alto   Tenor   Baritone   Bass

Concert Pitch

EXAMPLES (TRANSPOSITION BY CLEF)

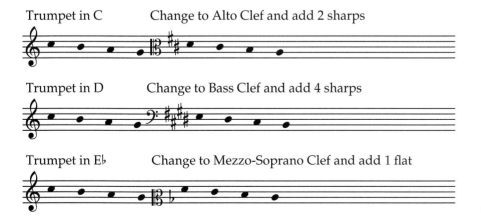

Trumpet in C   Change to Alto Clef and add 2 sharps

Trumpet in D   Change to Bass Clef and add 4 sharps

Trumpet in E♭   Change to Mezzo-Soprano Clef and add 1 flat

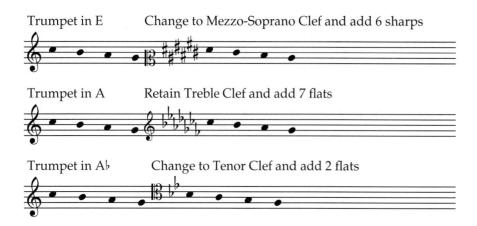

Trumpet in E   Change to Mezzo-Soprano Clef and add 6 sharps

Trumpet in A   Retain Treble Clef and add 7 flats

Trumpet in A♭   Change to Tenor Clef and add 2 flats

Other Uses of Clef Transposition   If the trumpet player knows bass clef baritone fingering, transposition of E-flat or E parts with a B-flat trumpet can be done by the following method.

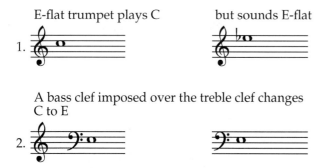

1. E-flat trumpet plays C   but sounds E-flat

2. A bass clef imposed over the treble clef changes C to E

3. The player adds three flats and plays the E-flat trumpet part as though he were playing a bass clef baritone part.

TRANSPOSITION BY INTERVAL

The second form of transposition is accomplished through intervallic relationships. The composer and conductor normally use concert C as a reference point in transposing.

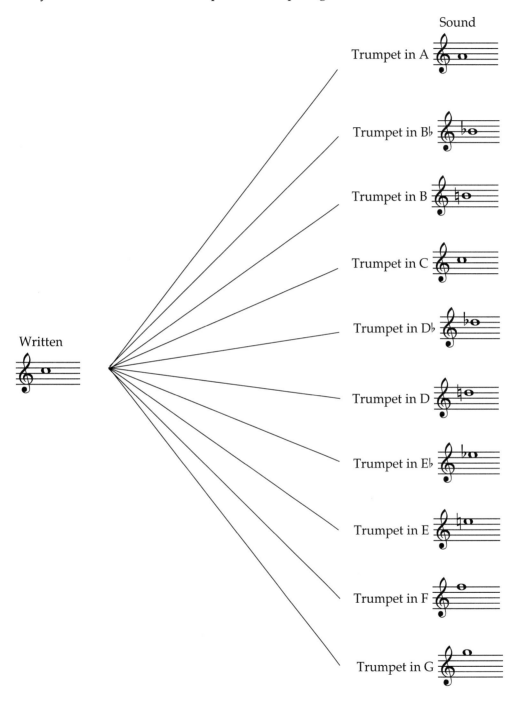

Transposition by Interval

Transposition by interval is a two-step process:

1. You must transpose up or down by the appropriate interval.
2. You must change the key signature by the same interval.

The following is a list of the transpositions most commonly called for in the trumpet literature.

Step 1: Calculate the interval from the key of your trumpet (e.g., B-flat trumpet) to the requested transposition (e.g., C trumpet).			Step 2: Transpose the key signature up or down by the same interval.	
Key of Trumpet Being Played	*Requested Transposition*	*Interval to move up or down*	*Printed Key Signature*	*New Key Signature*
	Trumpet in C	M2 up	C	D
	Trumpet in D	M3 up	C	E
	Trumpet in E♭	P4 up	C	F
B♭	Trumpet in E	aug4 up	C	F♯
	Trumpet in F	P5 up	C	G
	Trumpet in A	m2 down	C	B
	Trumpet in A♭	M2 down	C	B♭
	Trumpet in B♭	M2 down	C	B♭
	Trumpet in D	M2 up	C	D
	Trumpet in E♭	m3 up	C	E♭
C	Trumpet in E	M3 up	C	E
	Trumpet in F	P4 up	C	F
	Trumpet in A	m3 down	C	A
	Trumpet in A♭	M3 down	C	A♭

Examples:

If you are playing a **B-flat trumpet** and the music says:

If you are playing a **C trumpet** and the music says:

Even though the trumpet in C is the traditional orchestral instrument, the average high school trumpet student is restricted to the B-flat instrument. The student is frequently called on to play parts written for one of the previously listed trumpets, in which case transposition from the score to the B-flat trumpet is necessary.

The following examples feature excerpts from standard repertoire for trumpets in various keys with their transpositions to B-flat trumpet.

EXCERPTS FROM ORCHESTRAL REPERTOIRE

B♭ Trumpet playing a C part

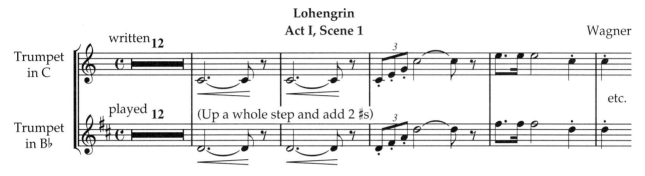

B♭ Trumpet playing an E part

B♭ Trumpet playing an E♭ part

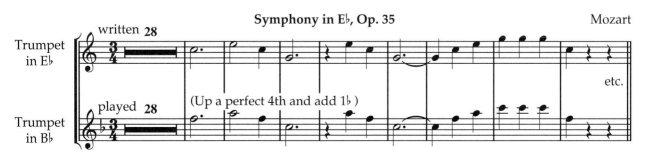

B♭ Trumpet playing an F part

B♭ Trumpet playing an A part

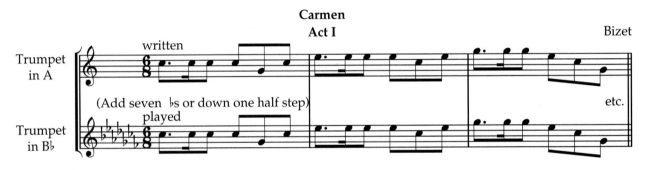

PLAYING POSITIONS FOR MEMBERS OF THE TRUMPET FAMILY

Students should exercise extreme care in developing correct playing position on the trumpet, because the position of the instrument in relation to the body determines not only appearance but also, to a great extent, the tone quality and fluency. The chest should be high, the head erect, and the elbows away from the body. The trumpet normally will be pointed a few degrees below horizontal, determined by the dento-facial characteristics of the student. Posture should be relaxed and the stance always conducive to maximum breath support (Figure 8.16).

The left hand should be placed firmly (without being tense or rigid) around the valve casings, with the ring finger inserted in the third valve slide, if the trumpet is so equipped (Figure 8.17). When the trumpet is equipped with a first valve trigger, the fleshy part of the thumb should rest on the trigger.

The right thumb should be placed between the first and second valve casings under the mouthpiece tube. The first three fingertips of the right hand should rest on the valves in a comfortable manner (Figure 8.18). The hand should be curved as though a ball were held in the palm, while the fingers—neither straight nor excessively curved—should be in the most relaxed position that affords

FIGURE 8.16
Playing position for trumpet, standing

FIGURE 8.17
Left hand position, trumpet

FIGURE 8.18
Right hand position, trumpet

the greatest speed. The little finger should rest lightly on the finger rings. Many trumpet teachers suggest inserting the little finger in the rings; however, this practice leads to using the ring as a way of exerting pressure on the embouchure. The use of the little finger should be restricted to turning pages and inserting or removing mutes. For most performers the freedom of the little finger greatly improves third-valve fingering problems.

A player should avoid unnecessary movements when playing. Positions should not be rigid; some natural movement of the instrument is desirable. However, movements up and down on the first beat of the bar, movements of the eyebrows for high notes, and the like should be avoided. When seated, the trumpet player should not cross the legs or slouch in the chair.

Intonation Problems

As discussed in Chapter One, a definite shortcoming of the three-valve, seven-combination system is that there are serious problems in playing all notes equally in tune. With the three-valve, seven-combination system, the length of the valve crooks must be calculated in relation to the length of the main tube. As long as single valves are used, the harmonics remain in correct relationship to the main tube.

Because of the overtone series characteristics and the deficiencies of the three-valve, seven-combination system, all notes are not equally in tune. In all instances in which valves are used in combination, the resultant tones will be sharp. The more valves used in combination, the sharper the pitch will become. When valves 1–2–3 are used in combination, the pitch will be approximately 28 cents sharp. Many brass instruments are equipped with compensating devices (i.e., third- and first-valve slides on the trumpet), and the student should be given an opportunity to practice using these devices, since they form an integral part of the technique of brass instrument playing.

The intonation chart presents an analysis of out-of-tune notes on brass instruments. It should be kept in mind, however, that degrees of out-of-tuneness vary with each individual instrument. The chart below shows the discrepancies inherent in the three-valve, seven-combination system.

Means of lengthening the tube through the use of valve slides (Figures 8.19 and 8.20) illustrate the most effective way to improve intonation on today's brass instruments. It should be emphasized that none of these devices takes the place of discriminative listening by the performer.

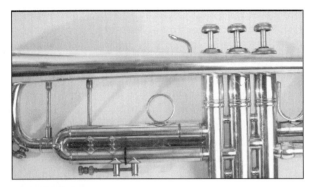

FIGURE 8.19
Third valve slide (Courtesy—David Brown)

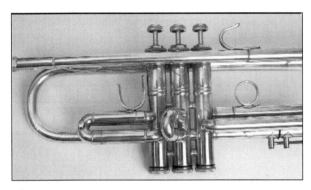

FIGURE 8.20
First valve slide (Courtesy—David Brown)

MUTES

Figure 8.21 shows the most frequently used trumpet mutes. The cup and straight mutes are the standard mutes used in most solo and ensemble playing. If a piece requests a mute "con sordino," the trumpet player would use a straight mute.

Straight Mute—used in jazz, solo, ensemble, orchestra, and band. It has a more strident quality and plays sharp.
Cup Mute—used for special effects in jazz, ensemble, solos, orchestra, and band. It has a mellow sound.

Harmon Mute or "Wa-Wah"—used almost exclusively in jazz and for special effects in all other idioms. It comes in two parts, with the stem and without. The stem inserted gives the instrument a second bell. Using the hand to open and close the stem bell, a "wa-wah" effect is produced. If the stem is taken out, the tone has a "buzzy" quality.
Whisper Mute—used to play extremely softly, allowing a musician to practice "on the road" in motel rooms or other places where normal volume would be prohibitive. It looks like a straight mute with holes.
Plunger Mute—used in jazz and all idioms of music to open or close the sound. It is often a small toilet plunger without the handle. In a piece of music, a "+" means to close the plunger over the bell, while an "o" means to open the plunger by pulling it away from the bell.
Bucket Mute—used strictly in jazz to produce a mellow sound.

FIGURE 8.21
Trumpet mutes (straight, cup, harmon, whisper, plunger, and bucket) (Courtesy—David Brown)

Roman numerals beneath the notes indicate the degree to which the pitch is out of tune.

I slightly out of tune
II moderately out of tune
III greatly out of tune
IV drastically out of tune

INTONATION CHART
Trumpet

B♭ Trumpet, Cornet, Flügelhorn, Baritone 𝄞

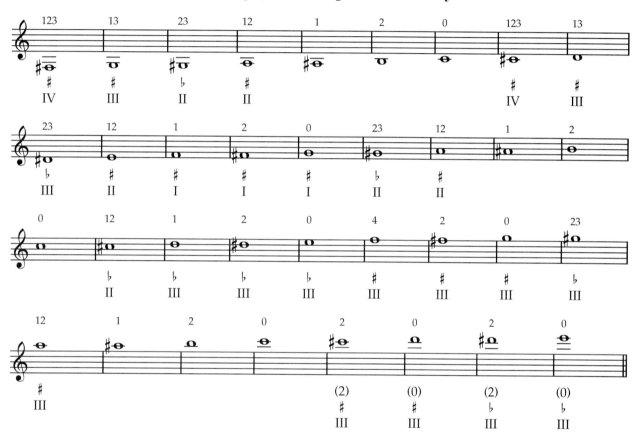

Summary of Notes Affected

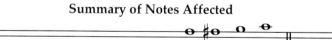
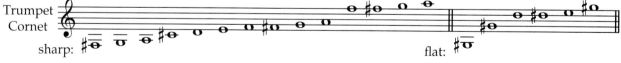

DAILY EMBOUCHURE AND FLEXIBILITY STUDIES

1.

2.

3.

4. To establish attack and tuning, attack with full MP tone. Round the end of each note. Never allow the tone to become brassy, and do not increase the volume after attack.

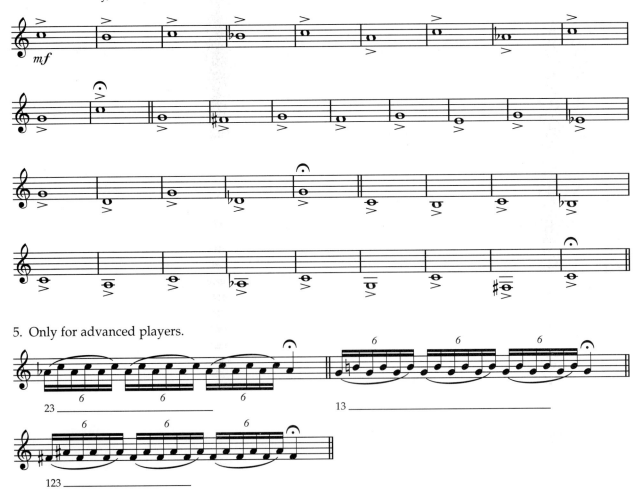

5. Only for advanced players.

6. Legato (da) tongue. Never have the tongue between the lips.

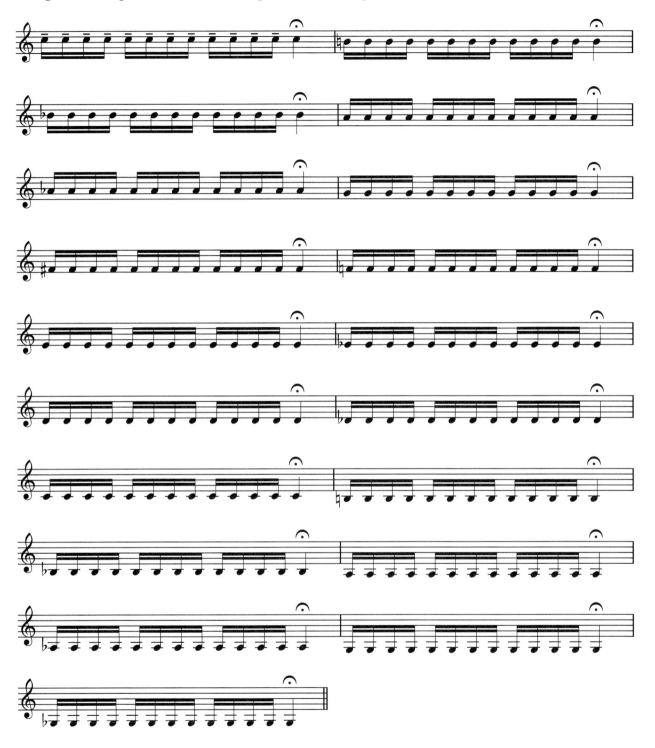

Because of the small cup diameter and lip tension needed to play the trumpet, it is essential that flexibility exercises be approached cautiously to avoid tension and undue lip pressure.

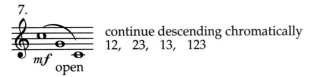

continue descending chromatically
12,   23,   13,   123

Do not move to new exercise until #7 is accomplished without tension.

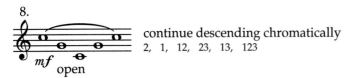

continue descending chromatically
2,   1,   12,   23,   13,   123

Master 8 before moving to 9.

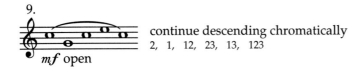

continue descending chromatically
2,   1,   12,   23,   13,   123

Master 9 before moving to 10.

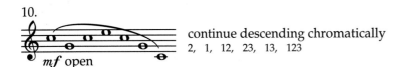

continue descending chromatically
2,   1,   12,   23,   13,   123

Master 10 before moving to 11.

continue descending chromatically
2,   1,   12,   23,   13,   123

13. Soft tongue only an initial attack. Use no tongue for the remainder of the phrase. Play three times in one breath, making certain there are no accents. Keep tone constant.

14.

15. Breath control and legato. Take normal speaking breath for first phrase and increase gradually for each succeeding phrase. Do not breathe in the middle of a ligature. Articulate each note with a soft legato tongue. Maintain strict tempo. The following model should be played in all major and minor keys.

etc., in all major
and minor keys

16.

17.

18.

Alternate between

Vary dynamics

TO DEVELOP HIGH RANGE

19. Overtone series over two octaves with added ninth. As embouchure grows stronger, add tenth, etc., to overtone series. Play relaxed, with no pressure, and as smoothly as possible.

For advanced players:

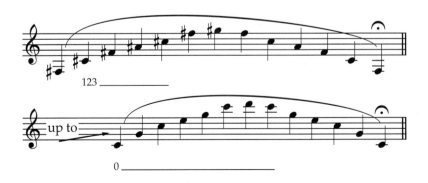

20. Do not breathe or relax embouchure during pause. Start note after pause with a very soft tongue. Don't push with lips. Try to hear tone before attack. Play in one breath.

21. Play completely relaxed. Round the end of each tone.

22. Make all notes equal in value, tone, etc. No accents. No pressure for high note. Be sure that the seventh is not allowed to replace the ninth in the overtone series, in descending from highest note.

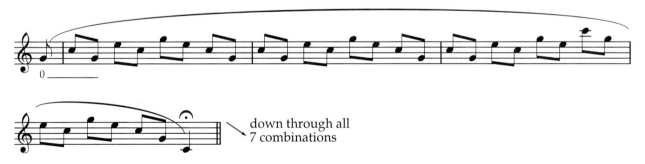

down through all
7 combinations

SELECTED LITERATURE FOR TRUMPET

Prepared by Neal Woolworth and printed with his permission. Additions to the list were provided by David Brown.

Level 1 = beginning
Level 2 = 2 and 3 years
Level 3 = junior high, early high school
Level 4 = advanced high school, early college
Level 5 = junior/senior in college
Level 6 = graduate/professional

Methods and Studies

Level 1

Edmondson, *Developing Band Book 1*, Edmondson & McGinty

Edwards-Hovey, *Method Book 1*, Belwin

Hering, *The Advancing Trumpeter*, Fischer

Lillya, *Method for Trumpet and Cornet, Book 1*, Balquhidder Music

O'Reilly, *Accent on Achievement, Book 1*, Alfred Pub. Co.

O'Reilly, *Yamaha Band Ensembles, Book 1*, Alfred Pub. Co.

Pearson, *Standard of Excellence, Book 1*, Kjos Music Co.

Rubank, *Elementary Method*

Rusch, *Hal Leonard Elementary Band Method*, Hal Leonard Pub. Co.

Level 2

Brandt, *Thirty-Four Studies*, International

Clarke, *Technical Studies*, Fischer

Edmondson, *Developing Band Book 2*, Edmondson & McGinty

Edwards-Hovey, *Method Book 2*, Belwin

Hering, *Fifty Recreational Studies*, Fischer

Hering, *Forty Progressive Etudes*, Fischer

Hering, *The Progressing Trumpeter*, Fischer

Lautzenheiser, *Essential Elements 2000*

Lillya, *Method for Trumpet and Cornet, Book 2*, Balquhidder Music

O'Reilly, *Accent on Achievement, Book 2*, Alfred Pub. Co.

O'Reilly, *Yamaha Band Ensembles, Book 2*, Alfred Pub. Co.

Ostling, *Time Out for Ensembles*, Belwin

Pearson, *Standard of Excellence, Book 2*, Kjos Music Co.

Ployhar, *Recommended Warm-Up Technique Book*, Belwin

Ployhar, *Tone and Technique*, Belwin

Rusch, *Intermediate Band Method*, Hal Leonard Pub. Co.

Ryden, *Classical Quartets for All*, Belwin

Skornicka, *Rubank Intermediate Method*, Rubank

Voxman, *Selected Studies*, Rubank

Level 3

Arban, *Complete Method*, Fischer

Clarke, *Characteristic Studies*, Fischer

Colin, *Lip Flexibilities, Volumes I–II*, Colin

Edmondson, *Developing Band Book 3*, Edmondson & McGinty

Elledge, *Band Technique Step by Step*, Kjos Music Co.

Erickson, Frank, *Technique through Performance*, Alfred Pub. Co.

Getchell, *Second Book of Practical Studies for the Cornet and Trumpet*, Belwin

Goldman, *Practical Studies for the Trumpet*, Fischer

Gower and Voxman, *Rubank Advanced Methods*, Rubank

Hering, *Thirty-two Etudes*, Fischer

Hering, *Twenty-four Advanced Etudes*, Fischer

Nagel, *Rhythmic Studies*, Mentor

O'Reilly, *Accent on Achievement, Book 3*, Alfred Pub. Co.

Pearson, *Standard of Excellence, Book 3*, Kjos Music Co.

Ployhar, *Recommended Warm-Up Technique Book*, Belwin

Ployhar, *Tone and Technique*, Belwin

Rusch, *Hal Leonard Advanced Band Method*, Hal Leonard Pub. Co.

Ryden, *Classical Quartets for All*, Belwin

Schlossberg, *Daily Drills and Technical Studies*, Baron

Smith, *Symphonic Warm-ups*, Hal Leonard Pub. Co.

Stamp, *Warm-ups and Studies*, Editions BIM

Level 4

Bartold, ed., *Orchestral Studies, Volumes I–V*, International

Borgogni, *Twenty-four Vocalises*, Leduc

Bousquet, *Thirty-six Celebrated Studies*, Fischer

Hickman, *Music Speed Reading*, Wimbledon

Irons, *Twenty-seven Groups of Exercises*, Southern

Sachse, *One Hundred Studies*, International

Level 5

Charlier, *Thirty-six Transcendental Etudes*, Leduc

Gates, *Odd Meter Etudes*, Gornston

Gordon, *Daily Trumpet Routines*, Fischer

Gordon, *Systematic Approach to Daily Practice*, Fischer

Harbison, *Technical Studies for the Modern Trumpet*, Aebersold

Hickman, *The Piccolo Trumpet*, Tromba

Longinotti, *Studies in the Modern and Classical Style*, International

Lin, *Lip Flexibilities*, Balquhidder Music

Shew, *Exercise and Etudes*, Balquhidder Music

Smith, *Lip Flexibility on the Trumpet*, Sicher

Vizzutti, *Book 1, Technical Studies*, Alfred Pub. Co.

Vizzutti, *Book 2, Harmonic Studies*, Alfred Pub. Co.

Vizzutti, *Book 3, Melodic Studies*, Alfred Pub. Co.

Voisin, ed., *Orchestral Studies, Volumes VI–X*, International

Weast, *Keys to Natural Performance*, Brass World

Level 6

Arban-Maire, *Célèbre Méthode Complète, Volume III*, Leduc

Blatter, Zonn, Hickman, *Contemporary Trumpet Studies*, Tromba

Nagel, *Speed Studies*, Mentor

Orchestral Studies—Strauss, International

Orchestral Studies—Wagner, International

Pietzel, *Die Trompete*, University Music Press

Smith, *Top Tones for the Trumpeter*, Fischer

Wade, *Virtuoso Works for Trumpet*, Colin

Webster, *The Piccolo Trumpet*, Brass Press

Solos

Level 1

Bach-Fitzgerald, *Bist du bei mir* (Aria), Belwin

Belwin-Mills, *B♭ Trumpet Solos*, Belwin

Buchtel, *Czech Dance Song*, Kjos Music Co.

The Canadian Brass Book of Beginning Trumpet Solos, The Canadian Brass on the Companion CDs, Hal Leonard Pub. Co.

The Canadian Brass Book of Easy Trumpet Solos, The Canadian Brass on the Companion CDs, Hal Leonard Pub. Co.

Feldstein, *First Solo Songbook*, Belwin

Hering, *Miniature Classics*, Fischer

Snell, *Belwin Master Solos (Easy)*, Belwin

Vandercook, *Sirius*, Rubank

Weber, *Cornet Soloist*, Belwin

Level 2

Althouse, *Trumpet Soloist*, Alfred

Anderson, *A Trumpeter's Lullaby*, Belwin

Beeler, *Solos for the Trumpet Player*, Schirmer

The Canadian Brass Book of Intermediate Trumpet Solos, The Canadian Brass on the Companion CDs, Hal Leonard Pub. Co.

Clarke, *Maid of the Mist*, Warner Brothers

Corelli-Fitzgerald, *Sonata VIII*, Presser

Lethridge, *A Handel Solo Album*, Oxford University Press

Meyer, *Four Miniature Classics*, Fischer

Nagel, *Baroque Music Collection*, Belwin

Snell, *Belwin Master Solos (Intermediate)*, Belwin

Vandercook, *Regal*, Rubank

Voxman, ed., *Concert and Contest Collection*, Rubank

Level 3

Balay, *Petite Piece Concertante*, Belwin

Barat, *Andante et Scherzo*, Leduc

Barat, *Fantasie en mi bémol*, Leduc

Clarke, *The Carnival of Venice*, Warner Brothers

Handel-Fitzgerald, *Aria con Variazioni*, Fischer

Lamb, *Classic Festival Solos*, Warner Brothers

Levy, et al., *Ideal Collection of Famous Cornet Solos*, Fischer

Ropartz, *Andante et Allegro*, Fischer

Rubank, *Book of Trumpet Solos*, Rubank

Soloist Folio (cornet solos), Rubank

Voxman, *Concert and Contest Collection*, Rubank

Level 4

Arutiunian, *Aria et Scherzo*, Leduc

Balay, *Prélude et Ballade*, Belwin

Bennett, *Rose Variations*, Presser

Chance, *Credo*, Boosey & Hawkes

Charlier, *Solo de Concours*, Belwin

Clarke, *The Debutante*, Warner Brothers

Dello Joio, *Sonata*, Hal Leonard Pub. Co.

Gabaye, *Boutade*, Leduc

Gaubert, *Cantabile et Scherzetto*, Cundy-Bettoney

Goedicke, *Concert Etude*, MCA

Haydn, *Concerto in E-flat*, Universal

Hovhaness, *Prayer of Saint Gregory*, Peer International

Kaminski, *Concertino*, Israeli Music

Kennan, *Sonata*, Warner Brothers

Latham, *Suite*, Presser

Purcell, *Sonata No. 1*, King

Riisager, *Concertino*, Wilhellm Hansen

Simon, *Willow Echoes*, Fischer

Vizzutti, *20 Dances for Trumpet*, Hal Leonard Pub. Co.

Vizzutti, *Trumpet Solos for the Performing Artist* (includes CD or tape), Alfred Music Co.

Level 5

Arutiunian, *Concerto*, International

Bellstedt, *La Mandolinata*, Southern

Bozza, *Caprice*, Leduc

Brandt, *Concertpiece No. 1*, International

Ewazen, *Sonata*, Southern

Hindemith, *Sonata*, Schott

Hummel, *Concerto in E-flat*, Universal

Ibert, *Impromptu*, Leduc

Peeters, *Sonata*, C. F. Peters

Stevens, *Sonata*, C. F. Peters

Stradella, *Sonata*, King

Tartini, *Concerto*, Selmer

Torelli, *Concerto in D, G. 1*, Musica Rara

Torelli, *Concerto in D, G. 8*, Musica Rara

Level 6

Bitsch, *Four Variations on a Theme by Scarlatti*, Leduc

Campo, *Times*, Dario Music

Casterede, *Sonatine*, Leduc

Davies, *Sonata*, Schott

Enesco, *Legend*, International

Freidman, *Solus*, Brass Press

Hertel, *Concerto*, Brass Press

Honegger, *Intrada*, Leduc

Jolivet, *Concertino*, Editions Durand

Lovelock, *Concerto*, Southern

Molter, *Concerto in D, No. 1*, Brass Press

Mozart, L., *Concerto in D*, Billaudot

Neruda, *Concerto in E-flat*, Musica Rara

Planel, *Concerto*, Editions Musicale Transatlantiques

Telemann, *Concerto in D (di Melante)*, Sikorski

Tomasi, *Concerto*, Leduc

Turrin, *Caprice*, Brass Press

Texts

Altenburg-Tarr, *Trumpeter's and Kettledrummer's Art*, Band Press

Baines, *Brass Instruments, Their History and Development*, Faber

Bate, *The Trumpet and Trombone*, Ernest Benn

Bendinelli-Tarr, *Entire Art of Trumpet Playing*, Brass Press

Cardoso, *Playing Trumpet in the Orchestra*, Cardoso

Clarke, *How I Became a Cornetist*, Holton

Dahlquist, *The Keyed Trumpet and Its Greatest Virtuoso, Anton Weindinger*, Brass Press

Eliason, *Early American Brass Instrument Makers*, Brass Press

Eliason, *Graves and Co., Instrument Makers*, Brass Press

Eliason, *Keyed Bugles in the United States*, Smithsonian Institution Press

Fantini-Tarr, *Modo per imparare*, Brass Press

Farkas, *Art of Brass Playing*, Wind Music

Farkas, *Art of Musicianship*, Musical Publishers

Johnson, *Art of Trumpet Playing*, University of Iowa Press

Mendez, *Prelude to Brass Playing*, Fischer

Smithers, *Music and History of the Baroque Trumpet before 1721*, Oxford University Press

LIST OF RECORDINGS
(Compiled by David Brown)

Album Title	Contents	Performer/s	Label
The Best of Timofey Dokshitser	Arutiunian, *Konzert* Hummel, *Konzert* Haydn, *Konzert* Tartini, *Konzert* Handel, *Larghetto* Bach/Gounod, *Ave Maria*	Timofey Dokshitser	Marcophon CD 954-2
Bret Jackson, Trumpet	Pierce, *Danza Comique* Bitsch, *Capriccio* Arnold, *Fantasy for Trumpet* Arutiunian, *Aria et Scherzo* Agafonikov, *Sonata* Plog, *Four Concert Duets* Ritter, George, *Sonata* Vizzutti, *Cascades* Gabaye, *Boutade*	Bret Jackson	Summit Records DCD153
Carnaval	Arban, *Variations sur "Le Carnaval de Venise"* Clarke, *The Debutante* Traditional, *Believe Me, If All Those Endearing Young Charms* Levy, *Grand Russian Fantasia* Paganini, *Moto Perpetuo* Traditional, *'Tis the Last Rose of Summer* Rimsky-Korsakov, *The Flight of the Bumblebee* Bellstedt, *Napoli* Arban, *Fantaisie Brillante* Traditional, *Sometimes I Feel like a Motherless Child* Clarke, *Valse Brillante*	Wynton Marsalis	CBS Records MK 42137
Cornet Favorites	Clarke, *From the Shores of the Mighty Pacific* Clarke, *Sounds of the Hudson* Simon, *Willow Echoes* Arban, *Fantaisie and Variations on the "Carnival of Venice"* Thomson, *At the Beach—Concert Waltz* Clarke, *The Debutante* Höhne, *Slavische Fantasie* Clarke, *The Bride of the Waves* Clarke, *Cousins* Clarke, *Maid of the Mist* Smith, *The Cascades-Polka Brilliant*	Gerard Schwarz	Elektra Nonesuch 79157-2
David Hickman, Trumpet	Chance, *Credo* Stevens, *Sonata* Bennett, *Rose Variations* Presser, *Suite for Trumpet* Turrin, *Caprice* Kennan, *Sonata* Dello Joio, *Sonata* Mendez, *Scherzo in D Minor*	David Hickman	Crystal Records CD668

LIST OF RECORDINGS (cont.)
(Compiled by David Brown)

Album Title	Contents	Performer/s	Label
Famous Classical Trumpet Concertos	Hummel, *Concerto in E* Hertel, *Concerto in C* Stamitz, *Concerto in D* Haydn, *Concerto in E♭* Richter, *Concerto in D* Mozart, *Concerto in D* Hertel, *Concerto No. 1 in E♭* Molter, *Concerto No. 1 in D* M. Haydn, *Concerto No. 2 in C* Corelli, *Sonata in D for Trumpet,* *2 Violins and Continuo* Albinoni, *Concerto in B♭* Albinoni/Giazotto, *Adagio in G minor* Clarke, *Trumpet Tune* Bach, *Chorale Preludes* Gounod, *Ave Maria*	Hakan Hardenberger	Philips 289 464 028-2
In Gabriel's Garden	Mouret, *Rondeau* Clarke, *The Prince of Denmark's March* Torelli, *Sonata in D Major* Clarke, *The King's March* Torelli, *Sinfonia in D Major* Clarke, *An Ayre* Purcell, *Sonata No. 2 in D Major* Purcell, *Rondeau from Abdelazar* Torelli, *Sonata á 5 No. 1 in D Major* Dandrieu, *Rondeau* Torelli, *Sonata in D Major* Charpentier, *Prelude from Te Deum* Torelli, *Sinfonia con Tromba in D Major* Stanley, *Trumpet Voluntary* Bach, *Brandenburg Concerto No. 2*	Wynton Marsalis	Sony Classical SK 66 244
The London Concert	Haydn, *Concreto in E♭* L. Mozart, *Concerto in D* Fasch, *Concerto in D* Hummel, *Concerto in E*	Wynton Marsalis	Sony Classical SK 57 497
Thomas Stevens, Trumpet	Hindemith, *Sonata* Bozza, *Caprice* Ropartz, *Andante and Allegro* Barat, *Andante and Scherzo* Bozza, *Lied* Bozza, *Badinage* Poulenc, *Sonata* Borden, *Six Dialogues for Trumpet and* *Trombone* Lewis, *Monophony VII*	Thomas Stevens	Crystal Records CD761
Trumpet Concertos	Bach, *Brandenburg Concerto No. 2 in* *F major* Handel, *Suite in D major* Telemann, *Concerto in D* Stoelzel, *Concerto in D* M. Haydn, *Concerto in D* J. Haydn, *Concerto in E♭* Torelli, *Concerto in D* Albinoni, *Concerto in D minor* Tartini, *Concerto in D* Vivaldi, *Concerto for 2 Trumpets*	Maurice Andre	EMI Classics CDZB 7 69152 2

LIST OF RECORDINGS (cont.)
(Compiled by David Brown)

Album Title	Contents	Performer/s	Label
	Marcello, *Concerto in C minor* Cimerosa, *Concerto in C major*		
Trumpet Concertos	Manfredini, *Concerto for 2 Trumpets in D* Vivaldi, *Concerto for 2 Trumpets in C* Torelli, *Concerto in D Major* Corelli, *Sonata in D Major* Albinoni, *Concerto in B♭ Major* Hertel, *Concerto in E♭ Major* Hummel, *Concerto in E♭ Major*	Helmut Hinger and Andre Bernard	Sony Classical SBK 47633
Trumpet in Our Time	Rouse, *The Avatar* Korf, *The Living Daylights* Sampson, *The Mysteries Remain* Ketting, *Intrada* Wolpe, *Solo Piece for Trumpet* Sampson, *Solo* Kennan, *Sonata* Blacher, *Divertimento for Trumpet, Trombone, and Piano*	Raymond Mase	Summit Records DCD148
20th Century Settings for Trumpet	Stevens, *Sonata* Tull, *Profiles for Solo Trumpet* Petrassi, *Fanfare for 3 Trumpets* Campo, *Two Studies for Trumpet and Guitar* Plog, *Animal Ditties* Erickson, *Kryl* Hindemith, *Sonata*	Anthony Plog	Crystal Records CD663

: HORN

HISTORY AND DEVELOPMENT OF THE HORN

The primitive horn was more conical and less cylindrical than the primitive trumpet (Figures 9.1 and 9.2).

The Alphorn, a type of primitive horn, was sounded in some Catholic cantons in Switzerland to signify the commencement of evening prayer (Figure 9.3).

One of the earliest examples of a hornlike instrument was the Scandinavian lur, dated to the sixth century B.C. and used militarily. The cup-shaped mouthpiece may have accounted for its spreading popularity throughout Europe (Figure 9.4).

The traditional hunting horn, used in Europe during the Middle Ages, had a great effect on the development of the horn. Hunting horns were used to conduct the hunt in an orderly fashion. Horn calls identified animals, started and ended the hunt, and celebrated the successful completion of the chase. These calls are musically significant because they gradually increased the number of notes that the horn player had to play.

The sixteenth-century hunting horn was made of wood and metal and covered with leather or some other material. As the hunting horns became longer, there was a natural tendency to curve them for ease of handling. The hunting horn curve, circular rather than S-shaped like the trumpet, was a necessity because a long, straight tube—or even a semicircular instrument—would be extremely difficult to handle during a hunt. The circular development of the horn placed the bell of the instrument where the player could modify the tone quality. The hunting horn, like all other brass instruments at this period of development, was capable of playing only the natural harmonic series made possible by the total length of the tube (Figure 9.5).

The French were the first to lengthen the tube of the circular horn so that many notes were available from the harmonic series. The English hunting horn was shorter and consequently had fewer notes at its disposal.

FIGURE 9.1
End blown

FIGURE 9.2
Side blown

FIGURE 9.3
Alphorn (as long as 12 feet)

By the eighteenth century, the horn was used in orchestras in France, England, and Italy. Operas by Reinhard, Keiser, Galliard, Handel, and Scarlatti used the hunting horn before the second half of the eighteenth century. In these works, the horn was treated much the same as when playing the calls and fanfares of the hunt. Handel, Keiser, and others gradually wrote horn parts calling for melodic passages in combination with other instruments. The eighteenth-century hunting horn had greater tube length and bell flare than the sixteenth-century hunting horn (Figure 9.6).

FIGURE 9.4
Lur

FIGURE 9.5
The sixteenth-century hunting horn had a shorter length and less bell flare than that of the eighteenth-century hunting horn.

FIGURE 9.6
Eighteenth-century hunting horn

Crooks expanded the length of the instrument and were an early mechanical improvement of brass instruments. These crooks, consisting of coiled or bent brass tubes, were inserted into the main tube of the instrument and made possible the use of the natural horn in all keys. The composer indicated the desired key, and the performer supplied the necessary crook (Figures 9.7 and 9.8).

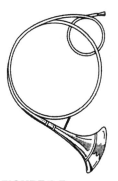

FIGURE 9.7
This is one version of the eighteenth-century natural horn used in orchestras.

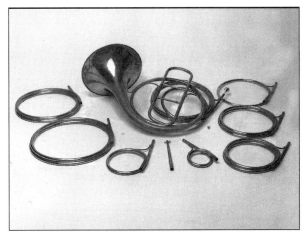

FIGURE 9.8
Natural horn with crooks, owned by Llewellyn B. Humphreys, Utah Symphony Personnel Manager. Photographed with his permission.

A. J. Hampel of the Royal Orchestra in Dresden developed crooks and made other important discoveries that contributed to the development of the horn. For example, while trying to devise a system to soften the rather harsh tone quality of the open horn, he found that by inserting his hand in the bell of the horn, he could obtain a note one half-tone lower, and that by completely stopping the bell with his hand, he could make the tone fall a full step and more. This discovery made possible, for the first time, a complete chromatic scale. The notes in the harmonic series of the open horn, combined with the notes from the half and completely stopped horn, resulted in many new uses of the horn. Although this scale was not perfect—the tone quality of the open tones differed from the quality of the stopped tones—just having these notes available contributed a great deal to the use of the instrument. It is possible that during this period good performers could control the difference in tone quality between the stopped tones and the open tones (Figure 9.9).

The concertos of Mozart and Haydn use the natural horn and represent the most highly developed musical scores for this instrument in the eighteenth century. Neither composer made extensive use of hand stopping, using almost exclusively the notes available in the natural harmonics of crooked horns.

The development of the valve by Bluehmel in 1813 made possible the eventual development of the horn in use today (Figure 9.10).

FIGURE 9.9
Hand horn

FIGURE 9.10
This is an early-nineteenth-century two-valve horn, an ancestor of the modern horn.

THE MODERN HORN

Like the trumpet, the horn in use today bears little resemblance to its predecessors, with the exception of its circular shape. Despite the common background of the horn and the trumpet, today's instruments are quite different. These differences include the following: 1) The bore of the horn is conical throughout most of its length, whereas that of the trumpet is cylindrical. The horn is cylindrical only in the valve and tuning slides. This difference in construction lends a more mellow sound to the horn. (2) The horn contains approximately twice as much tubing as the trumpet. 3) The mouthpiece of the trumpet is cupped with a sharp edge, while that of the horn is conical or funnel-shaped. The sharp edge of the trumpet mouthpiece contributes to brilliance, while the conical shape of the horn mouthpiece has the opposite effect.

The modern horn is a flexible instrument. It blends well with other instruments of the orchestra—so well with the woodwinds that it is sometimes referred to as a woodwind instrument. It is a regular member of the woodwind quintet, and much of the outstanding literature for the horn was written for this combination of instruments.

The tone quality of the horn varies from a mellow, full sound to a bright, brassy sound when the bell is stopped with the hand or a mute. It is capable of playing all types of musical passages. When the horn uses the upper harmonics, its open notes are very close together; this requires a very well-trained embouchure. Probably even more important is a well-trained ear that can readily distinguish intervals.

Modern orchestral scores usually call for four horns and occasionally for as many as eight. Because four horns are the standard instrumentation of the orchestra and the band, parts are usually written in four-part harmony. Unlike the trumpets, the horns are not given high to low parts from first to fourth horns, but are generally written for in an interlocking manner, the higher pitches being given to the first and third horns, with the lower pitches written for second and fourth horns. This interlocking of parts has become so traditional among composers that horn players sometimes designate themselves as first or third horn players if they are proficient in the upper register, and as second or fourth horn players if proficient in the lower register. However, this tradition is disappearing, since most hornists today are well trained in the entire register of the instrument.

Three horns have found general acceptance among performers today: the single horn in F, the single horn in B-flat, and the double horn in F and

B-flat. Most hornists prefer the double horn, which provides the best features of both single horns. The basic instrument is the instrument in F, which is most satisfactory in tone production and range. The nomenclature is the same for all three instruments. Shown in Figure 9.11 is the double horn in F and B-flat.

The tube lengths of the horn are controlled in the same manner as those of the trumpet. The various valves may be used independently or in combination, resulting in seven different tube lengths. The first valve adds tubing that allows a pitch a whole step down, putting the horn in E-flat and adding approximately 20 inches to the horn length. The second valve adds approximately 10 inches of tubing, resulting in a pitch a half-step lower. The third valve—which for acoustical reasons mentioned in Chapter One is a little longer than the combination of the first and second valves—adds a little more than a step and a half downward, putting the horn in the rather low key of D and lengthening the tube approximately 31½ inches.

The double horn in F and B-flat has two sets of valve shanks and a thumb valve to change from one set to the other. The valves are usually rotary rather than piston type. When the thumb valve is depressed on a double instrument, approximately four feet of tubing are eliminated, and the harmonic series on the open horn is raised a perfect fourth in pitch from F to B-flat. The B-flat side of the double horn, being 48 inches shorter than the F horn, has valve shanks that are shorter than those of the F.

The seven different harmonic series for the horn in F and the horn in B-flat (see below) result in a complete chromatic scale that covers the entire range of the instrument. All parts are transposed a fifth above concert pitch. Since many notes appear in more than one series, they may be played with more than one valve combination and on either the F or B-flat horn. The chromatic fingering chart that follows gives all fingerings for both F and B-flat horn.

Note the usually accepted change from F to B-flat horn indicated by the asterisk. Most teachers will give the inexperienced student on the double horn only one set of fingerings. They indicate only F fingerings below the indicated change point and only B-flat fingerings above. Because each horn may

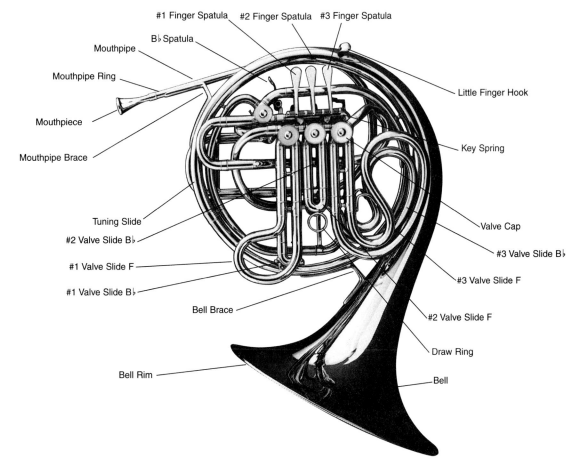

FIGURE 9.11
Horn nomenclature (Courtesy of C. G. Conn Division of United Musical Instruments, USA, Inc., www.unitedmusical.com)

HARMONIC FINGERING CHART

Horn in F

---

*The fundamental is impossible to play on the horn in F.
**This set of partials is generally so out-of-tune as to be unusable.

HARMONIC SERIES
Horn in B♭

*This set of partials is generally so out-of-tune as to be unusable.
**These notes are generally unplayable on the B-flat horn.

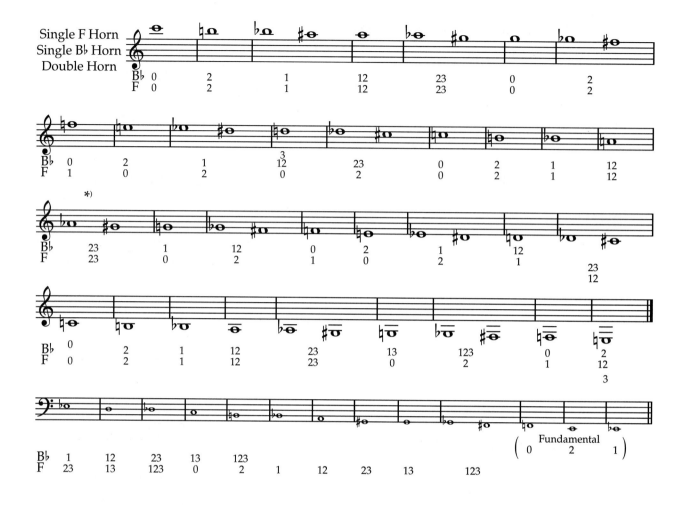

respond better on one key than the other, the ultimate goal is to develop a fingering chart for the individual instrument being played. This, however, remains for the student as he or she progresses from an inexperienced performer to one with more skill.

The instrument used by professional hornists and advanced students is almost without exception the double horn in F and B-flat. However, many have extolled the advantages in the upper register which the single horn in B-flat affords. The B-flat horn provides greater security in attack in the upper register, since, for equivalent sounds, the harmonics do not lie so close together as on the single horn in F.

Many single horns in B-flat come equipped with a fourth valve that is operated by the thumb. It is often called a "muting" valve, and this leads to misconceptions about its use. The fourth valve does not mute the horn; it simply lowers the pitch enough so that the player can stop the instrument by hand

without transposing. This valve simply adds tubing to the instrument, lowering the pitch slightly more than one half-step, and the length of the valve tube must be adjusted for muting, according to the distance the performer extends his hand into the bell. The fourth valve may also be used in conjunction with the other three valves to obtain good intonation.

TRANSPOSITION

The horn family has its ancestry in the natural horn. Because the natural horn is now obsolete, many writings of the early composers need to be transposed. Examples in various keys of written and sounding notes are shown on the following chart.

Table 9.1, a list of keys indicated for horn with their French and German equivalents, may prove helpful.

TRANSPOSITION BY INTERVAL

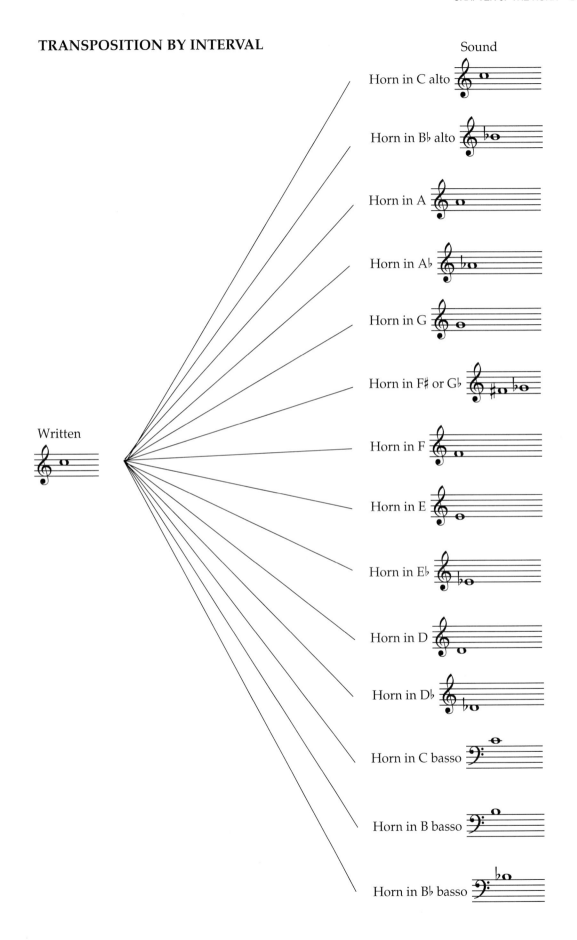

Examples from the standard literature may help the student become more familiar with transpositions from horn parts in different keys to that of the horn in F.

TABLE 9.1

FOREIGN LANGUAGE EQUIVALENTS

English	German	French
Horn in F	Auf F	Fa
Horn in E	Auf E	Mi
Horn in E♭	Auf Es	Mi-bémol
Horn in D	Auf D	Re
Horn in D♭	Auf Des	Re-bémol
Horn in F♯	Auf Fis	Fa-dièse
Horn in G	Auf G	Sol
Horn in A♭	Auf As	La-bémol
Horn in A	Auf A	La
Horn in C	Auf C	Ut
Horn in B♭	Auf B	Si-bémol
Horn in B	Auf H	Si

Transposition by Interval from F

While it is possible to transpose through the use of clefs (see the section on transposition for the trumpet family), the most common transposition practice is to read a note an interval away from the written pitch. Since a hornist learns the basic instrument from parts written in F, then uses this key as a point of departure to play the parts for the various horns, the following intervallic transpositions are used, starting from the basic instrument in F:

Transposition by interval is a two-step process.

1. You must transpose up or down by the appropriate interval.
2. You must change the key signature by the same interval.

The following is a list of the transpositions most commonly called for in the horn literature.

Step 1: Calculate the interval from the key of your horn (e.g., F horn) to the requested transposition.				Step 2: Transpose the key signature up or down by the same interval.	
Key of Horn Being Played		Requested Transposition	Interval to move up or down	Notes and Accidentals Assume the Key* of:	New Key* Signature
	1.	Horn in C alto	P5 up	C	G
	2.	Horn in B alto	aug4 up	C	F♯
	3.	Horn in B♭ alto	P4 up	C	F
	4.	Horn in A	M3 up	C	E
	5.	Horn in A♭	m3 up	C	E♭
	6.	Horn in G	M2 up	C	D
	7.	Horn in F♯–G♭	m2 up	C	C♯
F	8.	Horn in E	m2 down	C	B
	9.	Horn in E♭	M2 down	C	B♭
	10.	Horn in D	m3 down	C	A
	11.	Horn in D♭	M3 down	C	A♭
	12.	Horn in C basso	P4 down	C	G
	13.	Horn in B basso	dim5 down	C	G♭ or F♯
	14.	Horn in B♭ basso	P5 down	C	F

*Horns historically do not use key signatures; however, the application of a mental key signature will help with the transposition and accidentals.

Examples:

If you are playing an **F horn** and the music says:

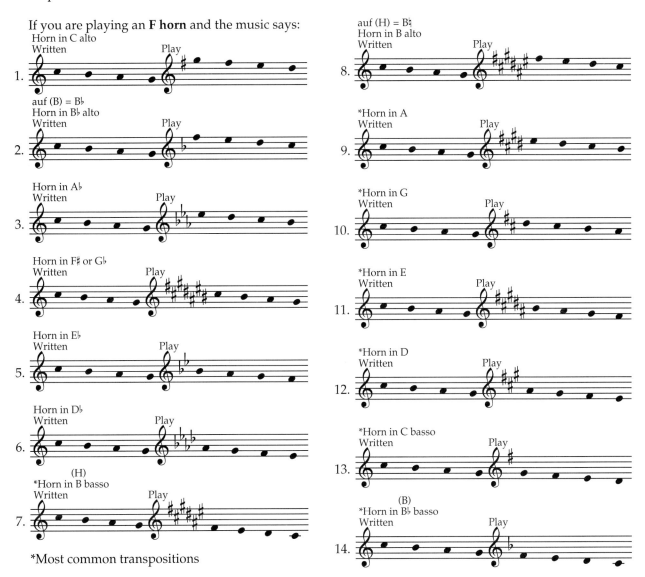

*Most common transpositions

EXCERPTS FROM ORCHESTRAL REPERTOIRE

(Horn in H is B in German) **Don Carlos** Verdi

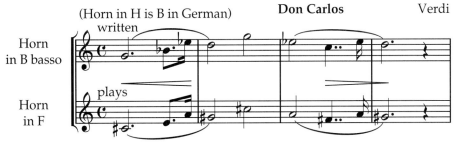

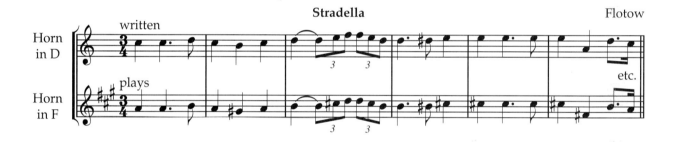

PLAYING POSITIONS FOR THE HORN

The horn is the only brass instrument on which the left hand manipulates the valves. Historically, the right hand was placed in the bell to act as a stop. After the invention of the valve, the practice of placing the right hand in the bell of the instrument continued in order to control tone quality and intonation, and for muting.

The horn is normally played while seated (Figure 9.12) but can be played while standing (Figure 9.13). Of primary concern should be a playing position that allows for maximum breath control, finger dexterity, intonation control, and tone quality. The hornist should hold the instrument so that the mouthpiece fits directly on the embouchure without having to move the head from its normal upright position. Most hornists prefer to rest the bell on the outside of the right upper thigh, while others prefer to hold the instrument entirely away from the body. The horn should not be pulled tightly against the thigh, since this tends to stifle the vibration of the bell and thus impairs the tone quality.

The left hand should be held in a fairly straight line extending from the forearm, with the fingers curved over the tubing and resting lightly on the valves. The fingers should not be excessively curved, nor too straight, and should rest lightly on the valve levers (Figure 9.14). The fleshy part of the thumb should rest on the B-flat change valve (Figure 9.15).

The most important aspect of holding the horn is the position of the right hand, used for muting, stopping, changing tone color, and intonation. The hand should be formed with the fingers held together and the thumb along the edge of the hand. The hornist should cup the hand slightly, with the thumb touching the index finger, taking care that there is not an opening between the thumb and the hand (Figure 9.16). The hand is inserted into the bell of the instrument so that the backs of the fingers and the top of the thumb touch the bell (Figure 9.17). The hand is now in a position to partially support the horn. In altering the tone quality or stopping the horn, the heel of the hand is held in such a way as to close or open the bell. The more the bell is closed, the darker the tone quality will be and the flatter the pitch will become. The less the bell is covered, the brighter the tone quality and the higher the pitch. The amount of closure each performer uses is a matter of personal taste or is dictated by the style of music played. It is important in the upper register that the hand be not too far out of the bell, or the notes may be unfocused.

FIGURE 9.13
Standing position, horn

FIGURE 9.14
Left hand position, horn

FIGURE 9.12
Seated position for horn

FIGURE 9.15
Left thumb position, horn

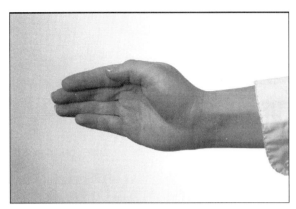

FIGURE 9.16
Right hand prepared for insertion in bell

FIGURE 9.17
Right hand inserted

Muting and Stopping the Horn

Muting the horn is accomplished by inserting a conical mute constructed of cardboard, metal, wood, or plastic with strips of cork to regulate the amount of muting. *Stopping* the horn is accomplished by inserting the hand into the bell of the instrument. The degree of insertion regulates the amount of stopping. There is a great deal of difference in tonal quality between a muted and a stopped horn; however, many players neglect to make the distinction between muting and stopping. Muting is referred to as follows: in English as *muted,* in German as *mit Dämpfer* or *gedämpft,* in French as *avec sourdine,* and in Italian as *con sordino.* Stopping by means of the hand is referred to as follows: in English as *stopped,* in German as *gestopft,* in French as *bouché,* and in Italian as *chiuso.* (There is a common misconception

concerning the German term *schmetternd* and the French *cuivre.* These terms refer to the player's ability to play a loud, "brassy" sound rather than to muting or stopping.)

Indications to remove the mute and return to open horn are as follows: in English as *open,* in German as *ohne Dämpfer,* in French as *ouvrez,* and in Italian as *senza.* Indications to return to open horn from stopped horn are as follows: in English as *open,* in German as *nicht gestopft,* in French as *ouvrez,* and in Italian as *aperto.* The sign "+" over a note indicates in all languages that the note is stopped, and the sign "o" that the note is open.

Hand-stopping the horn raises the pitch approximately one half-step; consequently, the notes must be played as though they were written for horn in E. A facile technique of hand-stopping the horn is difficult to master and requires much practice (Figure 9.18). The student must be sure to completely stop the instrument, since an almost-stopped instrument flattens the pitch almost a half-step. This leads to the mistaken belief that stopping the horn flattens rather than raises the pitch a half-step. When playing stopped notes correctly, the student must transpose down a half-step. Stopping should always be done on the F-horn, because stopping the B-flat side of the instrument raises the pitch farther than a half-step, which cannot be corrected by transposition.

The marching horn is in F without the double horn capabilities of B-flat. The marching horn's advantage is that the forward bell allows the sound to be projected directly toward the audience. It is held in the same way as the trumpet (Figure 9.19).

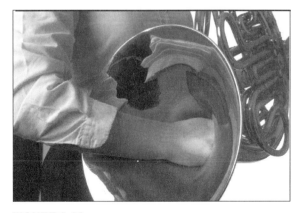

FIGURE 9.18
Right hand position for stopped horn

FIGURE 9.19
Marching horn

Two common mutes are manufactured for the horn—a transposing mute and a nontransposing one. The transposing mute requires the same transposition as the stopped horn; its value lies in its brilliant brassy tone. The nontransposing mute does not alter the pitch of the horn, and its tone is less brassy than the transposing mute. On both mutes the corks should be sandpapered until they fit the instrument and provide the desired tone quality.

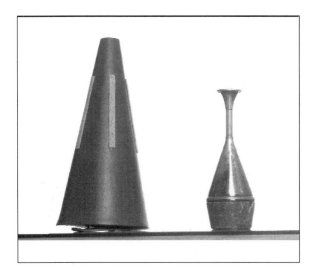

FIGURE 9.20
Horn mute (straight); horn mute (stopped)

Straight Mute is the standard mute for the horn and is designed to play in tune (Figure 9.20).

Stopped Mute is used as a substitute for stopping with the hand (Figure 9.20). This is usually designated with a "+," meaning to stop the horn, which produces the next ascending semi-tone and requires the horn player to play a half-step lower.

Tuning Horns

Single horns in F and B-flat have one main tuning slide, while the double horn in F and B-flat is equipped with two main tuning slides, one for each side of the instrument. Each horn, whether single or double, should be tuned first with this main tuning slide and with the right hand in the normal playing position in the bell. After the main tuning slide has been used to tune the open horn and after each valve slide has been used to tune the open horn, each valve slide should be tuned. Normally, manufacturers make the horn a little sharp with the valves all the way in; they must be pulled out in relation to their total length. For example, the second valve should have to be pulled out the least, the first a little more, and the third the most. Many hornists, for ease of replacement after emptying condensation, mark their main tuning slide and valve slides once they have the horn exactly in tune. A small change in the main tuning slide should not require any adjustment of the three valve slides, and the student should remember that tuning cannot be absolute. The performer must be able to hear beats and be able to tune them out quickly when playing with another performer. Playing in tune requires adjustment to the sounds of the other instruments and does not depend entirely on the way the instrument has been tuned, even though this can be a great help.

Intonation

For a discussion of intonation problems caused by characteristics of the overtone series and the three-valve, seven-combination system, see Chapters One and Eight.

The following example gives a chromatic scale that indicates whether the note is flat or sharp. The roman numerals show the degree. The hornist can adjust the pitch of the horn by closing the right hand in the bell to flatten or open the hand to sharpen.

INTONATION CHART B♭ AND F HORN

Roman numerals beneath the notes indicate the degree to which the pitch is out of tune.

I—Slightly out of tune
II—Moderately out of tune
III—Greatly out of tune
IV—Drastically out of tune

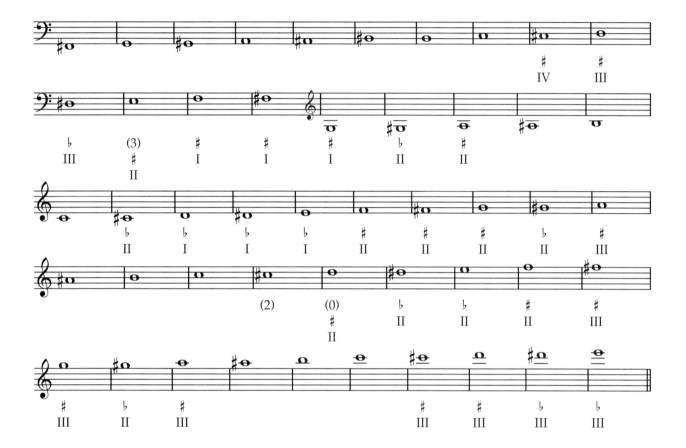

Summary of Notes Affected

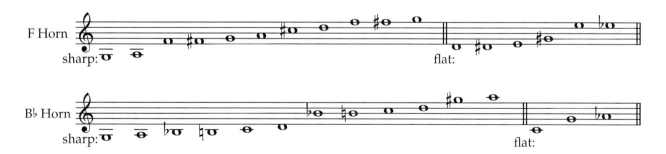

DAILY EMBOUCHURE AND FLEXIBILITY STUDIES

1. The first three exercises should be played chromatically descending for at least two octaves. Play with soft da or du tones.

4. To establish attack and tuning, attack with full MP tone. Round the end of each note. Never allow the tone to become brassy, and do not increase the volume after attack.

5. Use no tongue.

6. B♭ Horn

7. B♭ Horn

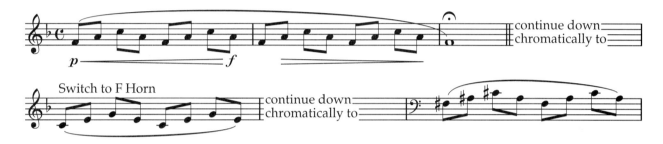

8. F Horn

To extend range upward, use more breath support and no pressure for upper note.

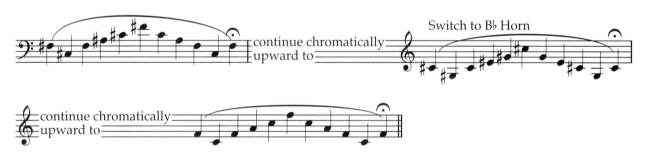

SELECTED LITERATURE FOR HORN

Methods and Studies

Level 1

Edmondson, *Developing Band Book 1*, Edmundson & McGinty

Howe, *Method for the French Horn*, Remick

Kopprasch, *Sixty Selected Studies*, Fischer

Maxime-Alphonse, *Deux cent Etudes Nouvelles*, 6 volumes, Leduc

O'Reilly, *Accent on Achievement, Book 1*, Alfred Pub. Co.

O'Reilly, *Yamaha Band Ensembles, Book 1*, Alfred Pub. Co.

Pearson, *Standard of Excellence, Book 1*, Kjos Music Co.

Rusch, *Hal Leonard Elementary Band Method*, Hal Leonard Pub. Co.

Yancich, *Method*, 2 vols., Wind Music

Level 2

Davies, *Scales and Arpeggios*, Belwin

Edmondson, *Developing Band Book 2*, Edmundson & McGinty

Kopprasch, *Sixty Selected Studies*, Fischer

Maxime-Alphonse, *Deux cents Etudes Nouvelles*, 6 volumes, Leduc

O'Reilly, *Accent on Achievement, Book 2*, Alfred Pub. Co.

O'Reilly, *Yamaha Band Ensembles, Book 2*, Alfred Pub. Co.

Ostling, *Time Out for Ensembles*, Belwin

Pearson, *Standard of Excellence, Book 2*, Kjos Music Co.

Ployhar, *Recommended Warm-up Technique Book*, Belwin

Ployhar, *Tone and Technique*, Belwin

Pottag-Andraud, *335 Selected Melodious Progressive and Technical Studies*, 2 vols., Southern

Rusch, *Hal Leonard Intermediate Band Method*, Hal Leonard Pub. Co.

Ryden, *Classical Quartets for All*, Belwin

Singer, *Embouchure Building*, Belwin

Yancich, *Method*, 2 vols., Wind Music

Level 3

Edmondson, *Developing Band Book 3*, Edmundson & McGinty

Elledge, *Band Technique Step by Step*, Kjos Music Co.

Erickson, *Technique through Performance*, Alfred Pub. Co.

Kopprasch, *Sixty Selected Studies*, Fischer

Maxime-Alphonse, *Deux cents Etudes Nouvelles*, 6 vols., Leduc

O'Reilly, *Accent on Achievement, Book 3*, Alfred Pub. Co.

Pearson, *Standard of Excellence, Book 3*, Kjos Music Co.

Ployhar, *Recommended Warm-up Technique Book*, Belwin

Ployhar, *Tone and Technique*, Belwin

Pottag-Andraud, *335 Selected Melodious Progressive and Technical Studies*, 2 vols., Southern

Rusch, *Hal Leonard Advanced Band Methods*, Hal Leonard Pub. Co.

Ryden, *Classical Quartets for All*, Belwin

Schantl, *Grand Theoretical and Practical Method for the Valve Horn*, Baldwin

Singer, *Embouchure Building*, Belwin

Smith, *Symphonic Warm-ups*, Hal Leonard Pub. Co.

Level 4

Huth, *Horn Etuden*, Schott

Kopprasch, *Sixty Selected Studies*, Fischer

Maxime-Alphonse, *Deux cent Etudes Nouvelles*, 6 vol., Leduc

Pottag-Andraud, *335 Selected Melodious Progressive and Technical Studies*, 2 vols., Southern

Schantl, *Grand Theoretical and Practical Method for the Valve Horn*, Baldwin

Singer, *Embouchure Building*, Belwin

Level 5

Chambers, *Orchestral Excerpts*, 7 vols., International

Huth, *Horn Etuden*, Schott

Jones, ed., *20th Century Orchestral Studies*, Schirmer

Kling, *Horn Schule*, Wind Music

Kopprasch, *Sixty Selected Studies*, Fischer

Maxime-Alphonse, *Deux cent Etudes Nouvelles*, 6 vols., Leduc

Moore, ed., *Operatic Horn Passages*, Presser

Pottag, *French Horn Passages*, 3 vols., Belwin

Pottag-Andraud, *335 Selected Melodious Progressive and Technical Studies*, 2 vols., Southern

Schantl-Pottag, *Preparatory Melodies to Solo Work*, Belwin

Singer, *Embouchure Building*, Belwin

Level 6

Chambers, *Orchestral Excerpts*, 7 vols., International

Jones, ed., *20th Century Orchestral Studies*, Schirmer

Kling, *Horn Schule*, Wind Music

Maxime-Alphonse, *Deux cent Etudes Nouvelles*, 6 vols., Leduc

Moore, ed., *Operatic Horn Passages*, Presser

Pottag, *French Horn Passages*, 3 vols., Belwin

Reynolds, *48 Etudes*, Schirmer

Solos

Level 1

Bakaleinikoff, *Canzona*, Belwin

Bakaleinikoff, *Cavatina*, Belwin

Belwin-Mills, *F Horn Solos*, Belwin

Bozza, *En Irelande*, Leduc

Bruch, *Kol Nidrei*, Columbia Pictures Pub.

The Canadian Brass Book of Beginning Horn Solos, The Canadian Brass on the Companion CDs, Hal Leonard Pub. Co.

The Canadian Brass Book of Easy Horn Solos, The Canadian Brass on the Companion CDs, Hal Leonard Pub. Co.

Chopin, *Cavatina*, Op. 10, No. 3, Kjos Music Co.

Clerisse, *L'Absent*, Leduc

Clerisse, *Chanson à Bercer*, Leduc

Feldstein, *First Solo Songbook*, Belwin

Goddard, *Berceuse*, from *Jocelyn*, Fischer

Gounod, *Ave Maria*, Fischer

Hauser, *At the Fair*, Fischer

Hauser, *Twilight Thoughts*, Fischer

Jarnefelt, *Berceuse*, Kendor

Kaplan, *Serenade*, Belwin

Martini, *Romance Célèbre*, Leduc

Mozart, *Sonata Theme*, Belwin

Ployhar, *Caprice*, Belwin

Ployhar, *The Hunt*, Belwin

Schubert, *Berceuse*, Elkan

Smith, *Nobility*, Belwin

Snell, *Belwin Master Solos* (Easy), Belwin

Strauss, *Allerseelen*, Op. 10, No. 8, Rubank

Level 2

Bakaleinikoff, *Canzona*, Belwin

Bakaleinikoff, *Cavatina*, Belwin

Bozza, *En Irelande*, Leduc

Bruch, *Kol Nidrei*, Columbia Pictures Pub.

The Canadian Brass Book of Intermediate Horn Solos, The Canadian Brass on the Companion CDs, Hal Leonard Pub. Co.

Chopin, *Cavatina*, Op. 10, No. 3, Kjos Music Co.

Clerisse, *L'Absent*, Leduc

Clerisse, *Chanson à Bercer*, Leduc

Corelli, *Adagio*, Wind Music

Fauré, *Après un rêve*, Music Press

Fauré, *Pie Jesu*, Fenetic Music

Gluck, "Melody" from *Orfeo*, Kendor Music

Goddard, *Berceuse*, from *Jocelyn*, Fischer

Gounod, *Ave Maria*, Fischer

Hauser, *At the Fair*, Fischer

Jarnefelt, *Berceuse*, Kendor Music

Jones, *First Solos for the Horn*, Schirmer

Kaplan, *Serenade*, Belwin

Lawton, ed., *The Young Horn Player*, 3 books, Editions Musicales

Lotti, *Ricercar*, Philarmusica Corp.

Luigini, *Romance*, Editions Billaudot

Mahler, "Primeval Light," from *The Youth's Magic Horn*, Editions Musicus

Martini, *Romance Célèbre*, Leduc

Mozart, *Sonata Theme*, Belwin

Ployhar, *Caprice*, Belwin

Ployhar, *The Hunt*, Belwin

Samazeuilh, *Evocation*, Editions Durand

Schubert, *Berceuse*, Elkan

Smith, *Nobility*, Belwin

Snell, *Belwin Master Solos* (Intermediate), Belwin

Solomon, *November Nocturne,* Southern

Strauss, *Allerseelen,* Op. 10, No. 8, Rubank

Yancich, ed., *15 Solos,* Western International

Level 3

Chabrier, *Larghetto for Horn,* Editions Salabert

Cherubini, *Concerto,* Editions Billaudot

Corelli, *Adagio,* Wind Music

d'Indy, V., *Andante,* Editions Billaudot

Glasunov, *Reverie,* Leeds

Jones, *Solos for the Horn Player,* Schirmer

Lamb, *Classic Festival Solos,* Warner Brothers

Mozart, *Adagio,* Sansone

Purcell, *Concerto,* Editions Billaudot

Ravel, *Pavane,* Editions Max Eschig

Romance, Schirmer

Samazeuilh, *Evocation,* Editions Durand

Solomon, *November Nocturne,* Southern

Strauss, *Allerseelen,* Op. 10, No. 8, Rubank

Strauss, "Andante" from *Concerto No. 2,* Boosey & Hawkes

Tchaikovsky, "Andante Cantabile" from *Symphony No. 5,* Fischer

Vivaldi, *Largo,* Marvin McCoy

Voxman, *Concert and Contest Collection,* Rubank

Yancich, ed., *15 Solos,* Western International

Level 4

Cherubini, *Concerto,* Editions Billaudot

Cooke, *Rondo in B♭,* Schott

Danzi, *Sonata in E♭,* Hofmeister

Dukas, *Villanelle,* Editions Durand

Frackenpohl, *Largo and Allegro,* Schirmer

Jones, *Solos for the Horn Player,* Schirmer

Mozart, *Four Horn Concertos,* Schirmer

Purcell, *Concerto,* Editions Billaudot

Romance, Schirmer

Rossini, *Prélude, Thème et Variations,* International Music Co.

Saint-Saëns, *Morceau du Concert,* Editions Durand

Strauss, F., *Concerto No. 1,* Op. 11, Belwin

Strauss, F., *Concerto No. 2,* Boosey and Hawkes

Yancich, ed., *15 Solos,* Western International

Level 5

Bassett, *Sonata for Horn and Piano,* Morris and Co.

Beethoven, *Sonata for Horn,* Editions Peters

Beversdorf, *Sonata,* Andraud

Bozza, *En Forêt,* Leduc

Donato, *Sonata,* Remick

Haydn, *Concertos No. 1 and 2,* Cundy-Bettoney

Heiden-Bernhard, *Sonata*

Hindemith, *Sonata for Horn,* Schott

Jacob, *Concerto for Horn,* Joseph Williams

Jones, *Solos for the Horn Player,* Schirmer

Mozart, *Four Horn Concertos,* Schirmer

Olson, *4 Fables, Hornists' Nest,* Hornseth Music Company

Strauss, *Concertos No. 1 and 2,* Boosey & Hawkes

Level 6

Bassett, *Sonata for Horn and Piano,* Morris and Co.

Beethoven, *Sonata for Horn,* Editions Peters

Beversdorf, *Sonata,* Andraud

Bozza, *En Forêt,* Leduc

Donato, *Sonata,* Remick

Haydn, *Concertos No. 1 and 2,* Cundy-Bettoney

Heiden-Bernhard, *Sonata,* Associated Music Publishers

Hindemith, *Sonata for Horn,* Schott

Jacob, *Concerto for Horn,* Williams

Strauss, *Concertos No. 1 and 2,* Boosey & Hawkes

LIST OF RECORDINGS
(Compiled by Claire Edwards Grover)

Album Title	Contents	Performer/s	Label
The Art of Dennis Brain	Dukas, *Villanelle* Beethoven, *Horn Sonata in F Major, Op. 17* Mozart, *Divertimento in E-flat Major, Op. 17* Dittersdorf, ed. Haas: *Partita in D Major* Schumann, *Adagio and Allegro, Op. 70* Haydn, *Symphony No. 31 in D Major* Mozart, *Concerto No. 2 in E-flat Major, K. 417*	Dennis Brain	Seraphim LP M-60040
Barry Tuckwell	Telemann, *Horn Concerto in D* Cherubini, *Sonata No. 2 in F for Horn and Strings* Förster, *Concerto in E-flat for Horn and Strings* Weber, *Horn Concertino in E Minor Op. 45* Mozart, L., *Concerto in D for Horn and Strings*	Barry Tuckwell	Angel LP S-36996
Dennis Brain	Strauss, *Concerto No. 1 in E-flat* Strauss, *Concerto No. 2 in E-flat* Hindemith, *Concerto*	Dennis Brain	EMI D 111294
Franz Joseph Haydn, Horn Concerti	Haydn, *Concerto No. 1 in D Major* Haydn, *Concerto No. 2 in D Major* Haydn, *Divertimento a Tré in E-flat major*	Michael Thompson	Musical Heritage Society CD 1718
Four American Sonatas for French Horn	Gates, *Sonata for Horn, op. 48* Stevens, *Sonata for Horn and Piano* Wilder, *Sonata No. 3 for Horn and Piano* Beversdorf, *Sonata for Horn and Piano*	Laurence Lowe	Tantara Records TCD 0799LL4
Richard Strauss, Horn Concerto	Strauss, *Horn Concerto No. 1 in E-flat major* Strauss, *Horn Concerto No. 2 in E-flat major*	Peter Dam	EMI Studio CD 1360
Mozart, Horn Concerti	Mozart, *Concerto in D-Major, K. 412* Mozart, *Concerto in E-flat Major, K. 447* Mozart, *Concerto in E-flat Major, K. 495* Mozart, *Rondo in E-flat for Horn and Orchestra, K. 371*	Peter Dam	Musical Heritage Society CD 5137591
Mozart, Horn Concertos Nos. 2 & 3	Mozart, W. A., *Concerto for Horn and Orchestra No. 3 in E-flat major, K. 447* Mozart, W. A., *Concerto for Horn and Orchestra No. 2 in E-flat major, K. 417*	William Purvis	Deutsche Grammophon CD 1100
Rössler-Rosetti, Horn Concertos No. 2 & 6	Rössler-Rosetti, *Concerto No. 2 in E-flat Major for French Horn and Orchestra* Rössler-Rosetti, *Concerto No. 6 in E-flat Major for French Horn and Orchestra*	František Langweil	Supraphony CD CO-72544
Thomas Bacon, "Fantasie"	Strauss, *Fantasie, Op. 2* Moscheles, *Theme Varie, Op. 138* Lorenz, C. D., *Fantasie, Op. 13* Rossini, *Introduction, Andante et Allegro*	Thomas Bacon	Crystal LP 5379

CHAPTER 10

THE TROMBONE

HISTORY OF THE TROMBONE

Like the trumpet, the trombone traces its ancestry to such primitive instruments as the shofar and buzine. After the development of the buzine, the trombone evolved by two distinct steps: the folding of the tube and the application of the movable slide. The principle of the movable slide has remained unchanged over the last five or six hundred years. Since the length of the tube is not fixed, the fundamental harmonics can be adjusted within the limits of the movable slide. The trombone, unlike the trumpet, is by nature a chromatic instrument and is the only brass instrument whose basic structure has remained the same.

The name *trombone* is derived from the Italian *tromba* (trumpet) and *one* (large)—which is exactly what the trombone is—a large trumpet. The term *slide trombone* as we know it retains the same connotation in nearly all languages. The French term for slide trombone is *trombone a'coulisse;* the German, *Zugposaune;* the Italian, *trombone a tiro* or *trombone dutule.* The early English name was *sackbut,* spelled, according to the custom of the time, in a very arbitrary manner as *sackbutte, sackbud, shagbushe, shagbolt,* and others. This term is said to have come from the Spanish *sacabuche,* which may be translated as "drawtube."

There are many ideas on the development of the slide principle. One is that the slide may have grown out of a movable crook that could be used as a tuning slide; on the other hand, the movable crook might have grown out of the trombone slide principle. At any rate, it seems probable that in the buzine's later stages, the straight buzine also had a sliding tube, by which the pitch of its sounds could be altered.

In a fourteenth-century manuscript, not only are the words *sacabuche* and *saquebute* found, but at its close an illustration of the instrument itself occurs on an ivory chessboard of Burgundian workmanship. The scene represented is a dance, the music being supplied by players on shawms and a trombone. The trombone was first used in England in the late fifteenth century; however, it was probably introduced in that country at an earlier date.

The first trombone slides probably made possible the extension of the instrument only a short distance, possibly enough for four or five semitones. This, along with the natural harmonics of the instrument, made possible a chromatic scale over most of the register of the trombone. In 1511, Virdung wrote about an instrument with a slide long enough to add five semitones to the natural scale.

By the close of the fifteenth and during the sixteenth century, the trombone remained a very popular instrument. While the trumpet was restricted to use in royal and military functions, the trombone was used extensively by the town musicians of this period. When the trombone was used in church and civic functions, the cornett was also used to supply the soprano voices (see Figures 10.1 and 10.2).

FIGURE 10.1
Cornett (Italian), zink (German)

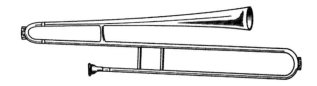

FIGURE 10.2
Sackbut

During the seventeenth century, trombones were used as a family or quartet: the alto trombone (alto or descant), which played the high parts; the tenor trombone (posaun ordinair), which is the instrument currently in favor today; the bass trombone; and the contrabass trombone (octave posaun or contrabass), which played in the register now given to the tuba. It was not until the end of the seventeenth century that the family of sackbuts, or trombones, was completed by adding a true descant or treble instrument. The descant trombone in B-flat was a fourth higher than the alto trombone, which to that point had been used for the highest part. This soprano instrument never became accepted as a member of the trombone family because the short slide made accurate playing extremely difficult.

The general changes in the trombone during the eighteenth century were these:

1. The bell size and conical shape increased.
2. The slide increased to seven positions, eliminating the necessity of crooks.
3. By the end of the century, flat, detachable stays replaced tubular braces.
4. The family of trombones were the E-flat alto, B-flat tenor, and E-flat or F bass. The soprano (not pictured) and contrabass were rarely used (Figure 10.3).

In keeping with the decline of brass instruments during the eighteenth century, the trombone was not used extensively by the composers of this period. Bach made some use of the trombone, as did Handel, but its life as a popular instrument, along with that of the cornett, seemed to be at an end. Mozart used the trombone as a solo instrument in his *Requiem,* while Beethoven used the trombone sparingly in his symphonic works, even though the instrument was a favorite of his.

Gluck was one of the first to realize the true potential of the trombone. His innovations set the style of trombone writing from that day on. The three trombones used were the alto, tenor, and bass, and they were used for the first time in a symphony in the last movement of Beethoven's *Fifth Symphony.*

The general changes in the trombone during the nineteenth century were two:

1. The trigger was invented toward the end of the century.
2. The trombones manufactured in Germany, France, and England had slight differences in style and design.

German
larger bores, tenor with F attachment

French
tenor replaced the alto
bass was tenor with F trigger
had narrower bore than German trombones

English
narrow bore, slightly larger than French
designed a bass trombone in G
designed contrabass with trigger in D

Early in the nineteenth century the demand for trombones increased, probably as a direct result of their use in opera and military bands. Trombone use in military bands brought about some rather odd-looking innovations. Some instruments with slides appeared with the bell turned over the shoulder in order to throw the sound behind the player. Some were made with ornamentations or elaborate bells in the shape of dragon and snake heads (Figures 10.4 and 10.5). Since the seventeenth century, when the trombones were used as a family, the symphonic literature has been written in three clefs: the alto, tenor, and bass. Contemporary composers seem to prefer the use of the tenor and bass; however, any competent trombonist must be well versed in the use of all three clefs. (See the Clef Comparison Chart, page 95.)

Trombones are nontransposing instruments with the pitch written exactly as it sounds. Most music for the school band, especially in America, has the trombone parts written in the bass clef. The same is true with most stage and dance band parts. This

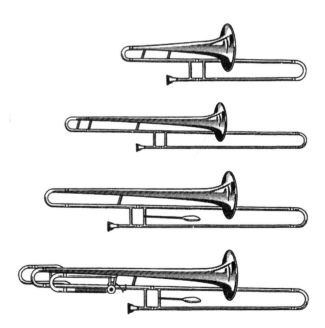

FIGURE 10.3
(a) alto; (b) tenor; (c) bass; (d) contrabass

FIGURE 10.4
Trombone with ornamental bows

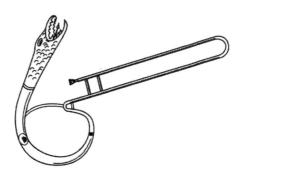

FIGURE 10.5
Ornamental bell in the shape of a dragon

practice necessitates writing many ledger lines above the staff for the tenor instrument and is not consistent with symphonic writing for the instrument.

The trombone in B-flat is generally the instrument in use today. Even the trombone referred to as the bass trombone is in reality a tenor instrument with a large bore, a flared bell, and added tubing, which may be brought into action by a rotary thumb valve (Figure 10.6a and Figure 10.6b).

Modern composers have scored the trombone for use in contemporary musical organizations such as the wind ensemble and dance band. Contemporary composers make use of all the trombone's resources and write for it as a melodic, rather than merely a

supporting, instrument. The range and technique required of the trombonist increases and no doubt the symphonic repertoire for the instrument will increase too. Even though the music and the technical demands made on the performer may change, the instrument has remained virtually the same for the past five or six hundred years.

THE MODERN TROMBONE

Like all other brass instruments, the trombone requires seven different harmonic series to complete the chromatic scale over the entire register of the instrument. When the slide is completely closed, the harmonic series on B-flat is possible. Hence the instrument is known as the B-flat tenor trombone. The 22-inch slide can then be extended into six lower positions, adding six half-steps to the open note. To produce each semitone, the slide must be extended about 3½ inches. (This figure is not always accurate, since the longer the slide, the larger the distance between positions.)

Theoretical positions on the B♭ Tenor Trombone (note that each position is slightly longer than the previous one)

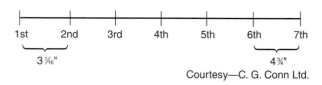

| 1st | 2nd | 3rd | 4th | 5th | 6th | 7th |

3 ¹⁄₁₆"   4¾"
Courtesy—C. G. Conn Ltd.

The harmonic series on each slide position is produced by changing lip and air pressure. In this manner, it is possible to produce all the notes in each harmonic series. The harmonic series playable in each of the seven slide positions is as follows:

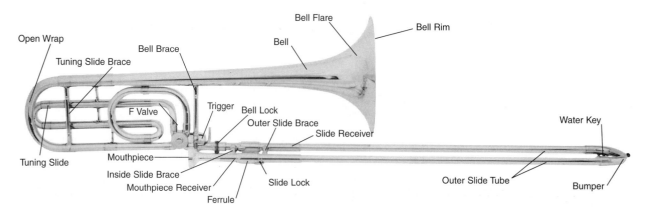

FIGURE 10.6a
Tenor trombone with F attachment (Courtesy of C. G. Conn Division of United Musical Instruments, USA, Inc., www.unitedmusical.com)

FIGURE 10.6b
Tenor trombone featuring the axio flow F valve (Courtesy—Edwards Trombone Co.)

---

*This set of partials is generally so out-of-tune as to be unusable.

The seven overtone harmonic series may be combined to produce the chromatic fingering scale for tenor trombone (see the Comparison Chromatic Fingering Slide Chart on page 96). Alternate fingerings are bracketed and valve positions are indicated for valve trombone, bass trumpet, and baritone horn.

The Alto Trombone

The alto trombone has recently returned as an integral part of the orchestra as well as a featured solo instrument. It is in E-flat with an optional trigger to B-flat. The B-flat side is equivalent to the B♭ tenor, while the E-flat is a perfect fourth higher. (See Figure 10.7, holding position, and Figure 10.8, playing position.)

Typical Problems of Switching from Tenor to Alto

Three typical problems are these:

1. If the trombonist attempts to play with the same air and tone that is achieved while playing the tenor, the alto tone will be uncharacteristically tubby and difficult to play. It is recommended that one play with good support, but with less air volume.
2. Since the alto responds more easily, there is a tendency to "overarticulate."
3. There is a tendency to inhale beyond the need of the phrase, thereby having too much air.

FIGURE 10.8
Playing position of alto trombone

FIGURE 10.7
Holding position of alto trombone

E-flat Alto Trombone

Most alto trombone music is written in alto clef. The position for the E-flat harmonic series is first position. See the Clef Comparison Chart for Trombone that follows. The E-flat positions are above the B-flat positions.

CLEF COMPARISON CHART FOR TROMBONE B♭ & E♭ ALTO

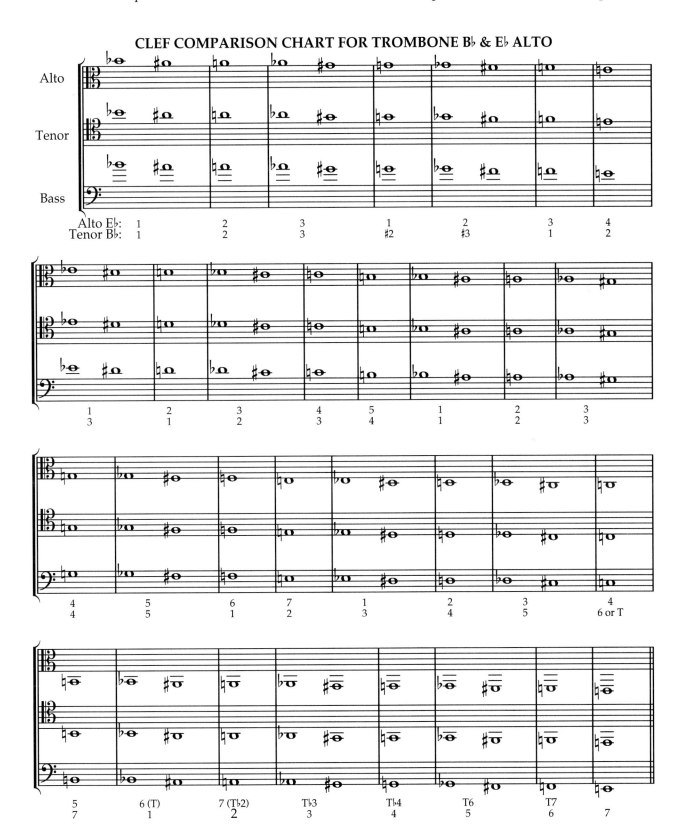

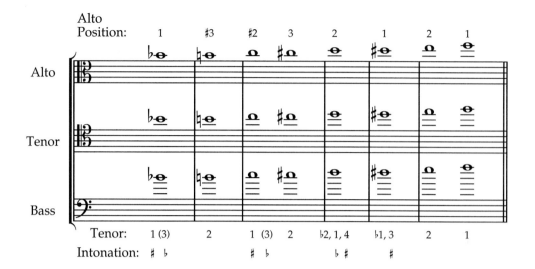

COMPARISON CHROMATIC FINGERING SLIDE CHART
Slide Trombone, Valve Trombone, Baritone 𝄢, Bass Trumpet

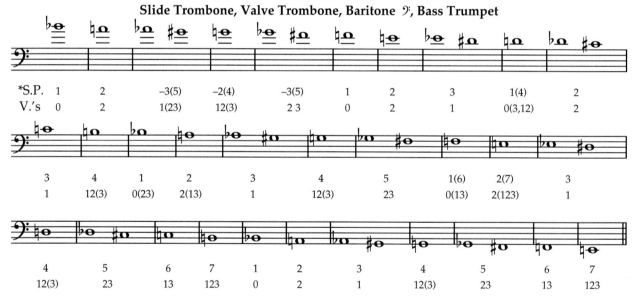

*Note: S.P. = Slide position, V.'s = Valves

The F Valve

The instrument referred to as the bass trombone is generally a tenor instrument with a rotary change valve to F. In most instances the instrument is made with a large bore and a large flared bell. As in the case of the horn, when the valve is activated, a separate set of tubing is brought into play. The trombone is the opposite of the horn; the primary pitch is in B-flat, with the rotary valve changing the pitch to F. Because the length of the instruments is the same in both instances, the difference in pitch is due to the bore size of the instrument rather than the length of the tube. When the F valve is used, the instrument is too short to accommodate seven positions or seven different harmonic series. With the valve activated, the slide is long enough for only six positions when the entire length, including the stockings of the slide, is used. As explained earlier, the distance between positions increases as the slide is extended, and the greater distance required on the bass (or tenor with valve) makes possible only six positions.

Theoretical positions on the B♭ Tenor Trombone (note that each position is slightly longer than the previous one)

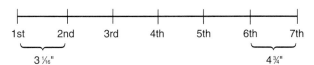

Theoretical positions with the F valve in use.

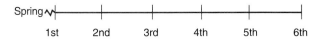

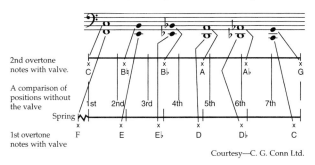

Courtesy—C. G. Conn Ltd.

Tenor-bass trombone slide positions

Notes usually obtained with the F valve in these positions are as follows:

1st position.
Slide closed. If instrument has a spring in the slide, it may be necessary to push it in in order to get the low F in tune.

♭ 2nd position.
Approximately 1 inch beyond the regular 2nd position.

♭ 3rd position.
Approximately 2¼ inches beyond the regular third position. This position may be thought of as a short fourth if this is easier for the performer.

♯ 5th position.
About an inch short of the regular fifth position. (Fourth position has been dropped.)

♭ 6th position.
Approximately 1 inch below normal sixth position.

♭ 7th position.
As far as it is possible to reach. It is likely that the pitch will still be sharp.

The bass trombone with change valve to F is not a complete chromatic instrument, since the low B-natural is not available on the instrument. This is usually provided for by a special tuning slide on the F valve, which, when extended to its proper length, allows the tuning of the instrument down to E. With the tuning slide pulled out to tune the E-natural, the following notes are possible:

1st position.

  If instrument is equipped with a spring in the slide, it will be necessary to push the slide in to get the low E in tune.

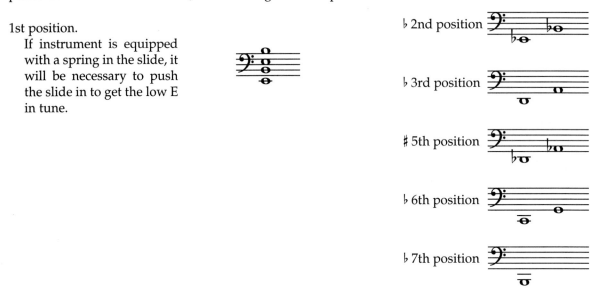

The advantage of using the F valve tuned to F, rather than pulled out to E, lies in the similarity of positions between the B-flat and F instruments, as well as the availability of the low F and C, which are not playable on the instrument when tuned to E. When tuned to F, the first and second positions correspond to sixth and seventh positions on the B-flat instrument. The notes most often used on the F valve are the following:

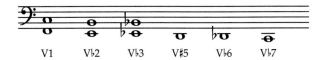

Notes most often employed on the bass trombone when tuned to E are as follows:

To tune the F valve, play open F on the B-flat instrument and tune the same pitch with the F valve activated. Remember that the low C in seventh position will most likely still be sharp. To tune the E valve, follow the same procedure; tune to E in the first position. Again, the low B-natural will be sharp. On most instruments, the low B-natural will be so sharp that many performers prefer to tune to a flat E-flat, enough so that the low B will be in tune, and then adjust positions to get D-flat, D, and E-flat in tune. The same procedure may be used to get the low C in tune on the F valve; however, this eliminates the use of the valve for C and F.

Double-Valved Bass Trombone

The independent valve system can produce three separate pitches: F with the thumb, G-flat with the middle finger, and D when combined. A picture of the Edwards independent valve system is shown in Figure 10.9. Note the axio flow valve system and interchangeable lead pipes.

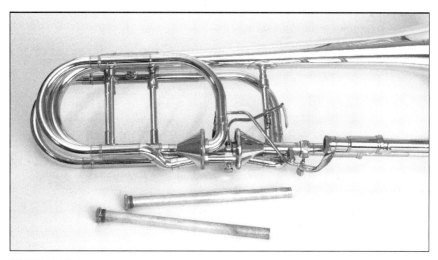

FIGURE 10.9
Double-valved bass trombone (Courtesy of Mark Philbrick BYU)

Below are shown the bass trombone position charts for the independent valve system.

G♭ VALVE AND D COMBINATION

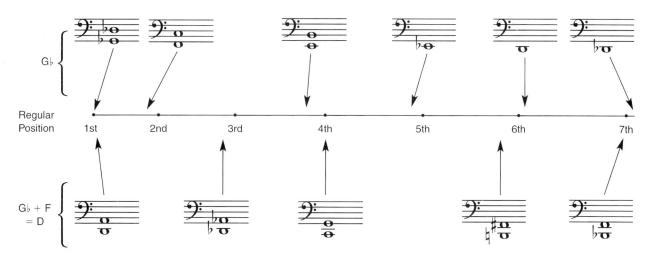

Below is shown the independent valve system with three tunings: F with the thumb, G with the middle finger, and E-flat when the two are combined. The independent system allows the trombonist the greatest flexibility.

G VALVE AND E♭ COMBINATION

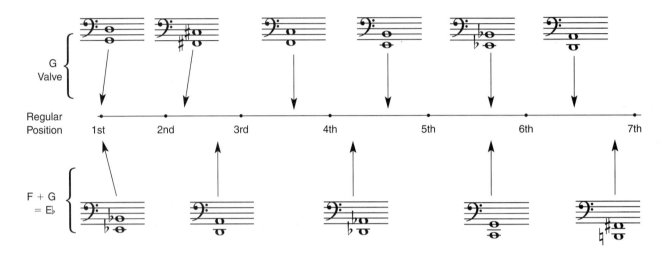

The double-valved bass trombone that is still used extensively has an F valve which, when used in combination with the secondary valve, produces the pitch of E-flat (the side-by-side system). The chart below serves as a guide to E-flat tuning.

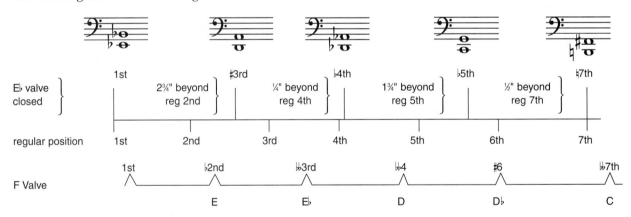

The trigger necessary to produce E-flat with the combination of the F trigger cannot be played separately. (See Figure 10.10.)

FIGURE 10.10
Double trigger bass trombone side-by-side system (F and E♭)

The contra bass trombone plays in the same register as the BB♭ tuba and uses a tuba mouthpiece. Because of this similarity, tuba players often double on this instrument. The pictured contra bass trombone also has an FF valve (an octave below tenor F valve). This valve is used primarily for 6th (T) and 7th positions (Tb2). (See Figure 10.11)

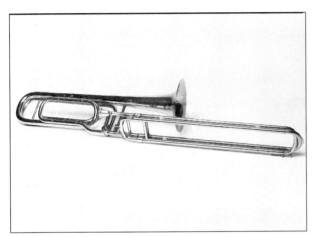

FIGURE 10.11
Contra bass trombone (Courtesy—Steve Call)

FIGURE 10.12
Playing position for trombone, seated

PLAYING POSITIONS FOR THE TROMBONE

Sitting and Standing Posture

Since the trombone requires a greater lung capacity to play than either the trumpet or the horn, it is essential that good posture be maintained while playing. This is especially true when performing the low register of the bass trombone, which requires the greatest lung capacity of any brass instrument.

While seated, the trombonist should have an arched back and a high chest, and no muscular tension. The elbows should be at a comfortable 45 degree angle to the body (not too high, which causes tension in the shoulders). The head and chin must be in a natural position, neither raised nor lowered, in order to allow maximum opening of the throat. If muscular tension is produced in the back, shoulders, arms, or neck while in the holding position, a posture adjustment is needed (Figure 10.12).

Standing posture has the same upper torso position as sitting (Figure 10.13). The back is arched, providing a good balance without excessive muscular tension. To assure proper balance, the feet should be placed three or four inches apart, balancing between the heels and balls of the feet.

The knees are not locked, so that the legs will be flexible. In a performance, the tension, if allowed,

FIGURE 10.13
Playing position for trombone, standing

can spread throughout the entire body, making breath control and performance accuracy difficult. If a student never practices a solo standing, he or she may have difficulty in performance if standing is required.

Left Hand Position

Most of the trombone weight is supported by the heel of the left hand (Figures 10.14 and 10.15). By having the weight primarily on the heel of the left hand, the pressure on the thumb and middle finger of the left hand can be minimized. The index finger of the left hand is placed on the lead pipe for the purpose of balance (Figure 10.16). The thumb is placed against the valve lever or around the cross bar, while the middle finger provides the leverage against the stationary brace of the slide, keeping the instrument properly balanced.

FIGURE 10.14
Left hand position for trombone, in rest position without F attachment

FIGURE 10.15
Left hand position, trombone, with F attachment

FIGURE 10.16
Left hand position with instrument in playing position with F valve

Some teachers prefer having three fingers on the slide cross bar and one below the slide tube. By having three fingers on the cross bar, there is less tendency to roll the hand over as the slide is brought towards first position. Some teachers believe the disadvantage of having just the little finger below the bottom slide tube is a possible lack of control when the fingers are used for the slide motion.

Right Hand Position and Slide Technique

Proper hand position of fingers, wrist, and arm while moving the slide is essential for slide accuracy and technique. Opinions differ on the correct way to hold the trombone slide. Even though many professionals have an outstanding technique in their ways of holding the slide, one approach is currently favored and taught. This approach is discussed and illustrated in Figure 10.17.

FIGURE 10.17a
Right hand playing positions, trombone

FIGURE 10.17b
Right hand playing positions, trombone

The right hand holds the slide cross bar with the palm of the hand facing the body, not toward the floor. Two fingers hold the cross bar, with the ring finger and middle finger straddling the bottom slide tube. The reason for having the hand and fingers in this position are as follows:

1. The fingers can control the slide without having the thumb in contact with the slide cross bar.
2. The wrist and fingers can move the slide with the least restriction.
3. Tension of the hand is minimized because slide stability does not depend on the thumb.
4. Slide motion can be accomplished by the wrist, arm, and fingers, allowing the greatest speed and accuracy.

Elbow and Arm Movement

Since the most accurate slide placement is accomplished by bending the arm from the elbow, many teachers prefer to minimize the amount of wrist and finger movement until it is necessary for technical requirements. In order to keep consistency and accuracy with the right arm movement, the elbow needs to be kept at a 45 degree angle from the body in first position and should not be allowed to droop down next to the body. The forearm moves from the elbow in a line with the slide, keeping the palm of the hand toward the body. This prevents the tendency to roll the hand and arm. In other words, the knuckles are always perpendicular to the slide tubes.

MUTES

Trombone mutes, like the other brass mutes, change the tone color or timbre of the instrument. Following is a list of trombone mutes and their general uses.

Plunger—often a standard toilet plunger without the handle, used in jazz and all idioms of music to produce the effect of opening and closing the sound. A "+" above the notes tells the performer to close the plunger over the bell, while an "o" means to open the plunger by pulling it away from the bell.

Pixy Mute—used exclusively for jazz; produces a softer, strident tone quality. Its smaller size allows the use of a plunger.

Cup Mute—produces a mellow sound and is used for special effect in jazz, ensembles, solo, orchestra, and band. It usually plays slightly flatter when inserted.

Straight Mute—used as the standard mute in all idioms of music. It has a strident quality and plays sharp when inserted. If music calls for unspecified muted section, "con sordino," the straight mute is used.

Harmon Mute—used almost exclusively in jazz and for special effects in all other idioms. It comes in two parts with an inserted stem that gives the instrument a secondary bell. By using the hand open and closed over the stem bell, a "wa-wah" effect is produced. If the stem is taken out, the tone has a "buzzy" quality.

Whisper Mute—looks like a straight mute with holes in it. It is designed to play extremely softly, allowing the musician to practice in situations where normal volume is prohibited.

FIGURE 10.18
Mutes: plunger, cup, straight (pixy, harmon, and whisper not pictured)

DAILY EMBOUCHURE AND FLEXIBILITY STUDIES

For further information on double valves and practice material, see Alan Raph's method for the double-valve trombone. For further information on all aspects of trombone playing, see Reginald Fink's *Trombonist's Handbook*.

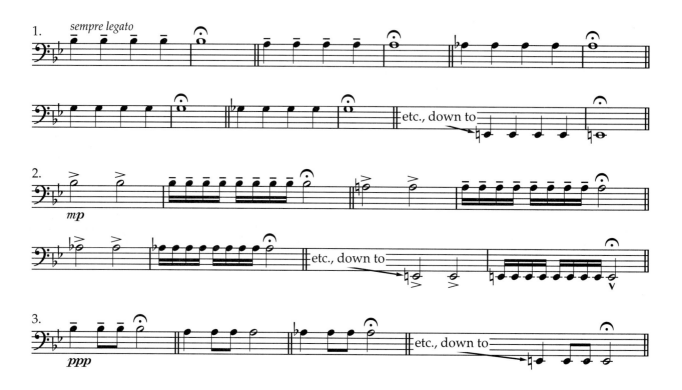

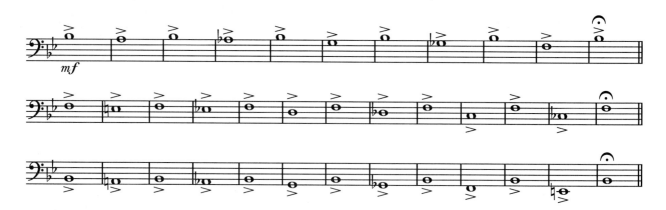

4. To establish attack and tuning, attack with full MP tone. Round the end of each note. Never allow the tone to become brassy and do not increase the volume after attack.

5. Use no tongue after initial attack.

6–7–8. Trill slurs. Play completely relaxed. Use horn as a megaphone with no resistance. Never allow tone to become brassy. Keep rhythm steady.

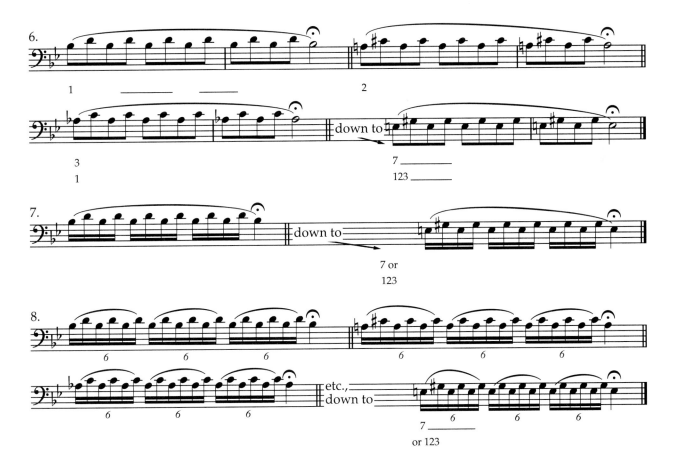

9. Legato (da) tongue.

10. Lip slurs. Do not accent top notes. Make slurs as smooth and even as possible. Keep same tone through-out exercise. Play in a relaxed manner and use tongue only on initial attack. Avoid unnecessary facial movement, i.e., chewing the notes.

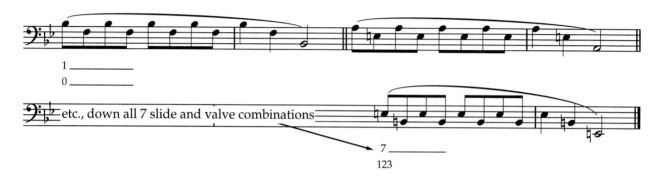

11–12–13. Full, round tone on each note.

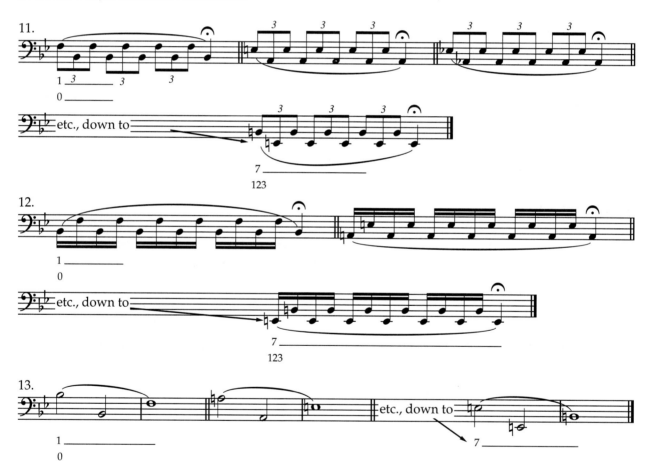

14. Soft tongue only on initial attack. Use no tongue for the remainder of the phrase. Play three times in one breath, making certain there are no accents. Keep tone constant.

15. Play with soft (da) legato tongue.

16. Triad slur. No tongue.

17. Lip massage. Play in a relaxed manner with full round tone on each note.

18. Overtone slur in two octaves. Do not use excessive pressure in order to obtain high note. Use bunching of the embouchure rather than a stretch (or smile) embouchure. Use no tongue after initial attack. Play as smoothly as possible.

7 ————
123

1 ————
0

19. Breath control and legato. Take normal speaking breath for first phrase and increase gradually for each succeeding phrase. Do not breathe in the middle of a ligature. Delay slide until note is stopped and then move quickly, but smoothly, to next position. Articulate each note with a soft legato tongue. Maintain strict tempo. The following model should be played in all major and minor keys.

etc., in all major and minor keys

20–21–22. Smooth, even slur. Attack first note in each group. Play in a strict orchestral style. Full, even tone.

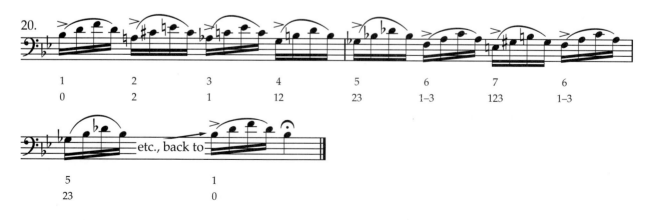

| 1 | 2 | 3 | 4 | 5 | 6 | 7 | 6 |
| 0 | 2 | 1 | 12 | 23 | 1–3 | 123 | 1–3 |

etc., back to

5
23

1
0

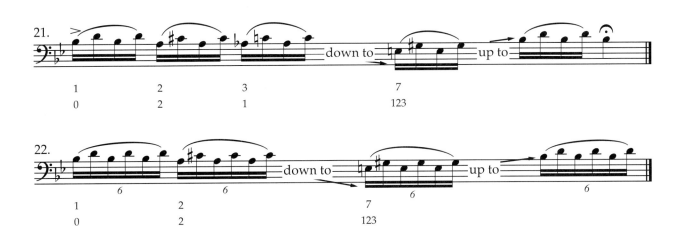

23–24–25. Play the following scale model in the following keys; E, F♯, G, A♭, B♭, A, C, and higher if possible. Use a firm legato (da) tongue. Separate between notes and keep constant throughout. Breathe after each eighth note. Use fast, even slide movement. Try for control of slide without stiffness. Maintain smooth, firm legato.

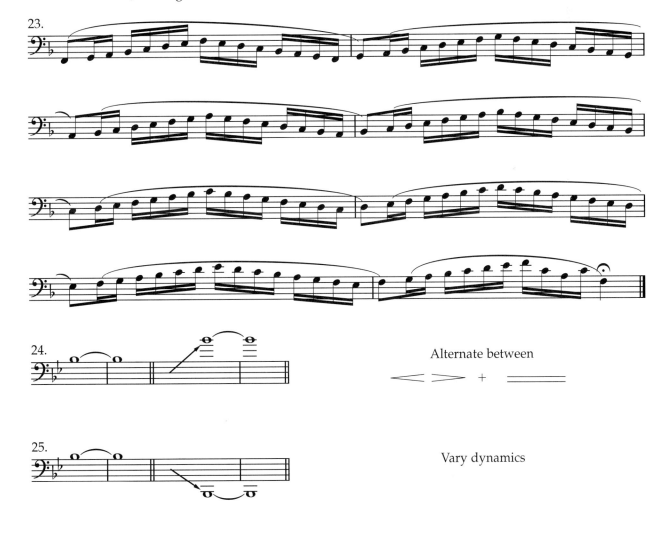

26. Do not breathe during exercise, and do not remove mouthpiece from lips. Keep rhythm steady.

To Develop High Range

27. Overtone series over two octaves with added ninth. As embouchure grows stronger, add tenth, etc., to overtone series. Play in a relaxed manner, with no pressure, and as smoothly as possible.

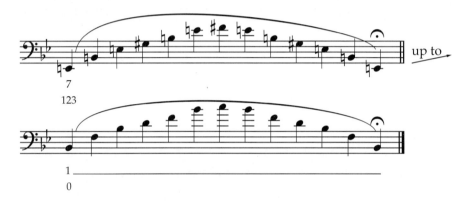

28–29. Do not breathe or relax embouchure during pause. Start note after pause with a very soft tongue. Don't push with lips. Try to hear tone before attack. Play in one breath.

28.

up all slide and valve combinations to 1st and open

29.

up to

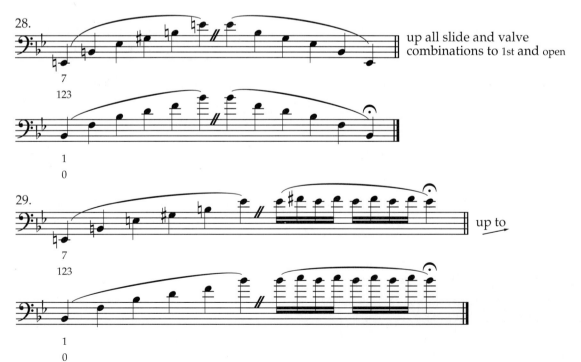

30. Make all notes equal in value, tone, etc. No accents. No pressure for high note. Be sure that the seventh is not allowed to replace the fifth in the overtone series, in descending from highest note, i.e., in first position (B♭ overtone series) A♭ instead of F, which is the fifth.

1
0   down through all 7 combinations

31. As relaxed as possible.

1
0   down to 7th or 123

32. No pressure on high slur. Full, round tone on each note. On all remaining exercises try for complete relaxation.

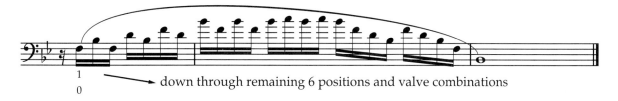

1
0   down through remaining 6 positions and valve combinations

33. Not playable on valve instruments. Use a firm, supple movement of the slide and play all notes possible within the octave during glissando. Do not pause on top note. Play with one quick movement.

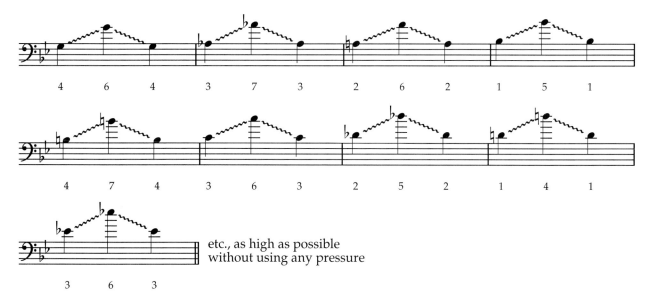

4   6   4   3   7   3   2   6   2   1   5   1

4   7   4   3   6   3   2   5   2   1   4   1

3   6   3   etc., as high as possible
without using any pressure

SELECTED LITERATURE FOR TENOR AND BASS TROMBONE

Methods and Studies: Tenor Trombone

Level 1

Anderson, *Best in Class, Books 1 & 2*, Kjos Music Co.

Beeler, *Walter Beeler Method, Book 1*, Warner Brothers

Belwin, *First Division Band Method*, Belwin

Edmondson, *Developing Band Book 1*, Edmundson & McGinty

Feldstein, *Alfred's New Band Method, Book 1*, Alfred Pub. Co.

Feldstein, *Alfred's Basic Solos and Ensembles, Book 1*, Alfred Pub. Co.

Kinyon, *Breeze Easy Method*, Warner Brothers

Leonard, *Learning Unlimited—Level 1*, Hal Leonard Pub. Co.

Leonard, *Let's Play Baritone Horn—Level 1 (Audio-visual Band Series)*, Hal Leonard Pub. Co.

Leonard, *Let's Play Baritone Horn—Level 2 (Audio-visual Band Series)*, Hal Leonard Pub. Co.

Long, *Elementary Method for Trombone or Baritone*, Rubank

O'Reilly, *Accent on Achievement, Book 1*, Alfred Pub. Co.

O'Reilly, *Yamaha Band Ensembles, Book 1*, Alfred Pub. Co.

Pearson, *Standard of Excellence, Book 1*, Kjos Music Co.

Rusch, *Hal Leonard Elementary Band Method*, Hal Leonard Pub. Co.

Level 2

Beeler, *Walter Beeler Method, Book II*, Warner Brothers

Clarke-Gordon, *Technical Studies for Bass Clef Instruments*, Fischer

Edmondson, *Developing Band Book 2*, Edmondson & McGinty

Feldstein, *Alfred's Basic Solos and Ensembles, Book 2*, Alfred Pub. Co.

Hunsberger, *The Remington Warm-up Studies*, Accura

O'Reilly, *Accent on Achievement, Book 2*, Alfred Pub. Co.

O'Reilly, *Yamaha Band Ensembles, Book 2*, Alfred Pub. Co.

Ostling, *Time Out for Ensembles*, Belwin

Pares, *Pares' Scales for Trombone or Baritone*, Rubank

Phillips, *Silver Burdett—Instrumental Series*, Silver Burdett

Pearson, *Standard of Excellence, Book 2*, Kjos Music Co.

Ployhar, *Recommended Warm-up Technique Book*, Belwin

Ployhar, *Tone and Technique*, Belwin

Rubank, *Rubank Soloist Folio for Trombone or Baritone with Piano Accompaniment*, Rubank

Rusch, *Hal Leonard Intermediate Band Method*, Hal Leonard Pub. Co.

Ryden, *Classical Quartets for All*, Belwin

Level 3

Arbans, *Method*, Fischer

Bordogni, *Melodious Etudes for Trombone*, Fischer

Clarke-Gordon, *Technical Studies*, Fischer

Edmondson, *Developing Band Book 3*, Edmondson & McGinty

Elledge, *Band Technique Step by Step*, Kjos Music Co.

Erickson, *Technique through Performance*, Alfred Pub. Co.

Fink, *From Treble Clef to Bass Clef Baritone*, Accura

Gower, *Rubank Advanced Method, Book II*, Rubank

O'Reilly, *Accent on Achievement, Book 3*, Alfred Pub. Co.

Pares, *Pares' Scales for Trombone or Baritone*, Rubank

Pearson, *Standard of Excellence, Book 3*, Kjos Music Co.

Phillips, *Silver Burdett—Instrumental Series*, Silver Burdett

Ployhar, *Recommended Warm-up Technique Book*, Belwin

Ployhar, *Tone and Technique*, Belwin

Rubank, *Rubank Soloist Folio for Trombone or Baritone with Piano Accompaniment*, Rubank

Rusch, *Hal Leonard Advanced Band Method*, Hal Leonard Pub. Co.

Ryden, *Classical Quartets for All*, Belwin

Schlossberg, *Daily Drills and Technical Studies for Trumpet*, *for Trombone*, Baron

Smith, C., *Symphonic Warm-ups*, Hal Leonard Pub. Co.

Voxman, *Selected Duets, Books I and II*, Rubank

Voxman, *Selected Studies for Baritone*, Rubank

Level 4

Arbans, *Method*, Fischer

Blume, *Thirty-one Studies for Trombone*, Fischer

Bordogni-Rochut, *Melodious Etudes, Book I*, Fischer

Charlier, *Trente-Six Etudes Transcendantes*, Leduc

Clarke, *Technical Studies*, Fischer

Fink, *Introducing the Alto Clef*, Accura

Fink, *Introducing the Tenor Clef*, Accura

Gower, *Rubank Advanced Method for Trombone or Trombone with F Attachment*, International

Grigoriev, *24 Studies for Bass Trombone or Trombone with F Attachment*, International

Pares, *Pares' Scales for Trombone or Baritone*, Rubank

Phillips, *Silver Burdett—Instrumental Series*, Silver Burdett

Rubank, *Rubank Soloist Folio for Trombone or Baritone with Piano Accompaniment*, Rubank

Schlossberg, *Daily Drills and Technical Studies for Trumpet*, *for Trombone*, Baron

Voxman, *Selected Studies for Baritone*, Rubank

Level 5

Amsden, *Duets*, Barnhouse

Arbans, *Method*, Fischer

Blazhevich, *Clef Studies*, Fischer

Bodet, *Seize Etudes de Virtuosité d'après J. S. Bach pour Trompette*, Leduc

Bordogni-Rochut, *Melodious Etudes, Book I*, Fischer

Charlier, *Trente-Six Etudes Transcendantes*, Leduc

Clarke, *Technical Studies*, Fischer

Gillis, *20 Etudes for Bass Trombone with F Attachment*, Southern

Gillis, *70 Progressive Studies for the Modern Bass Trombonist*, Southern

Gower, *Rubank Advanced Method for Trombone or Baritone, Vol. II*, Baron

Kopprasch, *Six Selected Studies*, Fischer

Remington, *Warm-up Studies*, Accura

Schlossberg, *Daily Drills and Technical Studies for Trumpet*, *for Trombone*, Baron

Tyrell, *Forty Progressive Etudes for Trombone*, Boosey

Voxman, *Selected Studies for Baritone*, Rubank

Level 6

Arbans, *Method*, Fischer

Bach, *Six Cello Duets*, International

Blazhevich, *Concert Duets*, Belwin

Bodet, *Seize Etudes de Virtuosité d'après J. S. Bach pour Trompette*, Leduc

Bordogni-Rochut, *Melodious Etudes, Book III*, Fischer

Bousquet, *Thirty-six Celebrated Studies*, Fischer

Charlier, Trente-deux Etudes de Perfectionnement, Lemoine

Clarke, *Technical Studies*, Fischer

Dubois, *Quartorze Etudes*, Leduc

Kopprasch, *Sixty Studies, Book II*, Fischer

La Fosse, *School of Sight Reading, Book V*, Baron

Ostrander, *Shifting Meter Studies*, King

Remington, *Warm-up Studies*, Accura

Schlossberg, *Daily Drills & Technical Studies for Trumpet*, *for Trombone*, Baron

Solos: Tenor Trombone

Level 1

Belwin-Mills, *Trombone Solos*, Belwin

The Canadian Brass Book of Beginning Trombone Solos, The Canadian Brass on the Companion CDs, Hal Leonard Pub. Co.

The Canadian Brass Book of Easy Trombone Solos, The Canadian Brass on the Companion CDs, Hal Leonard Pub. Co.

Feldstein, *First Solo Songbook*, Belwin

Snell, *Belwin Master Solos* (Easy), Belwin

Weber, *Baritone (Trombone) Student*, Belwin

Level 2

Bach-Falcone, *Two Pieces*, Southern

The Canadian Brass Book of Intermediate Trombone Solos, The Canadian Brass on the Companion CDs, Hal Leonard Pub. Co.

Haydn-Stouffer, *Country Dances*, Kendor

Johnson, *Moods Varietal*, Rubank

Lethbridge, *A Handel Solo Album*, Oxford University Press

Mozart-Stouffer, *Air in E-flat Major*, Kendor

Porret, *15e Solo de Concours*, Elkan

Rubank, *Concert and Contest Collection for Cornet, Trumpet or Baritone with Piano Accompaniment*, Rubank

Smith-Falcone, *Cactus Jack*, Belwin

Smith-Falcone, *Cheyenne*, Belwin

Snell, *Belwin Master Solos* (Intermediate), Belwin

Tanner, *Song of the Woods*, Belwin

Level 3

Alary, *Contest Piece (Morceau de Concours)*, Cundy-Bettoney

Bach, *Arioso from Cantata No. 56*, Schirmer

Bach-Figert, *For He That Is Mighty*, Kendor

Bach-Fitzgerald, *Bist Du Bei Mir*, Belwin

Bach-Ostrander, *Patron of the Wind*, Edition Musicus

Beach, *Suite*, Associated Music Pub.

Berlioz-Smith, *Recitative and Prayer*, Presser

Handel, *Honor and Arms from Samson*, Edition Musicus

Handel, *Where'er You Walk from Semele*, Boosey & Hawkes

Handel-Ostrander, *Arm, Arm, Ye Brave*, Edition Musicus

Kreisler, *Sonatina*, Southern

McKay, *Arietta and Capriccio*, Boston

McKay, *Concert Solo Sonatine*, Boston

McKay, *Suite*, University Music Press

Mozart, *Ave Verum Corpus*, Elkan

Mozart, *Concert Rondo in E-Flat Major, K. 371*, Southern

Telemann, *Sonata in F Minor*, International

Level 4

Bach, *For He That Is Mighty from the "Magnificat,"* Kendor

Bach-Beversdorf, *Tis Thee I Would Be Praising*, Southern

Barat, *Andante et Allegro*, Cundy-Bettoney, International, and Southern

Barat, *Fantaisie*, Leduc

Barat, *Introduction et Serenade*, Leduc

Bernstein, *Elegy for Mippy II*, Schirmer

Blazewitch, *Concerto Piece No. 5*, Belwin

Boda, *Sonatina*, W. D. Stuart

Boutry, *Tubaroque*, Leduc

Cimera, *Waltz Helen*, Belwin

Dubois, *Cortège*, Leduc

Frescobaldi, *Canzoni*, Ludwig

Frescobaldi, *Toccata*, International

Guilmant, *Morceau Symphonique*, Warner Brothers

Handel, *Andante and Allegro*, Southern

Hartley, *Arioso*, Fema

Haydn, *Air and Allegro*, Rubank

Haydn-Schuman, *Adagio from the Cello Concerto*, Warner Brothers

Hindemith, *Drei Leichte Stücke*, Schott

Hutchinson, *Sonatina*, Fischer

Johnson, *Soliloquy in Three-Four*, Rubank

Kelly, *Sonatina for Trombone & Piano*, Josef Weinberger

La Fosse, *Trois Pièces de Style*, Leduc

Lieb, *Song and Dance*, Trombone with String Quartet, International

Marcello, *Sonata in F Major*, International

Marcello, *Sonata in G Minor*, International

Marcello, *Sonate for Tuba, Basse Solo, Baritone, or Euphonium in B♭ with Piano*, Elkan

Marcello-Ostrander, *Sonata in G Minor*, International

Martin, *Elegy*, Fischer

Müller, *Praeludium, Chorale, Variations, and Fugue*, Edition Musicus

Nestico, *Reflective Mood*, Kendor

Pryor, *Annie Laurie*, Ludwig

Pryor, *The Patriot*, Fischer

Pryor, *La Petite Suzanne*, Fischer

Rimsky-Korsakov, *Concerto*, International & Leeds

Rossini, "Inflammatus" from *Stabat Mater*, Fischer

Rousseau, *Pièce Concertante*, Cundy-Bettoney

Saint-Saëns, *Cavatine, Op. 144*, Editions Durand

Vivaldi, *Praeludium in C Minor*, Edition Musicus

Vivaldi, *Sonata No. 1 in B-flat Major*, International

Walter, *Jabberwocky*, Rubank

Weber, *Romance*, Belwin

White, *Dance and Aria*, Shawnee

Level 5

Barat, *Morceau de Concours*, Leduc

Barat, *Réminiscences de Navarre*, Leduc

Büsser, *Cantabile et Scherzando*, Leduc

Childs, *Sonata for Solo Trombone*, Tritone Press

Clarke, *The Bride of the Waves*, Witmark

Cope, *Three Pieces for Trombone with F Attachment*, Brass Press

Corelli, *Sonata in F Major*, International

Corelli, *Sonata No. 9 in A Major*, International

Corelli-Brown, *Sonata in F Major*, International

David, *Concertino, Op. 4*, International

Davison, *Sonata*, Shawnee

Dedrick, *Inspiration*, Almitra

Fasch, *Sonata*, McGinnis & Marx

Fesch, *Sonata in A*, M. Tezak

Galliard, *Sonata I*, McGinnis & Marx

Galliard, *Sonata III*, McGinnis & Marx

Galliard-Clark, *Sonata No. 2*, McGinnis & Marx

Galliard-Clark, *Sonata No. 4*, McGinnis & Marx

Handel, *Aria con Variazioni*, Leduc

Handel, *Concerto in F Minor*, Southern

Handel-Little, *Suite in A Flat*, Belwin

Jacob, *Concerto*, Mills

Jones, *Sonatina*, Fema

Lamb, *Classic Festival Solos*, Warner Brothers

Larsson, *Concertino, Op. 45, No. 7*, Carl Gehrmans Musikförlag

Lebedev, *Concert Allegro*, University of Michigan Press

Marcello, *Sonata in A Minor*, International

Marcello, *Sonata in F Major*, International

McKay, *Sonata*, Remick

Monaco, *Second Sonata for Trombone & Piano*, Shawnee

Pachelbel-Dorf, *Pachelbel Canon for Euphonium and Piano*, Presser

Presser, *Sonatina*, Tenuto

Pryor, *Blue Bells of Scotland, Air and Variations*, Fischer

Pryor, *Thoughts of Love*, Fischer

Rimsky-Korsakov, *Concerto for Trombone and Band*, International

Rubinstein (Ostrander), *Cantilenna*, Edition Musicus

Sanders, *Sonata in E-flat*, Warner Brothers

Shostakovitch (Ostrander), *Four Preludes, Two Trombones, or Trombone and Piano*, Edition Musicus

Senaille, *Introduction and Allegro Spiritoso*, Hinrichsen Edition

Serocki, *Sonatina*, Herman Moeck Verlag (Germany)

Stevens, *Sonatina*, Southern

Vivaldi, *Sonata No. 5 in E Minor*, International

Voxman, *Concert and Contest Collection*, Rubank

Watts, *The Canadian Brass Book of Intermediate Trombone (Baritone) Solos*, Hal Leonard Pub. Co.

Level 6

Bach, *Cello Suite No. 1 in G Major*, Schirmer

Bach, *Sonata No. 1*, Southern

Bach, *Suite No. 4, for Unaccompanied Cello*, Schirmer

Bach-Lafosse, *Cello Suite No. 1*, Leduc

Bach-Lafosse, *Cello Suite No. 2*, Leduc

Bassett, *Sonata*, Robert King

Bassett, *Suite*, Robert King

Berio, *Sequenza V for unaccompanied Trombone*, Universal Editions (Austria)

Bitsch, *Intermezzo*, Leduc

Bloch, *Symphony for Trombone & Orchestra*, Broude Brothers

Bonneau, *Capriccio*, Leduc

Bozza, *Ballad, Op. 62*, Leduc

Bozza, *New Orleans*, Leduc

Bozza, *Prélude et Allegro*, Leduc

Castérede, *Sonatine*, Leduc

Corelli, *Sonata in D Minor*, International

Corelli, *Sonata in D Minor for Cello and Piano*, International

Creston, *Fantasy for Trombone & Orchestra*, Schirmer

Dutilleux, *Choral, Cadence et Fugato*, Leduc

Greson, E., *Trombone Concerto*, Novello

Gröndahl, *Concert*, Giovanni

Hartley, *Sonata Concertante*, Fema

Hartley, *Suite*, Elkan-Vogel

Hindemith, *Sonata*, Schott

Jongen, *Aria and Polonaise*, Belwin

Martelli, *Dialogue, Op. 100*, Editions Max Eschig

Martin, *Ballade*, Universal Edition

Milhaud, *Concertino d'Hiver*, Associated Music Pub.

Mozart, *Concerto in B♭ Major, K. 191*, International

Peaslee, *Arrows of Time*, Marqun Music

Pergolesi (Saver), *Sinfonia*, Wimbledon Music

Persichetti, *Parable*, Elkan-Vogel

Salzedo, *Piece Concertante*, Leduc

Telemann, *Fantasie No. 2 in F Minor*, Fischer

Telemann, *Fantasie No. 3 in C Minor*, Fischer

Telemann, *Fantasie No. 12 in B Minor*, Fischer

Tomasi, *Concerto for Trombone & Orchestra*, Leduc

Vivaldi, *Sonata No. 1 in B♭ Major*, International

Vivaldi, *Sonata No. 6 in B♭ Major*, International

Wear, *Sonata for Trombone*, Ludwig Music Pub. Co.

White, *Sonata*, Southern

Methods and Studies: Bass Trombone

Aharoni, E., *New Method for the Modern Bass Trombone*, NOGA Music, Israel

Arbans (Randall and Mantia), *Famous Method for Trombone*, King Co.

Blume, *36 Studies for Trombone with F-Attachment*, International

Bordogni, *L13 Bel Canto Studies*, King Co.

Fink, *Studies in Legato for Bass Trombone*, Fischer

Gillis, *20 Etudes for Bass Trombone*, Southern

Gillis, *70 Progressive Studies for the Modern Bass Trombone*, Southern

Kopprasch, *Selected Kopprasch Studies*, Fischer

Ostrander, *The F-Attachment and the Bass Trombone*, King Co.

Ostrander, *Method for Bass Trombone*, King Co.

Ostrander, *Shifting Meter Studies*, King Co.

Pederson, *Elementary Etudes for Bass Trombone*, Belwin

Pederson, *Intermediate Etudes for Bass Trombone*, Belwin

Pederson, *Advanced Etudes for Bass Trombone*, Belwin

Stephanovsky-Brown, *20 Studies for Bass Trombone*, International Music Co.

Solos: Bass Trombone

Level 4

Lieb, *Concertino Basso*, Fischer

Müller, *Praeludium, Chorale, Variations, and Fugue*, Editions Musicus

Level 5

David-Göss, *Concerto for Bass Trombone and Piano*, Zimmermann-Frankfurt

Spillman, *Concerto for Bass Trombone or Tuba*, Editions Musicus

Spillman, *Two Songs*, Editions Musicus

Tomasi, *Etre ou ne pas Etre*, Leduc

Level 6

Adler, *Canto II*, Oxford University Press

Bozza, *Allegro et Finale*, Leduc

Casterede, *Fantaisie Concertante*, Leduc

George, *Concerto for Bass Trombone*, Accura

Hartley, *Sonata Brève*, Fenette Music

Jongen, *Aria and Polonaise*, Belwin

Lebedev, *Concerto in One Movement*, Editions Musicus

Steven, *Sonatina for Bass Trombone & Piano*, Southern

Vaughan Williams, *Concerto for Tuba (Bass Trombone)*, Oxford University Press

White, *Tetra Ergon*, The Brass Press

Wilder, *Sonata for Bass Trombone & Piano*, Margun Music, Inc.

LIST OF RECORDINGS

Album Title	Contents	Performer/s	Label
All the Lonely People	Rimsky-Korsakov, *Concerto for Trombone and Orchestra* Tomasi, *Concerto for Trombone and Orchestra* Rota, *Concerto for Trombone and Orchestra* Schnittke, *Dialogue for Cello and Seven Performers* Rabe, *All the Lonely People: Concerto for Trombone and Chamber Orchestra*	Christian Lindberg	BIS CD-568
American Trombone Concertos	Creston, *Fantasy for Trombone and Orchestra* Walker, *Concerto for Trombone and Orchestra* Schuller, *Eine kleine Posaunenmusik* (A Little Trombone Music) *For Trombone and Wind Ensemble* Zwilich, *Concerto for Trombone and Orchestra*	Christian Lindberg	BIS CD-628
At the End of the Century	Crespo, *Improvisation No. 1* for Trombone Solo Filas, *Sonata for Trombone and Piano* Bonde, *Ballade in Blue for Trombone and Piano* Bolter, *Arctic Emanations for Trombone and Piano* Premu, *Concertino for Trombone and Woodwinds* Hidas, *Movement for Trombone and Piano* Gabaye, *Special*	Joseph Alessi	ITA-1002
The Burlesque Trombone	Folke, *Basta* for Trombone Solo Serocki, *Sonatina* na puzon i fortepiano Bernstein, *Elegy for Mippy II* Defaye, *Deux Dances* Casterede, *Sonatine* pour trombone et piano Dutilleux, *Choral, Cadence et fugato* Chopin, *Valse, Op. 64 No. 1* Jacobsen, *Sonata Serioso* Pöntinen, *Camera* per trombone e fortepiano	Christian Lindberg	BIS CD-318
Concerto for Trombone and Orchestra	Wagenseil, *Concerto* for Alto Trombone and Orchestra David, *Concertino* for Trombone and Orchestra Tomasi, *Concerto* for Trombone and Orchestra Martin, *Ballade* for Trombone and Orchestra	Branimir Slokar	Claves CD 50-8407
The Criminal Trombone	Rossini, The Overture to *The Barber of Seville* Schumann, *Romance, Op. 94, No. 1, Romance, Op. 94, No. 2* Mozart, Variations on "Ah! vous dirai-je, Maman" Giazotto, *The "Albinoni" Adagio*	Christian Lindberg	BIS CD-328

LIST OF RECORDINGS (cont.)

Album Title	Contents	Performer/s	Label
	Schubert, *The "Arpeggiono" Sonata, First Movement* Bach, *"Badinerie"* from *Suite in B minor*, *"Air"* from *Suite in D Major*		
Divertimento for Trombone and Orchestra	Mozart, L., *Concerto in D Major* Albrechtsberger, *Concerto in D Major* Hummel, J. N., *Introduction, Theme and Variations Op. 102* Bellini, *Concerto in E-flat Major* Sinigaglia, *Romance Op. 3* Mendelssohn, *Four Songs Without Words*	Branimir Slokar	Claves CD 50-906
Orchestral Excerpts	Mozart, *Requiem* Berlioz, *Hungarian March, Symphonie Fantastique* Bartok, *Concerto for Orchestra* Schubert, *Symphony No. 8* Wagner, Prelude Act III, *Lohengrin, Ride of the Valkyries, Tannhäuser Overture* Ravel, *Bolero* Mahler, *Symphony No. 3* Brahms, *Symphony Nos. 1 and 2* Beethoven, *Symphony No. 5* Rossini, *William Tell, La Gazza Ladra* Saint-Saëns, *Symphony No. 3* Stravinsky, *Firebird Suite, Petrouchka* Rimsky-Korsakov, *Russian Easter, Scheherazade* Strauss, *Till Eulenspiegel, Ein Heldenleben, Also Sprach Zarathustra* Bruckner, *Symphonies No. 4 & 7* Hindemith, *Mathis der Maler, Symphonie Metamorphosis*	Ralph Sauer	Summit Recordings, DCD 14-3
The Romantic Trombone	Ropartz, *Piece in E-flat minor* Mercadante, *Salve Maria* Gombert, *Morceau Symphonique* Jongen, *Aria et Polonaise* Stojowski, *Fantaisie* Alfvén, *Vallfickans* von Weber, *Romance*	Christian Lindberg	BIS CD-298
Romantic Trombone Concertos	David, Trombone *Concertino Op. 4* Guilmant, *Morceau Symphonique* Grøndahl, *Concerto* for trombone and orchestra Gunnar, *Concerto* for trombone and orchestra	Christian Lindberg	BIS CD-378
The Russian Trombone	Goedicke, *Improvisation* Tchaikovsky, Suite from *The Queen of Spades* Okunev, *Adagio and Scherzo* Ewald, V., *Mélodie* Denisov, *Choral varie* Prokofiev, Suite from *Romeo and Juliet*	Christian Lindberg	BIS CD-478
The Sacred Trombone	Read, *Invocation* Liszt, *Hosannah* Hillborg, *U-Tangia-Na*	Christian Lindberg	BIS CD-488

LIST OF RECORDINGS (cont.)

Album Title	Contents	Performer/s	Label
	Eben, *Invocation I* Schnittke, *Schall und Hall* Eben, *Invocation II* Sandstrom, *Lacrimae* Liszt, *Cujus animam* Read, *De Profundis, Op. 71*		
Slide Area	Grøndahl, *Concerto for Trombone and Piano* Jongen, *Aria and Polonaise* Rachmaninoff, *Elegy in E-flat, Op. 3, No. 1* Besozzi, *Sonata in C Major* Saint-Saëns, "The Swan" from *The Carnival of the Animals* Defaÿ, *Deux Dances pour Trombone et Piano* Elkjer, *Tonal Recall*	Joseph Alessi	Summit DCD 130
The Solitary Trombone	Berio, *Sequenza V* for trombone solo Xenakis, *Keren* for trombone solo Kagel, *Atem für einen Bläser* Eliasson, *Disegno* per trombone Cage, *Solo for Sliding Trombone* Stockhausen, *In Freundschaft für Solo-Posaune*	Christian Lindberg	BIS CD-388
Trombone and Voice in the Habsburg Empire	Joseph I, *Alme ingrate* Eberlin, *Der verlorene Sahn* Mozart, L., *Agnus Dei* Eberlin, *Sigismundus* Zechner, *Aria Solemus, Volta Quinquagenalia* Albrechtsberger, *Aria De Passione Domine* Reutter, *Alma Redemptoris No. 5* Wagenseil, "Memoriam" from *Confitebor* Reutter, *Salve Regina*	Christian Lindberg	BIS CD-548
Trombone Favorites	Haydn, M. *Andantino* Reutter, Excerpts from the *Gloria* of the *Missa S. caroli* Frescobaldi, *Canzona Settima* Wagenseil, *Memoriam* Sulek, *Sonata* Dusapin, *Sly* Pryor, *Fantastic Polka* Ellington, *In A Sentimental Mood* Pryor, *Blue Bells of Scotland* Lagage, *Blue No. 1*	Alan Trudel	ITA WO-121294
Trombone Odyssey 20th Century Landmarks for Trombone and Orchestra	Martin, *Ballade* for trombone and orchestra Serocki, *Concerto* for trombone and orchestra Bloch, *Symphony* for trombone and orchestra Sandström, *Concerto* for trombone and orchestra	Christian Lindberg	BIS CD-538

LIST OF RECORDINGS (cont.)

Album Title	Contents	Performer/s	Label
The Virtuoso Trombone	Rimski-Korsakov, *Flight of the Bumblebee* Sulek, *Sonata* for trombone and piano Martin, *Ballade* pour trombone et piano Monti, *Csardas* Kreisler, *Liebesleid* Pryor, *Blue Bells of Scotland* Hindemith, *Sonata* für Posaune und Klavier Berio, *Sequenza V* for trombone solo	Christian Lindberg	BIS CD-528
The Winter Trombone	Vivaldi, "Inverno" ("Winter") from *The Four Seasons* Milhaud, *Concertino d'hiver* Larsson, *Concerto* for trombone and strings Telemann, *Concerto in C minor* Pöntinen, *Bla Vinter* (Blue Winter)	Christian Lindberg	BIS CD-348

CHAPTER 11

THE BARITONE HORN AND EUPHONIUM

HISTORY OF THE EUPHONIUM

Historically, the euphonium and baritone horn are related to the trumpet, trombone, horn, and tuba.

The key in the development of the modern instrument was the invention of the valve in 1813. This development made experimentation possible in brass instrument construction, and in 1828 Wilhelm Weiprecht produced a complete family of brass instruments using valves: a small cornet, an E-flat trumpet, a B-flat tenor, and a B-flat baritone, which was extremely important in the development of the tuba.

An instrument similar to the present-day euphonium was invented by a German, Sommer of Weimar, around 1840.

The saxhorns, developed by Adolphe Sax, are all instruments that apply the valve mechanism to instruments of the keyed bugle family. They are all played with a cup mouthpiece and have conical bores. Although they have had little significance in brass instrument performance, the saxhorns included an instrument of BB-flat pitch. The saxhorns should not be confused with the modern-day saxophone, even though their names are similar (Figure 11.1).

All the new mechanical innovation, coupled with the ability to work with brass, led to new, extraordinary brass instruments toward the middle of the nineteenth century. Instruments were being produced of *euphonium proportions* with three to six valves (Figure 11.2).

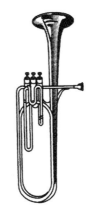

FIGURE 11.1
Baritone saxhorn in B♭, Adolphe Sax, Paris (1814–1894)

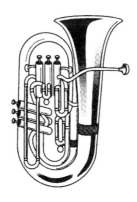

FIGURE 11.2
Six-valve euphonium

Euphonium—Baritone Horn

Because of the way they are currently being made, the difference between the baritone horn and euphonium is hard to define. In general, the euphonium has a greater proportion of conical tubes, and the bore size is larger (Figure 11.3). Both are large-bore conical instruments with the same pitch as the trombone. The euphonium has a darker, richer tone that, in the hands of a fine player, has an expressive and beautiful quality unlike any other instrument. It has been called the "cello of the band."

The euphonium mouthpiece has a larger shank, roughly halfway between the tenor trombone shank

121

Baritone horn   Euphonium

FIGURE 11.3
In general, the euphonium has a larger bore with greater proportion of conical tubes. (Courtesy of DEG Music Products Inc.)

and the bass trombone shank. Many of the new model euphoniums are constructed with the lead pipe receptacle equivalent to the bass trombone lead pipe. If performers are playing both euphonium and trombone, they should ensure that the

rim on both mouthpieces is identical. Cup size, back bore, and so on will make no difference on the embouchure; however, rim thickness must be the same to prevent "grooving." If the player is using two different rims, he or she will develop two different "grooves," and this feature will make the transfer from one to the other more difficult.

The baritone has less conical tubing and a smaller bore than the euphonium (Figure 11.4). Its open fundamental and overtone series are the same as those of the tenor trombone, and the three individual valves, like those of the euphonium, when depressed, lower the fundamentals, as do those of other three-valve instruments, such as the trumpet. The baritone, normally written in the bass clef, is a nontransposing instrument. Some band and brass ensemble arrangements include parts written in treble clef and transposed up a major 9th, read like a trumpet part, only sounding an octave lower. Many teachers transfer cornet or trumpet players to the treble clef baritone part, since it is fingered the same as the cornet or trumpet.

Upright or Bell Front

While the baritone horn is usually bell front, the euphonium is made in two models, bell front and upright. The bell front instrument projects the

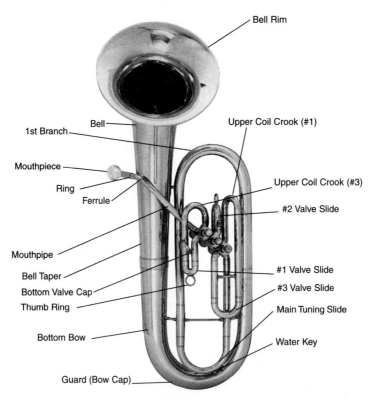

FIGURE 11.4
Baritone horn nomenclature (Courtesy of Conn Division of United Musical Instruments, USA, Inc., www.unitedmusical.com)

sound better than the upright model, which is good for outdoor playing conditions such as a marching band. However, most performers and conductors prefer the upright model for indoor performance. The upright model blends better with the group.

EMBOUCHURE FOR EUPHONIUM OR BARITONE HORN

The performer of euphonium or baritone produces the tone differently from that used while playing the trombone. In playing the trombone, the player maintains firm corners of the mouth and concentrates a fast airstream, thereby producing a directionally focused tone. The performer on the euphonium or baritone allows the corners of the mouth to be *slightly* softer and maintains a slower airstream, which produces a more open and mellow tone. If a player uses the trombone approach while playing the euphonium or baritone, the result is an undesired strident tone quality uncharacteristic of these instruments.

THE MODERN BARITONE HORNS AND EUPHONIUM

Present-day baritone horns and euphoniums are made with three and four valves (Figure 11.5). The fourth valve lowers the open fundamental from B-flat to F exactly as does the F rotary valve on the bass or tenor trombone.

Compensating Systems

A first or third valve slide is often used when playing the sharp 1–3 and 1–2–3 combinations. The player returns the slide inward on the 2–3 combination.

Euphoniums, baritones, and tubas are often manufactured with a fourth valve, to solve some of the intonation problems. The fourth valve is equal to an in-tune 1–3 combination and is also used in the combination 2–4 to substitute for 1–2–3.

Some large-bore instruments—euphoniums and tubas—use a compensating system to increase the length of tubing necessary for the lower register, which uses the fourth valve. When the first three valves are depressed separately or in combination, there are vibrations only in the valve tubes that are depressed and in the instrument. When the fourth valve is depressed in combination with any of the first three valves, the area inside the compensating tube is added to that of the valve tubes so that the total vibrating length includes the instrument length, the combined valve tube length, and the compensating tube length (Figure 11.6).

PLAYING POSITION FOR BARITONE HORN AND EUPHONIUM

The accepted method of holding the baritone in a standing position is with the instrument held diagonally across the body, which is erect, for maximum breath control (Figure 11.7). The left hand should grasp the bottom tubing wherever it is most comfortable for the student. When the performer is seated, the instrument is held in a similar manner and should not be lowered into the lap. A euphonium or baritone stand, a rod attached and extended below the instrument, can be purchased to help support the instrument while the player is in a seated position. This will promote better posture, breath control, and relaxation. As on all brass instruments, good posture is conducive to good performance. Fingers are curved over the valves; fingertips rest on the valves (Figure 11.8 and 11.9).

FIGURE 11.5
(a) Four-valve non-compensating euphonium; (b) four-valve compensating euphonium

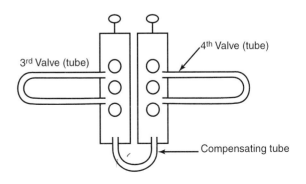

FIGURE 11.6
Compensating System

Comparison of low-registration fingerings: three-valve, four-valve non-compensating, and four-valve compensating.

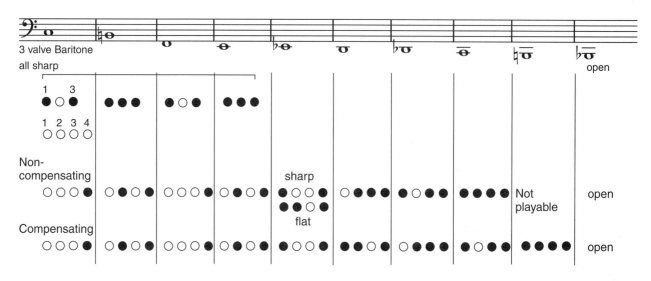

Note that the compensating system allows the performance of the B♮, which cannot be played on the noncompensating system.

FIGURE 11.7
Holding position of a baritone horn (standing)

FIGURE 11.8
Playing position for the euphonium. Note: A euphonium stand is used to maintain posture.

INTONATION

Since the intonation problems faced by the baritone and euphonium are the same as the trumpet's, please refer to Chapters One and Eight for a full discussion.

Solving Intonation Problems

There are three ways to solve intonation problems: use alternate fingerings, adjust the embouchure, and move the tuning slide. The tuning-slide adjustment is a better alternative, since it will not affect

FIGURE 11.9
Playing position for the euphonium (without euphonium stand)

the quality of the tone. A competent brass repairman can adapt a main tuning-slide trigger to a euphonium or baritone, which will extend the tuning slide when depressed, and return the tuning slide to its original position when released.

Moveable Tuning Slide

A main slide trigger device worked by the thumb of the left hand provides an additional means for adjusting the euphonium intonation. As the thumb is pushed inward, the turning slide is extended. This practical device was designed by Bob Dobson of Salt Lake City, Utah, and is pictured with his permission (Figure 11.10).

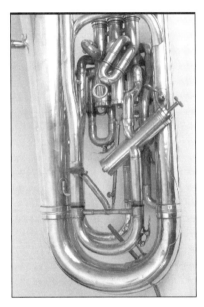

FIGURE 11.10
Slide trigger

	VALVE SLIDE TUNING ADJUSTMENTS (THREE-VALVE)			
Valve	Valve Slide Lengths (inches)	Actual Total Length of Instrument	Total Error (inches)	Tuning Discrepancy
0		100	0	0
2	6.25	106.25	0.30 long	5 cents ♭
1	12.57	112.57	0.32 long	5 cents ♭
3	20.35	120.35	1.43 long	21 cents ♭
1–2	18.82	118.82	0.10 short	1 cent ♯
2–3	26.60	126.60	0.61 long	8 cents ♭
1–3	32.92	132.92	0.56 short	7 cents ♯
1–2–3	39.17	139.17	1.25 short	28 cents ♯

The following examples present an analysis of out-of-tune notes on the euphonium and baritone.

I—Slightly out of tune
II—Noticeably out of tune
III—Decidedly out of tune
IV—Extremely out of tune

INTONATION CHART
Baritone and Euphonium

The following notes are most affected:

Courtesy—Conn Products Division of United Musical Instruments, USA, Inc.

MARCHING BARITONE (EUPHONIUM)

The marching baritone is comparable to a three-valved baritone, with the exception of the straight forward bell for the purpose of projecting the sound toward the audience. The holding position is comparable to the trumpet-holding position (Figure 11.11).

FIGURE 11.11
Holding position of the marching baritone

FIGURE 11.12
Euphonium mute (© Spencer Grant/Photo Edit)

MUTE

The standard euphonium mute resembles a straight mute (Figure 11.12). It is the only standard mute for the euphonium and is used in solos, ensembles, and band when muted sections are designated. When the mute is inserted, the pitch ascends 14 to 25 cents, depending on the thickness of the corks. With thin corks, the mute goes in further and causes the pitch to go even sharper. It is recommended that the euphonium player adjust the tuning slide outward upon insertion of the mute.

DAILY EMBOUCHURE AND FLEXIBILITY STUDIES

For further information on double valves and practice material, see Alan Raph's method for the double-valve trombone. For further information on all aspects of trombone playing, see Reginald Fink's *Trombonist's Handbook*.

4. To establish attack and tuning, attack with full MP tone. Round the end of each note. Never allow the tone to become brassy and do not increase the volume after attack.

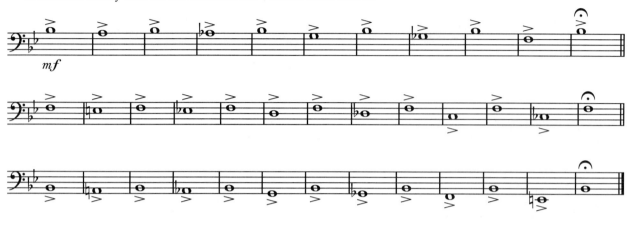

*These studies are numbered the same as the treble clef studies and with the exception of 33 (not given in treble clef section) may be played unison with these instruments.

5. Use no tongue after initial attack.

6–7–8. Trill slurs. Play completely relaxed. Use horn as a megaphone with no resistance. Never allow tone to become brassy. Keep rhythm steady.

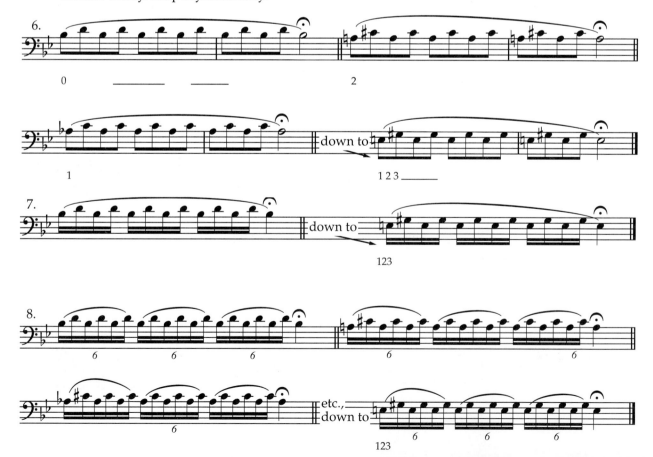

9. Legato (da) tongue.

10. Lip slurs. Do not accept top notes. Make slurs as smooth and even as possible. Keep same tone throughout exercise. Play relaxed and use tongue only on initial attack. Avoid unnecessary facial movement, i.e., chewing the notes.

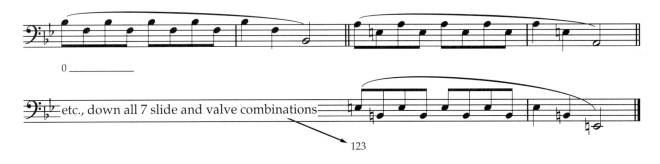

11–12–13. Full, round tone on each note.

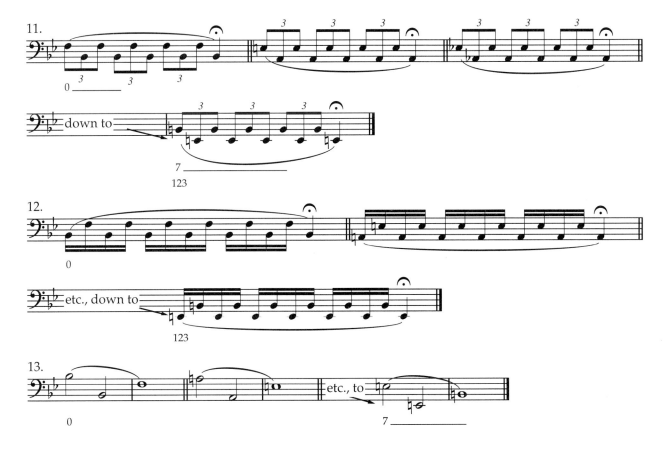

14. Soft tongue only on initial attack. Use no tongue for the remainder of the phrase. Play three times in one breath, making certain there are no accents. Keep tone constant.

0 _____ Repeat 3 times

123

15. Play with soft (da) legato tongue.

to 123

16. Triad slur. No tongue.

to 123

17. Lip massage. Play relaxed with full round tone on each note.

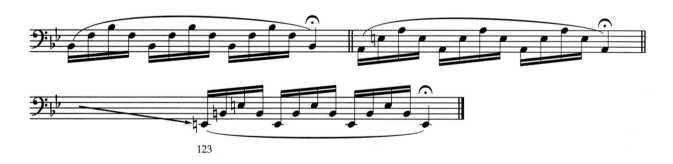

123

18. Overtone slur in two octaves. Do not use excessive pressure in order to obtain high note. Use bunching of the embouchure rather than a stretch (or smile) embouchure. Use no tongue after initial attack. Play as smoothly as possible.

123   0

19. Breath control and legato. Take normal speaking breath for first phrase and increase gradually for each succeeding phrase. Do not breathe in the middle of a ligature. Delay slide until note is stopped and then move quickly, but smoothly, to next position. Articulate each note with a soft legato tongue. Maintain strict tempo. The following model should be played in all major and minor keys.

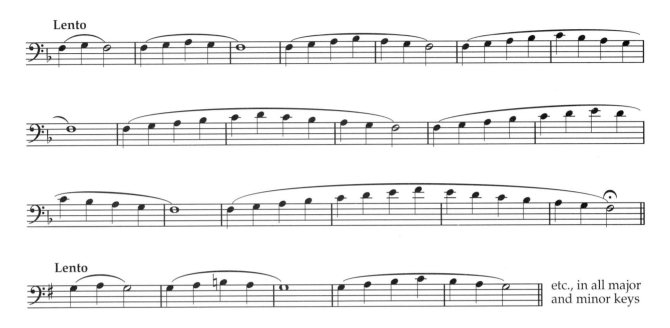

etc., in all major and minor keys

20–21–22. Smooth, even slur. Attack first note in each group. Play in a strict orchestral style. Full, even tone.

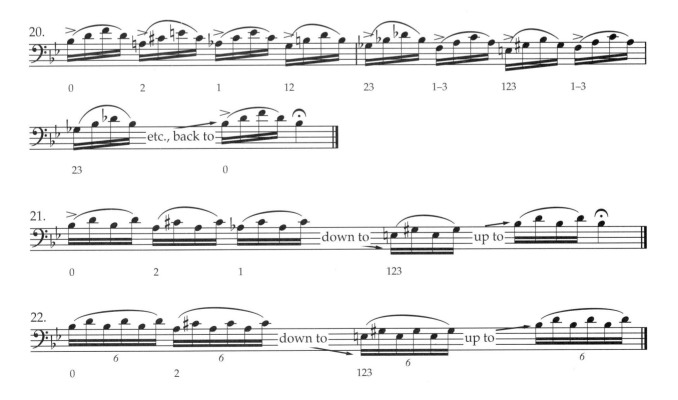

23–24–25. Play the following scale model in the following keys: E, F♯, G, A♭, B♭, A, C, and higher if possible. Use a firm, legato (da) tongue. Separate between notes and keep constant throughout. Breathe after each eighth note. Use fast, even slide movement. Try for control of slide without stiffness. Maintain smooth, firm, legato.

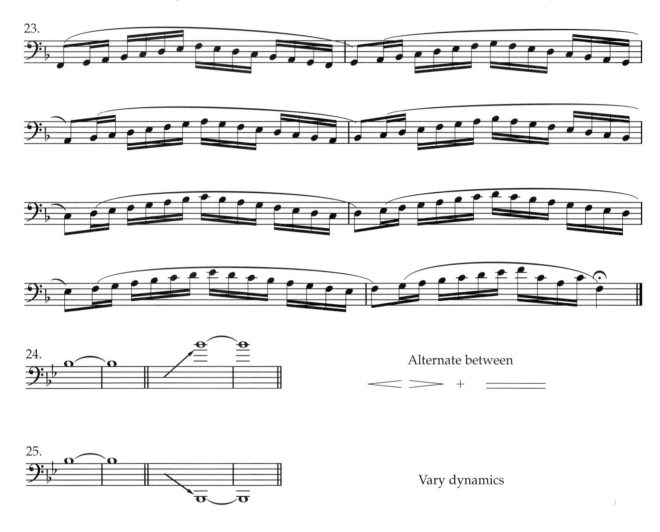

Alternate between

Vary dynamics

26. Do not breathe during exercise, and do not remove mouthpiece from lips. Keep rhythm steady.

To Develop High Range

27. Overtone series over two octaves with added ninth. As embouchure grows stronger, add tenth, etc., to overtone series. Play relaxed, no pressure, and as smoothly as possible.

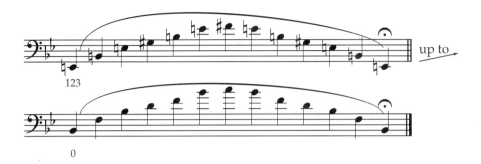

28–29. Do not breathe or relax embouchure during pause. Start note after pause with a very soft tongue. Don't push with lips. Try to hear tone before attack. Play in one breath.

30. Make all notes equal in value, tone, etc. No accents. No pressure for high note. Be sure that the seventh is not allowed to replace the fifth in the overtone series, in descending from highest note, i.e., in first position (B♭ overtone series) A♭ instead of F, which is the fifth.

31. As relaxed as possible.

32. No pressure on high slur. Full, round tone on each note. On all remaining exercises try for complete relaxation.

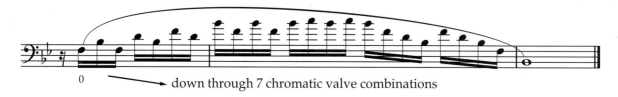

SELECTED LITERATURE FOR EUPHONIUM

Note: The euphonium can also play all of the trombone repertoire.

Methods and Studies

Level 1

Anderson, *Best in Class, Books 1 & 2*, Kjos Music Co.

Beeler, *Walter Beeler Method, Book I*, Warner Brothers

Belwin, *First Division Band Method*, Belwin

Edmondson, *Developing Band Book 1*, Edmondson & McGinty

Feldstein, *Alfred's New Band Method, Book 1*, Alfred Pub. Co.

Kinyon, *Breeze Easy Method*, Warner Brothers

Leonard, *Learning Unlimited Cassette Series*, Hal Leonard Pub. Co.

Leonard, *Learning Unlimited, Level One*, Hal Leonard Pub. Co.

Leonard, *Let's Play Baritone Horn, Level One* (Audio-Visual Band Series), Hal Leonard Pub. Co.

Leonard, *Let's Play Baritone Horn, Level Two* (Audio-Visual Band Series), Hal Leonard Pub. Co.

Long, *Elementary Method for Trombone or Baritone*, Rubank

O'Reilly, *Accent on Achievement, Book 1*, Alfred Pub. Co.

O'Reilly, *Yamaha Band Ensembles, Book 1*, Alfred Pub. Co.

Pearson, *Standard of Excellence, Book 1*, Kjos Music Co.

Rusch, *Hal Leonard Elementary Band Method*, Hal Leonard Pub. Co.

Level 2

Beeler, *Walter Beeler Method, Book II*, Warner Brothers

Edmondson, *Developing Band Book 2*, Edmondson & McGinty

Endreson, *Supplementary Studies*, Rubank

Feldstein, *Alfred's Basic Solos and Ensembles*, Book I

Gower, *Rubank Advanced Method, Book I*

Hunsberger, *The Remington Warm-up Studies*, Accura

O'Reilly, *Accent on Achievement, Book 2*, Alfred Pub. Co.

O'Reilly, *Yamaha Band Ensembles, Book 2*, Alfred Pub. Co.

Ostling, *Time Out for Ensembles*, Belwin

Pares, *Pares' Scales for Trombone or Baritone*, Rubank

Pearson, *Standard of Excellence, Book 2*, Kjos Music Co.

Phillips, *Silver Burdett—Instrumental Series*, Silver Burdett

Ployhar, *Recommended Warm-up Technique Book*, Belwin

Ployhar, *Tone and Technique*, Belwin

Rusch, *Hal Leonard Intermediate Band Method*, Hal Leonard Pub. Co.

Ryden, *Classical Quartets for All*, Belwin

Level 3

Arban, *Method*, Fischer

Edmondson, *Developing Band Book 3*, Edmondson & McGinty

Elledge, *Band Technique Step by Step*, Kjos Music Co.

Erickson, Frank, *Technique through Performance*, Alfred Pub. Co.

Fink, *From Treble Clef to Bass Clef Baritone*, Accura

Gower, *Rubank Advanced Method, Book II*, Rubank

Hunsberger, *The Remington Warm-up Studies*, Accura

O'Reilly, *Accent on Achievement, Book 3*, Alfred Pub. Co.

Pares, *Pares' Scales for Trombone or Baritone*, Rubank

Pearson, *Standard of Excellence, Book 3*, Kjos Music Co.

Phillips, *Silver Burdett—Instrumental Series*, Silver Burdett

Ployhar, *Recommended Warm-up Technique Book*, Belwin

Ployhar, *Tone and Technique*, Belwin

Rusch, *Hal Leonard Advanced Band Methods*, Hal Leonard Pub. Co.

Ryden, *Classical Quartets for All*, Belwin

Schlossberg, *Daily Drills and Technical Studies*, Baron

Smith, *Symphonic Warm-ups*, Hal Leonard Pub. Co.

Voxman, *Selected Duets, Books I and II*, Rubank

Level 4

Arban, *Method*, Fischer

Blume, *Thirty-one Studies for Trombone*, Fischer

Bordogni-Rochut, *Melodious Etudes, Book I*, Fischer

Charlier, *Trente-six Etudes Transcendantes*, Leduc

Fink, *Introducing the Alto Clef*, Accura

Fink, *Introducing the Tenor Clef*, Accura

Gower, *Rubank Advanced Method for Trombone or Baritone, Vol. 1*, Rubank

Level 5

Amsden, *Duets*, Barnhouse

Arban, *Method*, Fischer

Blazhevich, *Clef Studies*, International

Blume, *Thirty-Six Studies*, Fischer

Bodet, *Seize Etudes de Virtuosité d'après J. S. Bach pour Trompette*, Leduc

Bordogni-Rochut, *Melodious Etudes, Book I*, Fischer

Charlier, *Trente-six Etudes Transcendantes*, Leduc

Gillis, *70 Progressive Studies for the Modern Bass Trombonist*, Southern

Gower, *Rubank Advanced Method for Trombone or Baritone, Vol. II*, Rubank

Hunsberger, *The Remington Warm-up Studies*, Accura

Kopprasch, *Sixty Selected Studies for Trombone*, Fischer

Kopprasch, *Sixty Studies, Book I*, Fischer

Remington, *Warm-up Studies*, Accura

Tyrell, *Forty Progressive Etudes for Trombone*, Boosey & Hawkes

Level 6

Arban, *Method*, Fischer

Bach, *Six Cello Suites*, Fischer

Blazhevich, *Twenty-six Sequences*, International

Blazhevich, *Concert Duets*, Belwin

Bodet, *Seize Etudes de Virtuosité d'après J. S. Bach pour Trompette*, Leduc

Bordogni-Roberts, *Forty-three Bel Canto Studies*, King

Bordogni-Rochut, *Melodious Etudes, Book II*, Fischer

Bordogni-Rochut, *Melodious Etudes, Book III*, Fischer

Brasch, *The Euphonium and Four Valve Brasses*, Brasch

Charlier, *Thirty-two Etudes de Perfectionnement*, Lemoine

Clarke, *Characteristic Studies*, Fischer

Clarke, *Technical Studies*, Fischer

Hunsberger, *The Remington Warm-up Studies*, Accura

Kopprasch, *Sixty Studies, Book II*, Fischer

Lafosse, *School of Sight Reading, Book V*, Baron

Lehman, *The Art of Euphonium Playing, Books I and II*, Hoe

Ostrander, *Shifting Meter Studies*, King

Remington, *Warm-up Studies*, Accura

Schlossberg, *Daily Drills and Technical Studies*, Baron

Text

Bowman, *Practical Hints on Playing the Baritone*, Belwin

Solos

Levels 1–2

Belwin-Mills, *Trombone Solos*, Belwin

The Canadian Brass Book of Beginning Trombone Solos, The Canadian Brass on the Companion CDs, Hal Leonard Pub. Co.

The Canadian Brass Book of Easy Trombone Solos, The Canadian Brass on the Companion CDs, Hal Leonard Pub. Co.

The Canadian Brass Book of Intermediate Trombone Solos, The Canadian Brass on the Companion CDs, Hal Leonard Pub. Co.

Feldstein, *First Solo Songbook*, Belwin

Haydn-Stouffer, *Country Dances*, Kendor

Johnson, *Festive Ode*, Rubank

Lethbridge, *A Handel Solo Album*, Oxford University Press

Mozart-Stouffer, *Air in E-flat Major*, Kendor

Porret, *15e Solo de Concours*, Elkan

Rubank, *Concert and Contest Collections for B♭ Cornet, Trumpet or Baritone with Piano Accompaniment*, Rubank

Smith-Falcone, *Cactus Jack*, Belwin

Smith-Falcone, *Cheyenne*, Belwin

Smith-Falcone, *Two Pieces*, Southern

Snell, *Belwin Master Solos* (Easy), Belwin

Snell, *Belwin Master Solos* (Intermediate), Belwin

Weber, *Baritone (Trombone) Student*, Belwin

Levels 3–4

Alary, *Contest Piece (Morceau de Concours)*, Cundy-Betoney

Bach, *Ariosos*, Belwin

Bach-Figert, *For He That Is Mighty from the "Magnificat,"* Kendor

Barat, *Fantaisie*, Leduc

Barat, *Andante et Allegro*, Fischer

Berlioz-Voxman, *Air Gai*, Rubank

Blazhevich, *Concert Sketch No. 5*, Belwin

Cherubini-Pala, *2e Sonate*, Elkan

Clarke, *Carnival of Venice*, Warner Brothers

Clarke, *From the Shores of the Mighty Pacific*, Warner

Clarke, *Maid of the Mist*, Witmark

Corelli-Fitzgerald, *Sonata VIII*, Ricordi

Corelli-Ostrander, *Sarabande and Gavotte*, Rubank

Fauré, J.–Akers, *The Psalms*, Fischer

Galliard, *Six Sonatas*, International

Grafe, *Grand Concerto*, Fischer

Guilmant, *Morceau Symphonique*, Warner Brothers

Handel, *Andante and Allegro*, Southern

Handel, *Concerto in F Minor*, Southern

Handel-Little, *Suite in A Flat*, Belwin

Handel-Ostrander, *Arm, Arm, Ye Brave*, Edition Musicus

Haydn, *Air and Allegro*, Rubank

Haydn, *Adagio (from Cello Concerto)*, Warner Brothers

Hutchinson, *Sonatina*, Fischer

Johnson, *Soliloquy in Three-Four*, Rubank

Lamb, *Classic Festival Solos*, Warner Brothers

Marcello, *Sonata in A Minor*, International

Marcello, *Sonate for Tuba, Basse Solo, Baryton or Euphonium in B♭ with Piano*, Elkan

Marcello-Marriman, *Adagio and Allegro*, Southern

Mozart, *Concerto for Bassoon (K. 191)*, Southern

Mozart-Clulmen, *Ave Verum Corpus*, Elkan

Mozart-Ostrander, *Rondo from Concerto in B♭ (K. 191)*, Kendor

Mozart-Powell, *Arietta and Allegro*, Southern

Mozart-Voxman, *Concert Aria*, Rubank

Pachelbel-Dorf, *Pachelbel Canon for Euphonium and Piano*, Presser

Pryor, *Blue Bells of Scotland*, Fischer

Ropartz, *Andante et Allegro*, Fischer

Rossini-Sullivan, *Largo al Factotum*, Boosey & Hawkes

Schubert-Masso, "Entr'acte" from *Rosamunde*, Kendor

Smith, *First Solos for the Trombone*, Schirmer

Smith, *Solos for the Trombone Player*, Schirmer

Tomasi, *Danse Sacree*, Leduc

Verdi-Ostrander, *Aria* from *Don Carlos*, Edition Musicus

Vivaldi, *Sonatas I–VI (Cello Edition)*, Schirmer

Vivaldi-Sharrow, *Sonata No. 1 in B-flat Major*, International

Voxman, *Concert and Contest Collection*, Rubank

Watts, *The Canadian Brass Book of Intermediate Trombone (Baritone) Solos*, Hal Leonard Pub. Co.

White, *Dance and Aria*, Shawnee

Levels 5–6

Alder, *Four Dialogues*, Fischer

Bach, J. *Concert Variations for Euphonium and Piano*, Jan Bach

Bach, *Six Cello Suites*, International

Bach-LaFosse, *Cello Suites No. 1*, Leduc

Bach-LaFosse, *Cello Suites No. 2*, Leduc

Bach-Marsteller, *Sonata No. 1*, Southern

Bach-Marsteller, *Sonata No. 2*, Southern

Bach-Marsteller, *Sonata No. 3*, Southern

Bach-Marsteller, *Suites for Violoncello Alone*, 2 books, Southern

Bachelder, *Dialogue in Abstract, for Euphonium and Piano*, Tuba-Euphonium Press

Bachelder, *Lyric Piece for Euphonium*, Tuba-Euphonium Press

Bachelder, *Theatre Piece for Euphonium, Cello and Vibraphone*, Tuba-Euphonium Press

Beethoven-Bachelder, *Sonata Op. 17*, Tuba-Euphonium Press

Barat, *Introduction and Dance*, Southern

Barat, *Morceau de Concours*, Leduc

Bassett, *Suite*, King

Boda, *Sonatine*, Boda

Boutry, *Tubacchanale*, Leduc

Boutry, *Tubaroque*, Leduc

Bozza, *New Orleans*, Leduc

Bozza, *Prélude et Allegro*, Leduc

Casterede, *Fantasie Concertante*, Leduc

Clark, *The Southern Cross*, Warner Brothers

Clarke, *The Bride of the Waves (Polka Brillante)*, Witmark

Clarke, *Stars in a Velvety Sky*, Fischer

Corelli-Brown, *Sonata in F Major*, International

Corelli-Brown, *Sonata No. 9 in A Major (Op. 5)*, International

Corelli-Brown, *Sonata in D Major for Cello and Piano*, International

Corelli-Brown, *Sonata in F Major*, International

David, *Concertino*, Fischer

Dubois, *Suite*, Leduc

Frackenpohl, *Air and Rondo*, Doen Publishers

Galliard, *Sonata I*, McGinnis & Marx

Galliard, *Sonata III*, McGinnis & Marx

Galliard-Clark, *Sonata No. 2*, McGinnis & Marx

Galliard-Clark, *Sonata No. 4*, McGinnis & Marx

George, *Sonata*, Ensemble Pub.

George, *Sonata for Baritone Horn (Trombone) and Piano*, Ensemble Pub.

Gröndahl, *Concert*, Giovanni

Haddad, *Suite*, Shawnee

Handel, *Concerto in F Minor*, Southern

Handel-LaFosse, *Concerto in Fa Mineur*, Leduc

Handel-Sharrow, *Concerto in G Minor*, International

Hartley, *Sonata Euphonica*, Presser

Hartley, *Two Pieces for Euphonium (Trombone) and Piano*, Tenuto Pub.

Hogg, *Studies for Euphonium and Piano*, Music Graphic

Horovitz, *Euphonium Concerto* (Euphonium & Piano or Brass Band), Seven Oaks

Jacob, *Concerto for Trombone*, Galaxy

Jacob, *Fantasia for Euphonium and Piano* (band), Boosey

Jones, *Dialogue for Euphonium and Piano*, Jones

Jones, *Sonatina*, Fema

Krush, *Auroras for Euphonium and Organ*, Krush

Larsson, *Concertino, Op. 45, No. 7*, Carl Gehrmans Musik Fürlag

Latham, *Eidolons for Euphonium and Piano*, Shawnee

Liszt-Bachelder, *Oh quand je dors*, Tuba-Euphonium Press

Marcello, *Sonata in A Minor,* International

Martin, *Suite,* Canadian

McKay, *Sonata,* Remick

Mozart-Brown, *Sonata in B-flat Major (K. 292),* International

Mozart-Marcellus, *Sonata in B♭ Major (K. 292),* Kendor

Mozart-Weisberg, *Concerto in B♭ Major (K. 191),* International

Ponchielli, *Concerto for Euphonium,* Tuba-Euphonium Press

Presser, *Rondo for Baritone Horn and Piano,* Tenuto

Presser, *Sonatina,* Tenuto

Pryor, *Blue Bells of Scotland, Air & Variations,* Fischer

Rimsky-Korsakov–Gibson, *Concerto for Trombone and Band,* International

Rossini–Bachelder, *Duetto Buffo, For Euphonium and Voice,* Tuba-Euphonium Press

Saint-Saëns, *The Swan,* International

Sanders, *Sonata in E-flat,* Warner Brothers

Savard, *Morceau de Concours,* Fischer

Schubert, *Arpeggione Sonata,* Whaling Music Pub.

Schubert–Bachelder, *Auf dem Strom, for Euphonium and Voice,* Tuba-Euphonium Press

Serocki, *Sonatina,* Herman Moeck Verlag (Germany)

Smith, *Concert Piece,* Smith

Sparke, *Euphonium Concerto,* Studio Music Company

Sparke, *Pantomine,* Studio Music Company

Telemann, *Fantasie No. 2 in F Minor,* International

Townsend, *Chamber Concerto No. 2,* Presser

Uber, *Exhibitions,* Kendor

Vaughan Williams–Droste, *Six Studies in English Folksong,* Galaxy Music Co.

Vivaldi, *Sonata No. 1 in B-flat Major,* International

Vivaldi, *Sonata No. 5 in E Minor,* International

Vivaldi, *Sonata No. 6 in B-flat Major,* International

Whear, *Sonata,* Ludwig

Wilder, *Concerto,* Margun

Wilder, *Sonata,* Margun

LIST OF RECORDINGS

Album Title	Contents	Performer/s	Label
Childs Play	Farr (arr.), *Carnival of Venice* Wilkinson (arr.), *Deep Inside the Sacred Temple* Wilson (arr.), *Arrival of the Queen of Sheba* Jenkins (arr.), *Myfanwy* Wyss (arr.), *Ronda Alla Turca* Woodfield (arr.), *Double Bass* Snell (arr.), *Moto Perpetuo* Catheral (arr.), *Softly As I Leave You* Golland (arr.), *Childs Play* Fraser (arr.), *Perhaps Love* Wyss (arr.), *Viva Vivaldi* Ball (arr.), *Calon Lân* Child Brothers (arr.), *Parade of the Tin Soldiers* Howarth (arr.), *Grand Study No. 13* Graham (arr.), *Brilliante*	Child Brothers	Doyen CD: DOYCD 001
Elegance	Barat, *Morceau de Concours* Telemann, *Sonata in F minor* Schumann, "Ich grolle nicht" (No. VII of *Dichterliebe, Op. 48*) Cords, *Concert Fantasie* Uber, *Sonata for Euphonium and Piano* Wiedrich, *Reverie for Euphonium and Piano*	Roger Behrend	Coronet Recording Co. (No number)
Euphonium Music	Currow, *Rhapsody for Euphonium* Bowmen, *Euphonium Music* Phillips, *Romance* Stephens, *Solo Rhapsody* Gollard, *Euphonium Concerto No. 1*	Child Brothers	Doyen CD DOYCD 022

	Howarth, *Cantabile for John Fletcher* Sparke, *Fantasy for Euphonium*		
Premiere	Hummel, J. N., *Fantasy* Capuzzi, *Andante and Rondo* Mozart, W. A., *Adagio and Rondo* Fiocco, *Arioso and Allegro* Clark, *City in the Sea* Wilby, *Concerto for Euphonium*	Robert Childs	Doyen CD: DOYCD 016

A Shared Vision of Excellence	Curnow, *Symphonic Variants for
	    Euphonium and Band*
	Reed, *Seascape*
	Brubaker, *Rhapsody for Euphonium
	    and Band*
	Martino, *Introspect*
	Cords-Fabrizo, *Romanze*
	Gillingham, *Vintage*
	Nelhybel, *Concerto for Euphonium
	    and Band*
		Roger Behrend	IMPS Music
			  Ph: 1-800-234-2458

Welsh Wizards	Barry, *Fascinating Euphoniums* Brodsky-Farr, *Be My Love* Fraser, *Fantastic Fast Fingered Fandango* Swift-Catherall, *Elfried* Elgar-Wilson, *Salut d'amour* Powell, *Duo for Euphoniums* Catherall, *Song of the Seashore* Sparke, *Pantomime* Rimsky-Korsakov, *Flight of the Bumblebee* Catherall, *Only One* Newsome, *A Piece of Cake* Rossini, *Largo al Factotum* Ball, *Calon Lan* Monti-Wilson, *Czardas* Yamamoto, *Aka Tonbi Yamada* Sparke, *Two Part Invention*	Child Brothers	Doyen CD 022
The World of Euphonium	Marcello, *Sonata in F* Butterworth, *Partita Op. 89* Rachmoninov, *Vocalise* Wiggins, *Soliloquy IX* Hoshina, *Fantasy for Euphonium* Kummer, *Variations for Ophicleide* Hartley, *Sonata Euphonica* Faure, *Apres un Reve* Rimmer, *Weber's Last Waltz* Bosanko, *Heart in Heart* Offenbach, *Barcarolle* Arbans, *A New Carnival of Venice*	Roger Behrend	IMPS Music Ph: 1-800-234-2458

THE TUBA

HISTORY OF THE TUBA

Like that of the trumpet, trombone, and horn, ancestry of the tuba includes primitive instruments such as the shofar, the buzine, and the Roman tuba. Some claim the Roman tuba was the source of the name of this instrument, which is the lowest pitched of all brass instruments. The Roman tuba was a curved instrument, approximately 12 feet long, with a wide-angle taper. This instrument, closely related to the primitive trumpets of the Assyrians, Egyptians, and Jews, was called a *salpinx* by the Greeks. The Roman tuba was used as a signaling trumpet in the army and—except for its name—bears little resemblance to the present-day tuba (Figure 12.1).

Around the beginning of the seventeenth century, an instrument in the form of a letter S was developed. This instrument, known as the serpent, was approximately eight feet long and is generally accepted as the predecessor of the modern bass tuba (Figure 12.2). The serpent was played with a cupped mouthpiece and was usually constructed of wood and covered with leather. In its original form, the serpent was keyless, with six or eight holes drilled laterally into the instrument. However, keys were added in the last part of the eighteenth century. Toward the close of the eighteenth century, the instrument, after remaining in the S shape for over a hundred years, changed to resemble the present-day bassoon. Its eight feet of tubing were placed in two parallel lines, and the instrument became known as the military serpent or Russian bassoon (Figure 12.3).

FIGURE 12.2
Serpent

FIGURE 12.3
Military serpent or Russian bassoon

FIGURE 12.1
Roman tuba

By the middle of the nineteenth century, the military serpent evolved into an innovative instrument with an elaborate bell in the shape of a dragon (Figure 12.4).

The *ophicleide,* the bass instrument of the keyed bugle family, was the accepted bass of the military band until the middle of the nineteenth century (Figure 12.5). When assigned a part in the symphony orchestra, which rarely occurred, it was given parts that are now generally assigned to the tuba.

In 1835, Johann G. Moritz of Berlin constructed the first bass tuba for the Prussian army (Figure 12.6).

In 1847, Adolphe Sax of Paris developed a family of musical bass instruments called saxhorns (Figure 12.7). All these instruments had upright bells. Sizes included alto, tenor, baritone, and bass instruments.

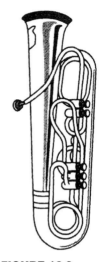

FIGURE 12.6
Bass tuba in F; earliest bass tuba known; Johann Gottfried Moritz, Berlin (1777–1840)

FIGURE 12.4
Military serpent or Russian bassoon (with dragon head)

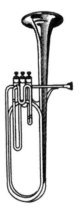

FIGURE 12.7
Baritone saxhorn in B♭; Adolphe Sax, Paris (1814–1894)

FIGURE 12.5
Ophicleide (Courtesy—Steve Call)

Toward the end of the nineteenth century, a circular form of the tuba, called a helicon, was invented in Russia. Its practical purpose was to accommodate tuba playing while marching or riding horseback—a difficult task with an upright instrument (Figure 12.8). The American helicon was constructed with a larger bore, and the bell had a greater flare (Figure 12.9).

In 1898, John Phillip Sousa asked C. H. Conn to construct a version of the helicon horn for the military. Like the helicon, it encircled the body and had an enlarged wide-flaring bell that was horizontal with the ceiling while being played, allowing its sound to fill the room. This was ideal for indoor concert playing, as the echo of the room enhanced the lowest bass tones, thus providing the best scenario for tuning. Marching outdoors, this instrument was moved to the back of the formation. For these occasions, the bell was designed to point forward in order to allow the sound to be heard by all.

FIGURE 12.8
Helicon (Courtesy—Steve Call)

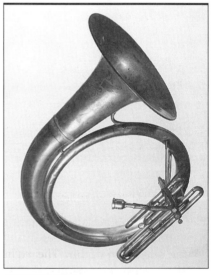

FIGURE 12.9
American helicon, enlarged wide-flaring bell

Richard Wagner was the first famous composer to include the tuba as a member of the orchestra. Wagner's parts written for tuba were performed by horn players on a modified horns called Wagner tubas. The instruments had slightly larger bores than the horns but were not as large as today's tuba. The instruments Wagner scored were in effect bass horns, called *tubens*. Wagner also scored for one *kontrabass tuba*, a large, four-valve instrument featuring a large cup mouthpiece and sounding in the register we now associate with the tuba (Figure 12.10).

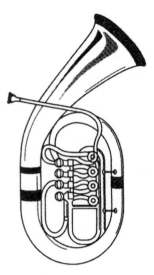

FIGURE 12.10
Wagner tuba

THE TUBA AND SOUSAPHONE

The tuba and sousaphone form the bass of the brass group and are made in a variety of models. The most common is the tuba in BB-flat, which is exactly one octave lower than the baritone and trombone. The BB-flat tuba is the preferred instrument for band. With the trumpets and trombones keyed in B flat, the tuning of the BB-flat tuba is more accurate and compatible with the harmonic series of these instruments. This is the open fundamental of the BB-flat tuba.

The sousaphone, another model of the bass horn or tuba, is characterized by its circular shape, which makes it suitable for use in marching bands. Unfortunately, many school groups, not supplied with both the regular tuba for concert work and the sousaphone for marching, must use only the sousaphone. If used for concert work, the instrument should be equipped with a stand because the sousaphone is extremely awkward for a player to hold when seated. Most sousaphones have three valves. See the nomenclature of the sousaphone in Figure 12.11.

THE E-FLAT TUBA

The E-flat tuba, pitched a perfect fourth higher than the BB-flat tuba, plays exactly the same music as the BB-flat, but is not as effective in the lower register because of its corresponding smaller bore. The

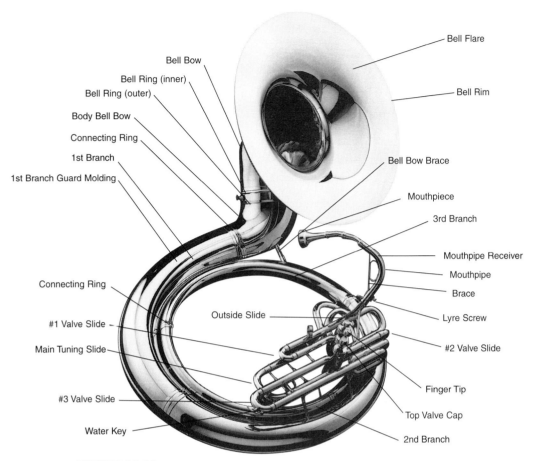

Bell Flare

Bell Rim

Bell Bow

Bell Ring (inner)

Bell Ring (outer)

Body Bell Bow

Connecting Ring

1st Branch

1st Branch Guard Molding

Bell Bow Brace

Mouthpiece

3rd Branch

Mouthpipe Receiver

Mouthpipe

Brace

Lyre Screw

Connecting Ring

Outside Slide

#1 Valve Slide

Main Tuning Slide

#2 Valve Slide

Finger Tip

#3 Valve Slide

Top Valve Cap

Water Key

2nd Branch

FIGURE 12.11
Sousaphone nomenclature (Courtesy of C. G. Conn Division of United Musical Instruments, USA, Inc., www.unitedmusical.com)

instrument is made in both the three- and four-valve models. The tuba's middle register has the strongest sound as well as the best intonation. The E-flat tuba is often played in parallel octaves with the BB-flat instrument and gives support to the trombone and baritone sections. It is also a popular chamber music instrument.

THE CC TUBA

The CC tuba is the preferred instrument of orchestral tubists. Its open fundamental and harmonic series start one step higher than the BB-flat tuba. Since different keyed tubas can all read the same music, the player must learn a new set of fingerings for each keyed instrument. One advantage of the CC tuba in orchestra is that it matches the pitches of the C trumpet's harmonic series more accurately. With the CC tuba's slightly smaller bore, its clarity and projection are superior to those of the BB-flat tuba. These factors are the primary reasons for the use of the CC tuba in orchestra. See the nomenclature of the CC tuba in Figure 12.12 on page 144.

HOLDING THE TUBA AND SOUSAPHONE

In holding the tuba or sousaphone, the musician's body and head should be erect and the feet firmly on the floor (Figures 12.13 and 12.14). The right hand should be curved and rest lightly on the valves (Figure 12.13). The left hand should support the instrument by grasping the inner tubing in as inconspicuous a manner as possible (Figure 12.14 and Figure 12.15).

For younger performers who find holding the tuba and sousaphone difficult, tuba and sousaphone stands are available at many music dealers. In the case of the sousaphone, a chair is manufactured with an attached stand that holds the sousaphone firmly in place.

MUTE

The standard tuba mute resembles a straight mute (Figure 12.16). The only standard mute for the tuba, it is used in solo, ensemble, band, and orchestra when muted sections are designated. The biggest

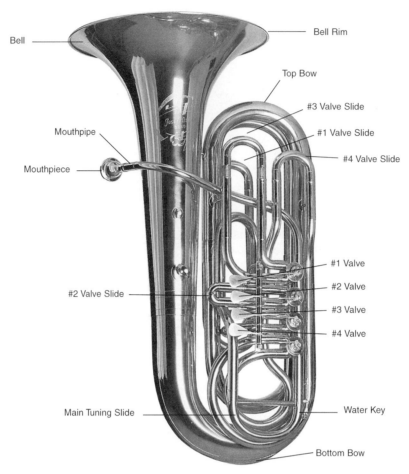

Bell

Bell Rim

Top Bow

#3 Valve Slide

#1 Valve Slide

#4 Valve Slide

Mouthpipe

Mouthpiece

#1 Valve

#2 Valve

#2 Valve Slide

#3 Valve

#4 Valve

Main Tuning Slide

Water Key

Bottom Bow

FIGURE 12.12
Meinl Weston CC (4-valve) tuba nomenclature

FIGURE 12.13
E♭ tuba, playing position

FIGURE 12.14
BB♭ sousaphone, playing position

FIGURE 12.15
CC tuba, playing position; the BB♭ tuba uses the same playing position

FIGURE 12.16
Tuba mute

challenge in playing with a tuba mute is adjusting the pitch, which is 14 to 25 cents sharp, depending on the thickness of the corks. With thin corks, the mute goes in farther and causes the tuba to play sharper. It is recommended that the tubist pull out the tuning side to the appropriate tuning while using the mute.

Use of the First Valve Slide

The first valve slide on most tubas is easy to reach with the left hand. Any note involving the first valve can be adjusted for intonation problems, providing the slide is prepared properly. To prepare the

first valve slide, lubricate it to move freely, and have a competent repairman vent it to eliminate any vacuum as it is moved.

Four, Five and Six-Valve Tubas

The four-valve tuba has an extended lower register. The fourth valve, when used alone, lowers the pitch of the instrument a fourth to F. This valve has the same advantages and limitations as explained in Chapter Eleven for the four-valve euphonium. The use of a fifth or sixth valve on the tuba allows for the extension of the range downward; see the example below.

FOUR-, FIVE-, AND SIX-VALVE TUBAS

The CC tuba is the favored instrument for most symphonic tuba players. Below is the fingering chart for CC tuba with four valves.

FINGERING CHART FOR CC TUBA WITH 4 VALVES

C	B	B♭	A♯	A	A♭	G♯	G	G♭	F♯	F	E	E♭	D♯	D	D♭	C♯	C
0	2	1		1–2	2–3		4	2–4		1–4 or 1–2–4	3–4 or 2–3–4	1–3–4		1–2–3–4	Not playable with 4 valves		

FINGERING CHART FOR CC TUBA WITH 5 VALVES

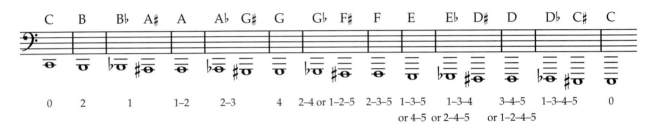

C	B	B♭	A♯	A	A♭	G♯	G	G♭	F♯	F	E	E♭	D♯	D	D♭	C♯	C
0	2	1		1–2	2–3		4	2–4 or or 4–5	1–2–5	2–3–5	1–3–5 or 2–4–5	1–3–4		3–4–5 or 1–2–4–5	1–3–4–5		0

CHROMATIC FINGERING CHART

BB♭ Tuba and Sousaphone, E♭ Tuba

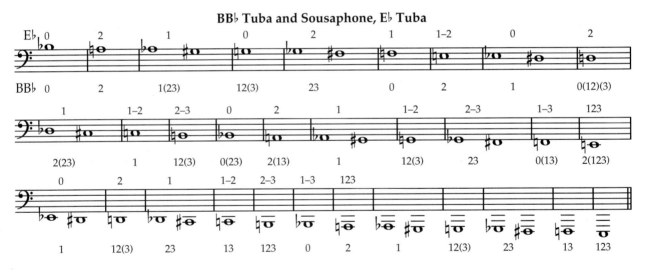

E♭	0		2		1		0		2		1		1–2		0		2
BB♭	0		2		1(23)		12(3)		23		0		2		1		0(12)(3)

	1	1–2	2–3	0	2	1	1–2	2–3	1–3	123
	2(23)	1	12(3)	0(23)	2(13)	1	12(3)	23	0(13)	2(123)

	0	2	1	1–2	2–3	1–3	123	0	2	1	1–2	2–3	1–3	123
	1	12(3)	23	13	123						12(3)	23	13	123

The following example gives the harmonic series for all seven valve combinations for BB♭ tuba and sousaphone.

HARMONIC SERIES

BB♭ Tuba, Sousaphone

Valve
Combinations

*This set of partials is generally so out-of-tune as to be unusable.

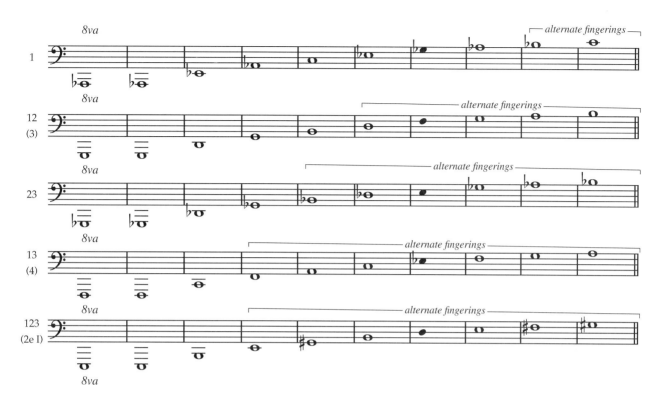

The CC tuba is used almost exclusively by orchestral players and the F tuba has gained popularity as a solo and chamber instrument. Since the CC tuba and F tuba usually have four and often five valves, the fingering chart includes their use.

CHROMATIC FINGERING CHART

F Tuba, CC Tuba

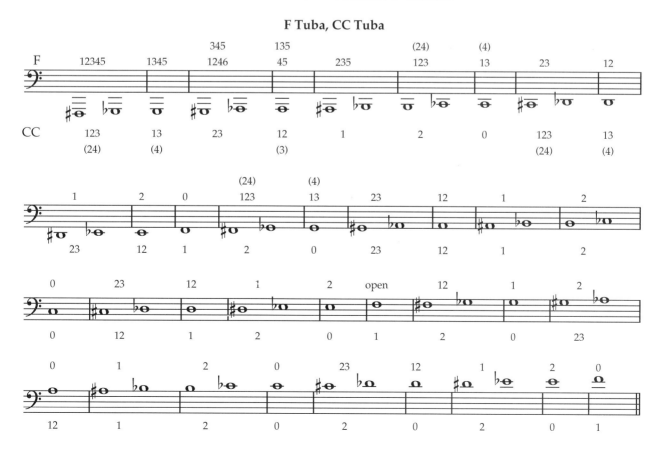

INTONATION PROBLEMS

The intonation problems of the baritone horn, tuba, and sousaphone are the same as for the trumpet, except that they are compounded by their larger size.

The intonation chart indicates the intonation tendencies for the BB-flat tuba. Tubas in any other key, F, CC, or E-flat, would have the same intonation tendencies on their chromatic scale.

In addition to the inherent intonation defects already discussed, brass instruments may acquire intonation defects through misuse, improper care, or conditions under which they are being played. It is important that brass instruments be kept in proper adjustment, since accumulation of foreign matter in the tubes or improper alignment of valve air passages can cause serious intonation problems. Dents in the tubing can alter the vibration form to a degree that affects the intonation of the instrument.

INTONATION CHART
BB♭ Tuba, Sousaphone

Roman numerals beneath the notes indicate the degree to which the pitch is out of tune.

   I—Slightly out of tune
  II—Moderately out of tune
 III—Greatly out of tune
 IV—Drastically out of tune

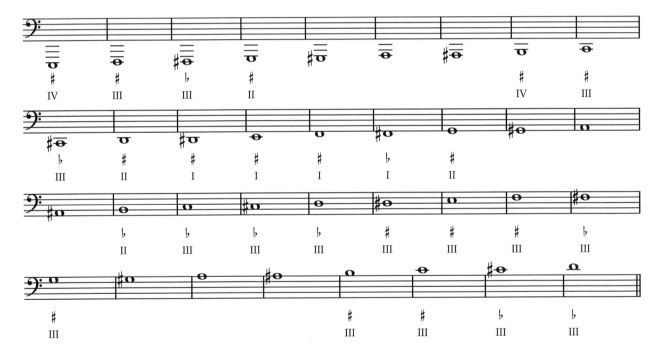

DAILY EMBOUCHURE AND FLEXIBILITY STUDIES

1. Use soft legato tongue.

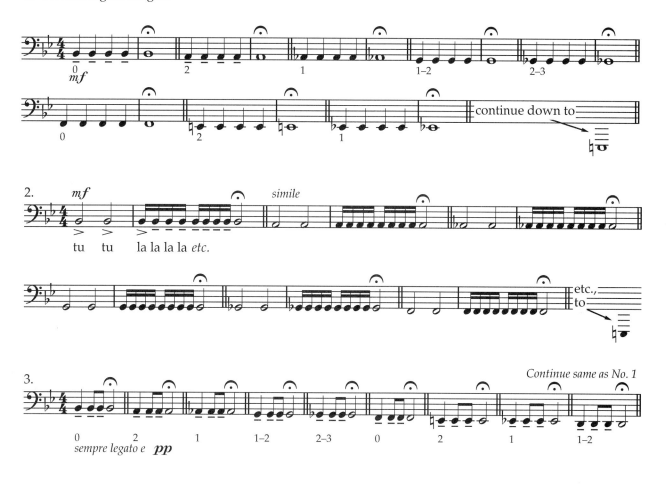

4. Attack and tuning. Attack with full MF tone. Be sure to round the end of each tone. Avoid cutting off the tone with the tongue as in "tut." Never allow the tone to become brassy and do not increase the volume after attack. *Support with the breath.*

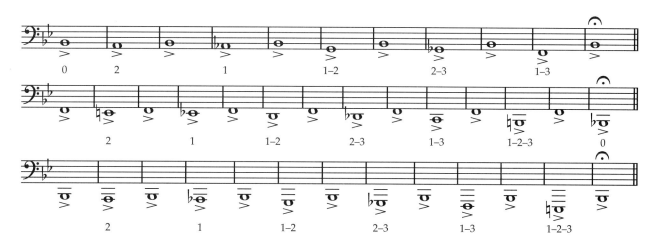

5. Use no tongue after initial attack.

6–7–8. Trill slurs. Play in a relaxed manner. Never allow the tone to become brassy. Keep rhythm steady.

9. Legato tongue.

10. Lip slurs. Do not accent top notes. Make slurs as smooth and even as possible. Keep same tone throughout exercise. Play relaxed and use tongue only on initial attack. Avoid unnecessary facial movement, i.e., chewing the notes.

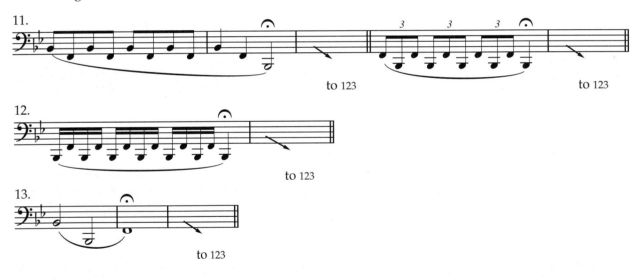

14. Soft tongue only on initial attack. Use no tongue for the remainder of the phrase. Play three times in one breath, making certain there are no accents. Keep tone constant.

15. Triad slur. No tongue after initial attack.

16. Play with soft legato tongue.

(tenuto sempre)

123

17. Lip massage. Play in a relaxed manner with full round tone on each note.

123

18. To extend range upward, use more breath support, and no excessive pressure for upper notes.

19. No breath during phrase.

20. Play the following scale model in the following keys: E, F♯, G, A♭, B♭, A, C, and higher if possible. Use firm legato tongue. Breathe after each eighth note. Maintain smooth, firm legato.

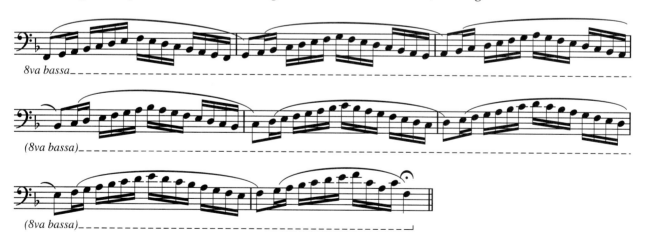

21. Overtone series with added ninth. As embouchure grows stronger, add tenth, etc. Play relaxed, no pressure, as smoothly as possible. Use exercises such as the following for increased flexibility.

123

SELECTED LITERATURE FOR TUBA

Methods and Studies

Level 1

Beeler, *Method for Tuba*, Remick

Beeler, *Play Away for Tuba or Sousaphone*, Schirmer

Bell, *Complete Method*, Colin

Blazhevich, *Seventy Studies*, 2 books, King Pub. Co.

Bordogni, *43 Bel Canto Studies*, King Pub. Co.

Cimera, *73 Advanced Studies*, Belwin

Gower-Voxman, *Rubank Advanced Method*, 2 books, Rubank

Herfurth, *A Tune a Day for Tuba*, Boston

Hovey, *Rubank Elementary Method for BB♭ and B♭ Tuba*, Rubank

Kinyon, *Breeze-Easy Method for BB♭ Tuba, Books I & II*, Witmark

Kopprasch, *60 Selected Studies*, King

Kuehn, *28 Advanced Studies*, Southern

Kuehn, *60 Musical Studies*, 2 books, Southern

Lass, *Studies and Melodious Etudes*, 3 books, Belwin

Little, *Embouchure Builder for BB♭ Bass (Tuba)*, Pro Arte

Little, *Practical Hints on Playing the Tuba*, Belwin

Pease, *Pro Arte E-flat or BB-flat Bass (Tuba) Method*, Pro Arte

Prescott, *Prep Band Method*, Schmitt, Hall & McCreary

Tyrrell, *Advanced Studies*, Boosey & Hawkes

Vasieliev, *24 Melodious Etudes*, King

Level 2

Adler, *Tubetudes*, Southern

Beeler, *Method for BB-flat Tuba, Book II*, Remlock

Getchell, *Practical Studies, Books 1 & 2*, Belwin

Hovey, *Rubank Elementary Method for BB♭ and B♭ Tuba*, Rubank

Kinyon, *Breeze-Easy Method for BB♭ Tuba, Book II*, Witmark

Kuehn, *60 Musical Studies for Tuba, Book I*, Southern

Lass, *Studies and Melodious Etudes, Books I–III*, Belwin

Little, *Embouchure Builder for B♭♭ Bass (Tuba)*, Pro Arte

Little, *Practical Hints on Playing the Tuba*, Belwin

Pares, *Pares' Scales*, Rubank

Vanders Cook, *Vanders Cook Etudes for Tuba*, Rubank

Level 3

Adler, *Tubetudes*, Southern

Arban, *The Arban-Bell Tuba Method*, Colin

Arban, *Complete Conservatory Method for Trombone and Euphonium*, Fischer

Arban-Prescott, *Arban-Prescott First and Second Year*, Fischer

Beeler, *Method for BB-flat Tuba, Book II*, Remlock

Bell, *Foundation to Tuba and Sousaphone Playing*, Fischer

Bell, *Tuba Warm-ups*, Colin

Cimera, *73 Advanced Tuba Studies*, Belwin

Fink, *Studies in Legato for Bass Trombone and Tuba*, Fischer

Getchell, *Practical Studies, Books 1 & 2*, Belwin

Knaub, *Progressive Techniques for Tuba*, M.C.A.

Kuehn, *60 Musical Studies for Tuba, Books 1 & 2*, Southern

Lass, *Studies and Melodious Etudes, Books I–III*, Belwin

Little, *Embouchure Builder for BB♭ Bass (Tuba)*, Pro Arte

Little, *Practical Hints on Playing the Tuba*, Belwin

Ostrander, *Shifting Meter Studies*, King Pub. Co.

Pares, *Pares' Scales*, Rubank

Tyrell, *Advanced Studies for BB-flat Bass (Tuba)*, Boosey & Hawkes

Vanders Cook, *Etudes for Tuba*, Rubank

Vasieliev, *24 Melodious Etudes for Tuba*, King Pub. Co.

Level 4

Adler, *Tubetudes*, Southern

Arban, *The Arban-Bell Tuba Method*, Colin

Arban, *Complete Conservatory Method for Trombone and Euphonium*, Fischer

Bell, *Tuba Warm-ups*, Colin

Cimera, *73 Advanced Tuba Studies*, Belwin

Clarke, *Technical Studies*, Fischer

Fink, *Studies in Legato for Bass Trombone and Tuba*, Fischer

Knaub, *Progressive Techniques for Tuba*, M.C.A.

Kopprasch, *60 Selected Studies*, King Pub. Co.

Kuehn, *60 Musical Studies for Tuba, Book 2*, Southern

Little, *Practical Hints on Playing the Tuba*, Belwin

Ostrander, *Shifting Meter Studies*, King

Roberts, *43 Bel Canto Studies for Tuba*, King

Sear, *Etudes for Tuba*, Cor

Tyrell, *Advanced Studies for BB-flat Bass (Tuba)*, Boosey & Hawkes

Vasieliev, *24 Melodious Etudes for Tuba*, King

Level 5

Arban, *Complete Conservatory Method for Trombone and Euphonium*, Fischer

Clarke, *Technical Studies*, Fischer

Knaub, *Progressive Techniques for Tuba*, M.C.A.

Kopprasch, *60 Selected Studies*, King

Lachmann, *Fünfundzwanzig Etuden für Bass Tuba*, Hofmeister

Sear, *Etudes for Tuba*, Cor

Solos

Level 1–2

Arnold, *Fantasy*, Faber

Bach, *Patron of the Wind*, Edition Musicus

Bach-Bell, *Gavotte*, Fischer

Bach-Ostrander, *Patron of the Wind*, Edition Musicus

Barnes, *Arioso and Caprice*, Robbins

Belwin-Mills, *Tuba Solos*, Belwin

Benson, *Arioso*, Belwin

Buchtel, *Londonderry Air*, Kjos Music Co.

The Canadian Brass Book of Beginning Tuba Solos, *The Canadian Brass on the Companion CDs*, Hal Leonard Pub. Co.

The Canadian Brass Book of Easy Tuba Solos, *The Canadian Brass on the Companion CDs*, Hal Leonard Pub. Co.

The Canadian Brass Book of Intermediate Tuba Solos, *The Canadian Brass on the Companion CDs*, Hal Leonard Pub. Co.

Delamarter, *Rocked in the Cradle of the Deep*, Rubank

Feldstein, *First Solo Songbook*, Belwin

Grieg, *In the Hall of the Mountain King*, Rubank

Handel, *Aria from "Judas Maccabaeus,"* Brodt

Handel, *Arm Ye Brave*, Edition Musicus

Handel, "Honor and Arms" from *Samson*, Belwin

Handel, *Larghetto and Allegro*, Belwin

Handel, *Revenge! Timotheus Cries!*, Ludwig

Harzell, *Egotistical Elephant*, Shawnee

Kinyon, *Breeze-Easy Recital Pieces*, Whitmark

Kriesler, *Rondo*, Southern

Masso, *Suite for Louise*, Kendor

Mendelssohn, "It Is Enough" from *Elijah*, Edition Musicus

Newton, *Modern Lullaby*, Boosey & Hawkes

Peter-Bell, *The Jolly Coppersmith*, Belwin

Presser, *Rondo*, Presser

Purcell, *Arise Ye Subterranean Winds*, Edition Musicus

Schubert, *Swan Song*, Edition Musicus

Schumann, *Jolly Peasant*, Rubank

Snell, *Belwin Master Solos (Easy)*, Belwin

Snell, *Belwin Master Solos (Intermediate)*, Belwin

Verdi, *Grand Air from "Masked Ball,"* Edition Musicus

Wagner, *Walther's Prize Song*, Rubank

Level 3–4

Bach, *Air and Bourree*, Fischer

Bach, *Patron of the Wind*, Edition Musicus

Bach, *Siciliano* (Sonata #2), Brodt

Bach-Bell, *Air and Bourée*, Fischer

Barat, *Introduction and Dance*, Southern

Barnet, *Four Segments*, Fema Music

Beach, *Lamento*, Southern

Beethoven, *Variations on a Theme by Handel (Judas Maccabaeus)*, Fischer

Bencriscutto, *Concertino*, Shawnee

Bernstein, *Waltz for Mippy II*, Schirmer

Beversdorf, *Sonata for Bass Tuba*, Southern

Boda, *Sonatina*, Kjos Music Co.

Capuzzi, *Andante and Rondo*, Hinrichsen

Catozzi, *Beelzebub*, Fischer

Childs, *Seaview*, Cole

Dedrick, *Touch of Tuba*, Kendor

Frackenpohl, *Concertino*, King

Frackenpohl, *Variations for Tuba*, Shawnee

Frackenpohl, *Variations (The Cobbler's Bench)*, Shawnee

Goltermann-Bell, *Concerto No. 4*, Fischer

Haddad, *Suite*, Shawnee

Haddad, *Suite for Tuba*, Shawnee

Handel, "Allegro" from *Concerto in F*, Ludwig

Handel, "Honor and Arms" from *Samson*, Schirmer

Handel, *Larghetto and Allegro*, Belwin

Handel, "Sarabande" from *Concerto in F Minor*, Ludwig

Handel, *Thrice Happy the Monarch*, Ludwig

Handel-Bell, *Variations on a Theme of "Judas Maccabaeus,"* Fischer

Hartley, *Aria*, Lekan-Vogal

Hayes, *Solo Pomposo* (H. Filmor), Fischer

Holmes, *Lento*, Shawnee

Lamb, *Classic Festival Solos*, Warner Brothers

Lebedev, *Concerto in One Movement*, Edition Musicus

Lebedev, *Konzert*, Hofmeister

Marcello, *Sonata No. 1*, Southern

McKay, *Suite for Bass Clef Instruments*, University Music Press

Mozart, *O Isis and Osiris*, Brass Press

Mozart, *Serenade*, Shawnee

Nelhybel, *Concert Piece*, Kerby

Ostrander, *Concert Piece in Fugal Style*, Edition Musicus

Presser, *Concertino*, Presser

Presser, *Second Sonatina*, Presser

Presser, *Sonatina*, Presser

Purcell, *Arise Ye Subterranean Winds*, Edition Musicus

Reed, *Fantasia a Due*, Belwin

Schmidt, *Serenade*, WIM

Schroen-Spencer, *Fantasie*, Fischer

Schumann-Bell, *Jolly Farmer*, Fischer

Sear, *Sonatina*, Cor

Sowerby, *Chaconne*, Fischer

Tcherepnine, *Andante*, King

Tcherepnine, *Andante*, Belaieff

Telemann, "Adagio and Allegro" (from *Trumpet Concerto*), Southern

Telemann, *Prelude and Allegro*, Southern

Tomasi, *Etre ou ne pas Etre*, Leduc

Uber, *A Deleware Rhapsody*, Kendor

Uber, *Summer Nocturne*, Southern

Vaughan, *Counterpiece No. 1*, Fema Music

Vaughan Williams, *Six Studies in English Folk Song*, Stainer and Bell

Vivaldi, *Concerto in A Minor*, Edition Musicus

Vivaldi, *Sonata No. 3 in A Minor*, Shawnee

Voxman, *Concert and Contest Collection*, Rubank

Walters, *Blow the Man Down*, Rubank

Wekselblatt, *First Solos for the Tuba Player*, Schirmer

Level 5–6

Bach-Bell, *Air and Bourée*, Fischer

Barat, *Introduction and Dance*, Southern

Beethoven, *Variations on a Theme by Handel*, Fischer

Benson, *Helix*, Fischer

Bernstein, *Waltz for Mippy III*, Boosey & Hawkes

Beversdorf, *Sonata*, Southern

Bozza, *Concertino*, Leduc

Broughton, *Sonata*, Masters Music Pub.

Capuzzi, *Andante and Rondo*, Hinrichsen Edition (UK)

Catozzi, *Beelzebub*, Fischer

Frackenpohl, *Concertino*, King Pub. Co.

Frackenpohl, *Concertino for Tuba*, Shawnee

Frackenpohl, *Sonata for Tuba and Piano*, Kendor

George, *Sonata for Tuba and Piano*, Manuscript

Goltermann, G., *Excerpts from Concerto No. 4*, Fischer

Gregson, *Concerto*, Novello

Hartley, *Double Concerto* (Tuba and Alto Sax), Presser

Hartley, *Suite*, Presser

Hindemith, *Sonata for Bass Tuba and Piano*, Schott

Jacob, *Bagatelles*, Emerson

Jacob, *Tuba Suite*, Boosey & Hawkes

Kellaway, *The Morning Song*, Editions BIM (Switzerland)

Kraft, *Encounters*, Editions BIM (Switzerland)

Lebedev, *Concertino*, Editions Musicus

Penderecki, *Capriccio,* Schott

Penn, *Three Essays,* Seesaw Music

Persichetti, *Parable,* Presser

Persichetti, *Serenade #12,* Presser

Plog, *Three Miniatures,* Editions BIM

Presser, *Capriccio,* Presser

Rachmaninoff, *Vocalises, Op. 34,* Ludwig Music Pub Co.

Russell, *Suite Concertante,* Accura Music

Roikjer, *Capriccio,* Imudico Musikforlaget

Schmidt, *Serenade,* Western International

Spillman, *Concerto,* Edition Musicus

Spillman, *Two Songs,* Edition Musicus

Stevens, *Sonatina,* Southern

Swann, *Two Moods,* Chamber Music Library

Vaughan Williams, *Concerto for Bass Tuba,* Oxford University Press

Vaughan Williams, *Six Studies in English Folksong,* Galaxy

Wekselblatt, *Solos for the Tuba Player,* Schirmer

White, *Sonata,* Ludwig

Wilder, *Elegy for the Whale,* Margun

Wilder, *Sonata,* Mentor

Wilder, *Suite No. 1 (Effie Suite),* Margun Music

Wilder, *Suite No. 4 (Thomas Suite),* Margun Music

LIST OF RECORDINGS

Album Title	Contents	Performer/s	Label
Bill Bell and his Tuba	Hupfeld, *When Yuba Plays the Rhumba on the Tuba Down in Cuba* Petrie, *Asleep in the Deep* Greig, *In the Hall of the Mountain King* Carr-Bell, *Tuba Man* Landes, *The Elephant Tango* Merle, *Mummers (Dance Grotesque)* Arban-Bell, *Carnival of Venice* Mozart, *O Iris and Osiris* Handel-Bell, *Variations on a Theme from "Judas Maccabaeus"* Schumann-Bell, *The Jolly Farmer Goes to Town*	William Bell	Golden Crest LP: CR4027/ CS: CRS4211
Bobissimo! The Best of Roger Bobo	Galliard, *Sonata No. 5 in D Minor* Barat, *Introduction and Dance* Hindemith, *Sonata for Bass Tuba and Piano* Wilder, *Suite No. 1 for Tuba and Piano (Effie)* Kraft, *Encounters II for Solo Tuba* Spillman, *Two Songs* Lazarof, *Cadence VI for Tuba and Tape* Wilder, *Encore Piece*	Roger Bobo	Crystal, 1991 CD: CD125
Changing Colors	Debussy, *Syrinx* Stevens, *Sonatina for Tuba and Piano* Kochan, *Sieben Miniaturen für Vier Tuben* Self, *Courante* Shumann-Self, *Scenes from Childhood, Op. 15* Rubinstein, *Bruegel—Dance Visions* Capuzzi-Self, *Rondo Allegro*	James Self	Summit, 1992 CD: DCD 132
Concert Works and Orchestral Excerpts: Wagner, Berlioz, Mahler and More	Berlioz, *Rakoczy (Hungarian) March* Brahms, *Chorale Prelude, Op. 122, No. 8 "Es is ein Ros' entsprungen"* Holst, "Mars" from *The Planets* Mahler, *Symphony No. 2 (fifth movement); Symphony No. 3 (first movement excerpts)*	Arnold Jacobs Chicago Symphony Orchestra trombone and tuba section	Educational Brass Recordings, 1971 LP: Stereo ERB 1000
Daniel in the Lion's Den	McBeth, *Daniel in the Lion's Den* Plog, *Three Miniatures*	Daniel Perantoni	Summit Records, 1994. CD: DCD 163

LIST OF RECORDINGS (cont.)

Album Title	Contents	Performer/s	Label
	Mahler-Perantoni and Yutzy, *Lieder eines Fahrenden Gesellen* Penderecki, *Capriccio for Solo Tuba* Arban-Domek, *Carnival of Venice* Rachmaninoff-Perantoni, *Vocalise, Op. 34, No. 14* Pinkard-Sellers, *Sweet Georgia Brown*		
The English Tuba	Vaughan Williams, *Concerto for Bass Tuba and Orchestra* Vaughan Williams, *Six Studies in English Folksong* Handel, *Air con Variazioni from Suite No. 5 in E Major* Elgar, *Romance* Gordon, *Tuba Suite*	Eugene Dowling	Fanfare, 1992 CD: CD D595
Harvey Phillips, Tuba	Wilder, *Sonata* Bach-Bell, *Air and Bourrée* Handel, *Andante* Corelli, *Gigue* Mozart, *O Isis and Osiris* Swann, *Two Moods for Tuba*	Harvey Phillips	Golden Crest LP: RE 7006
Harvey Phillips in Recital for Family and Friends	Hartley, *Suite for Flute and Tuba* Bach, *Invention No. 1 (flute and tuba)* Handel, *Selected Movements from Sonatas for Flute* Wilder, *Suite No. 1 for Tuba and Piano (Effie)* Wilder, *Suite No. 2 (Jessie)* Wilder, *Suite No. 3 (Little Harvey)* Wilder, *Suite No. 4 (Thomas)* Wilder, *Suite No. 5 (Ethan Ayer)* Wilder, *Song for Carol*	Harvey Phillips	Golden Crest LP: RE 7054
In at the Deep End	Bulla, *Quartet for Low Brass* Sousa-Morris, *Semper Fidelis*	British Tuba Quartet Steven Mead, Michael Howard, euphoniums; Ken Ferguson, Stuart Birnie, tubas	Heavyweight Records LTD, 1991 CD: HR008/D
Metamorphosis	Rossini-Davis, *Petite Caprice in the Style of Offenbach* Mehlan, *Bottoms Up Rag* Mozart-Fabrizio, "Overture" to *The Marriage of Figaro* Singleton, *Three Sixteenth-Century Flemish Pieces* Mozart-Mehlan, *Turkish Rondo* Martino, *Fantasy* Sherwin, *A Nightingale Sang in Berkeley Square* Sousa, *El Capitan* Dempsey, *Quatre Chansons* Massenet-Erickson: "Argonaise" from *Le Cid* Dempsey, *Now Hear This!* LeClair, *Carnival of Venice* Mehlan, *Londonderry Air* Taylor, *Fanfare No. 1* Mehlan, *Eine Kleine Schreckens Musik (A Little Fright Music)*	Monarch Tuba-Euphonium Quartet Roger Behrend, David Miles, euphoniums; Martin Erickson, Keith Mehlan, tubas	Campro Productions, 1993

LIST OF RECORDINGS (cont.)

Album Title	Contents	Performer/s	Label
Michael Lind Plays Tuba	Arban, *Fantasie and Variations on the "Carnival of Venice"* Koch, *Monolog No. 9 for Unaccompanied Tuba* Jacobsen, *Tuba Ballet* for tuba and woodwind quintet	Michael Lind	Four Leaf Records 1980 LP: FLC 5045/CD: FLC CD 102
Music for the Underdogs of the Orchestra	Vaughan Williams, *Concerto for Bass Tuba and Orchestra* Schuller, *Capriccio for Tuba and Orchestra*	Harvey Phillips New England Conservatory Orchestra; Gunther Schuller, director	GM Recording 1984 LP: GM2004
New York Tuba Quartet: Tubby's Revenge	Schuller, *Five Moods for Tuba Quartet* Heussenstamm, *Tubafour* Purcell, *Allegro and Air* Ross, *Fancy Dances for Three Bass Tubas* Steven, *Music 4 Tubas* Parker, *Au Privave*	Toby Hanks, Steven Johns, Sam Pilafian, Tony Price	Crystal, 1976 LP: 5221
The Romantic Tuba	Bach, *Sonata in E♭ Major* Brahms, *Vier Ernste Gesänge* Zindar, *Trigon* Russell, *Suite Concertante*	Floyd Cooley	Crystal, 1938 LP: S 120
Solo Pro: Contest Music for Tuba	Haddad, *Suite for Tuba* Holmes, *Lento* Gabrieli-Morris, *Ricercar* Frackenpohl, *Variations on "The Cobbler's Bench"* Vaughan, *Concertpiece No. 1* Bach-Bell, *Air and Bourrée* Sowerby, *Chaconne* Sear, *Sonatina* Martin, *Pompola* Little, *Lazy Lullaby*	Ronald Davis	Summit 1990 CS: DCD 106
Tuba! A Six-Tuba Musical Romp	Mozart, *Divertimento No. 2 in B-flat* Bach-Schmidt, *Fugue in G Minor* Couperin-Filafian, *Les Barricades Mystérieuses*	Gerhard Meinl's Tuba Sextet: Enrique Crespo, Warren Deck, Walter Hilgers, Samuel Pilafian, Jonathan Sass, Dankwart Schmidt	Angel, 1992 CD: CDC 754729 2 (USA): CDC 54729
Le Tuba Enchantée	Tchaikovsky, "Overture Miniature" from *The Nutcracker* Elgar, *Chanson de Matin* Wagner, "O Du Mein Holder Abendstern" from *Tannhäuser* Mussorgsky, *Song of the Flea* Mozart, "Non Più Andrai" from *Le Nozze di Figaro* Hartley, *Suite for Unaccompanied Tuba* Hindemith, *Sonata for Bass Tuba and Piano* Glass, *Sonatine for Bass Tuba and Piano*	John Fletcher	Seven Seas Records 1980 LP: K28C-65
Tuba Libera	Stevens, *Variations in Olden Style* Penderecki, *Capriccio for Solo Tuba* Madsen, *Sonata for Tuba and Piano* Plog, *Three Miniatures for Tuba and Piano* Arban-Berry, *Fantasie and Variations on the "Carnival of Venice"*	Roger Bobo European Tuba Octet	Crystal, 1994 CD: CD 690

LIST OF RECORDINGS (cont.)

Album Title	Contents	Performer/s	Label
	Dumitru, *Romanian Dance No. 2* Shostakovich, *Adagio* Stevens, *The Liberation of Sisyphus*		
Tuba in Recital	Stevens, *Sonatina for Tuba and Piano* Hindemith, *Sonata for Bass Tuba and Piano* Sibbing, *Sonata* Zonn, *Divertimento No. 1*	Daniel Perantoni	University Brass Recording Series LP: SN-101
Tuba Tracks	Handel, *Sonata in G Major* Bach, *Partita in A Minor for Flute Alone* Debussy-Schaefer, *General Lavine— Eccentric* Rachmaninoff, *Three Songs* Castèrède, "Serenade" from *Sonatine for Bass Saxhorn and Piano* Ravel, *Pavane pour une enfante défunte*	Gene Pokorny	Summit 1991 CD: DCD129; CS: DSD129
Tuba Tubissima	Bach-Hilgers, *Adagio from Toccata, Adagio and Fugue in C Major* Handel-Hilgers, *Sonata in C Major, Op. 1 No. 7 for Tuba and Organ* Bach-Hilgers, *"O Mensch Bewein' Dein Sünde Gross," BWV 622* Danielssohn, *"Capriccio da Camera" for Tuba and Brass Ensemble* Wilder, *Suite No. 1 for Tuba and Brass Quintet*	Walter Hilgers Hamburg Brass Soloists	Audite, 1993 CD: 368.403
Tubby the Tuba	Kleinsinger and Tripp, *Tubby the Tuba*	R. Steven Call	Macmillan/McGraw Hill Pub. 1994 General Music

EXERCISES FOR COMBINED BRASSES

CHROMATIC FINGERING CHARTS

Hunt

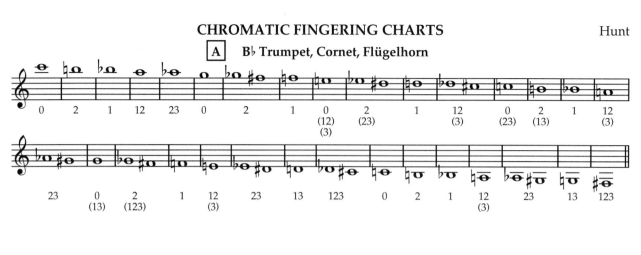

A   B♭ Trumpet, Cornet, Flügelhorn

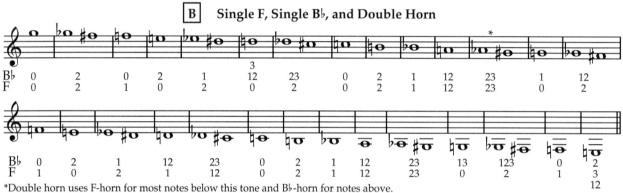

B   Single F, Single B♭, and Double Horn

*Double horn uses F-horn for most notes below this tone and B♭-horn for notes above.

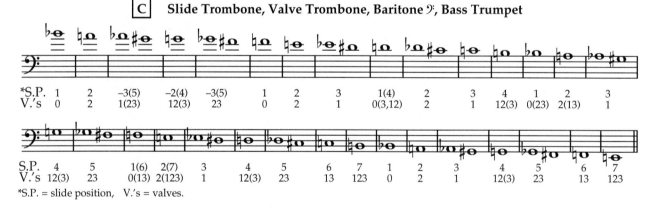

C   Slide Trombone, Valve Trombone, Baritone 𝄢, Bass Trumpet

*S.P. = slide position,   V.'s = valves.

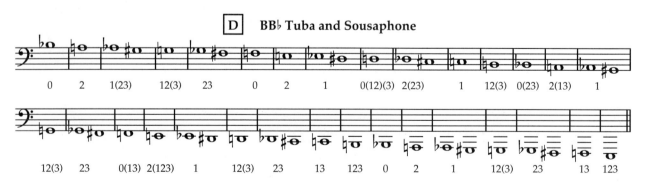

D   BB♭ Tuba and Sousaphone

SCALES
B♭ Trumpet, Cornet

Horn in F

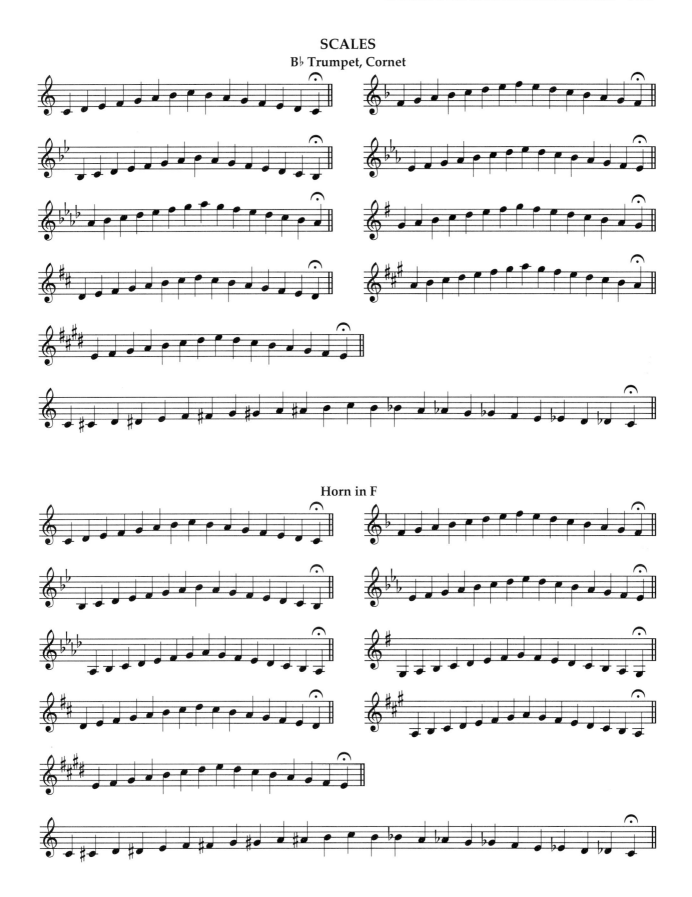

SCALES
Trombone, Baritone 𝄢

SCALES
Tuba, Sousaphone

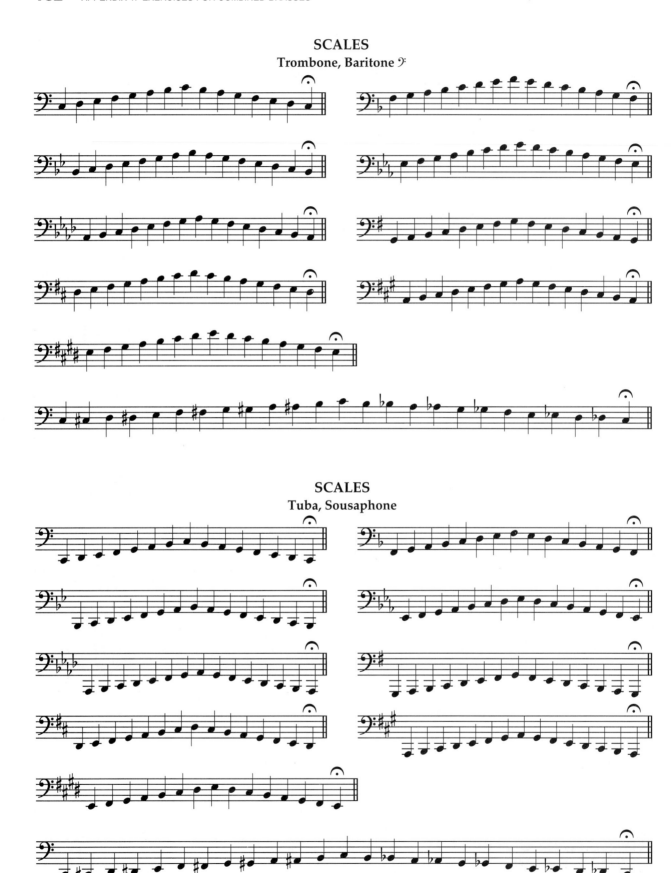

LONG TONES

Hunt

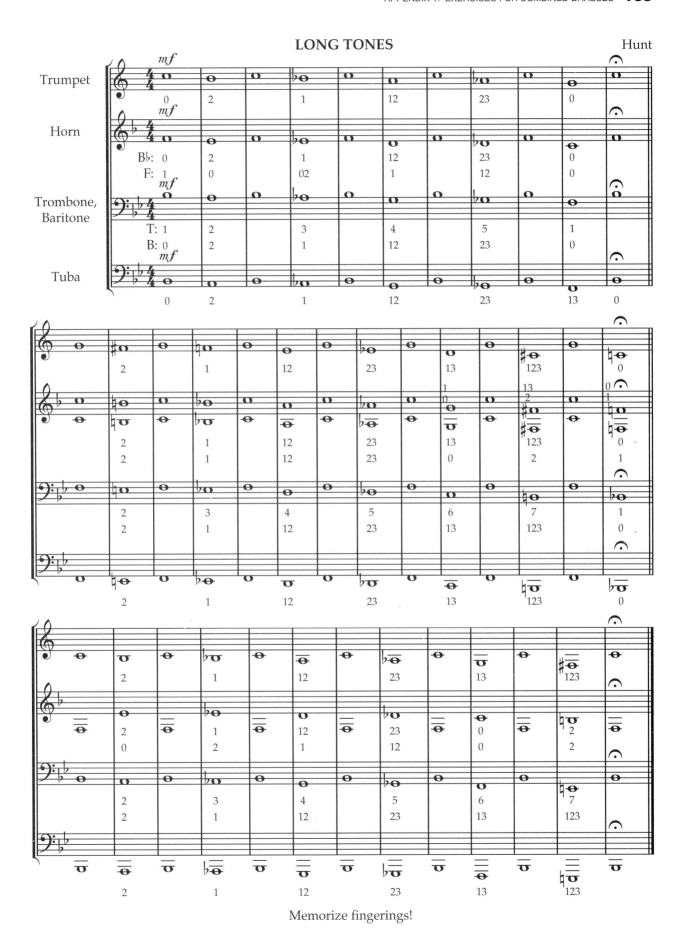

Memorize fingerings!

TONGUING

Hunt

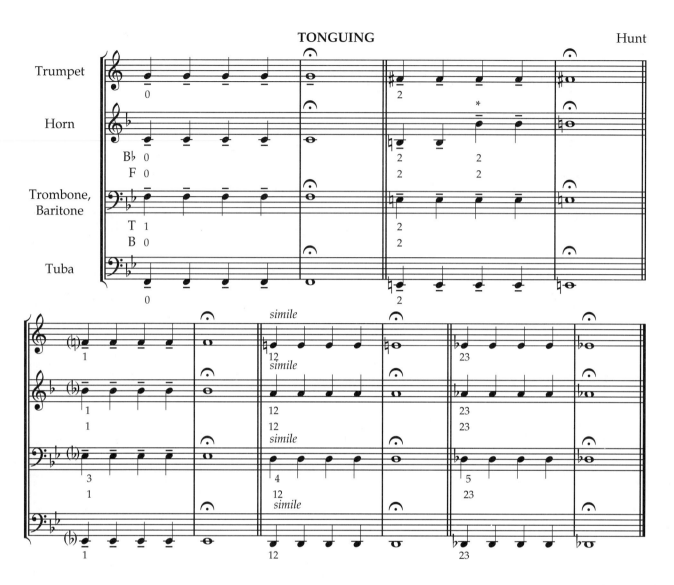

Trumpet:

Watch fingering chart and continue chromatically to

Memorize fingerings!

Horn:

Watch fingering chart and continue chromatically to

Memorize fingerings!

Trombone and Baritone:

Watch fingering chart and continue chromatically to

Memorize fingerings!

Tuba:

Watch fingering chart and continue chromatically to

Memorize fingerings!

---

*The octave jump is for convenience of range and can be placed wherever comfortable down to

TONGUING (CONTINUED)

Hunt

TONGUING (CONTINUED)
Combination of Fundamental and Legato Articulations—"tu" and "lu" or "la"

Hunt

Memorize fingerings!

TONGUING (CONTINUED)

Hunt

LIP SLURS

Hunt

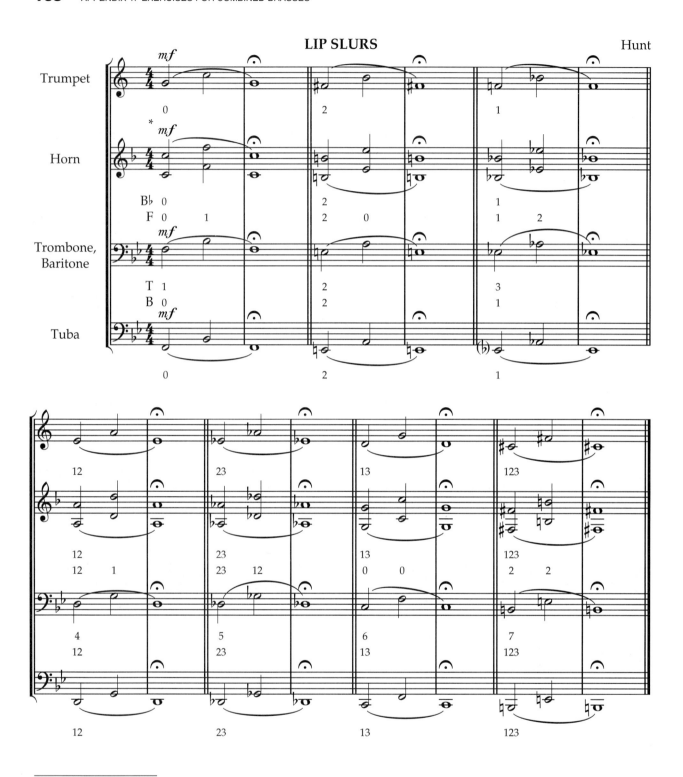

Trumpet

Horn

Trombone, Baritone

Tuba

*Note: Unless otherwise indicated, the fingerings given for this and the following slur exercises are for the duration of the phrase. (French horn in F is an exception.) By reading the trumpet part, the French horn in F may follow the normal sequence of fingerings with the resultant interval of a fourth. The interval is not objectionable, and many students prefer this technique to fingering the instrument while working on embouchure.

LIP SLURS

Hunt

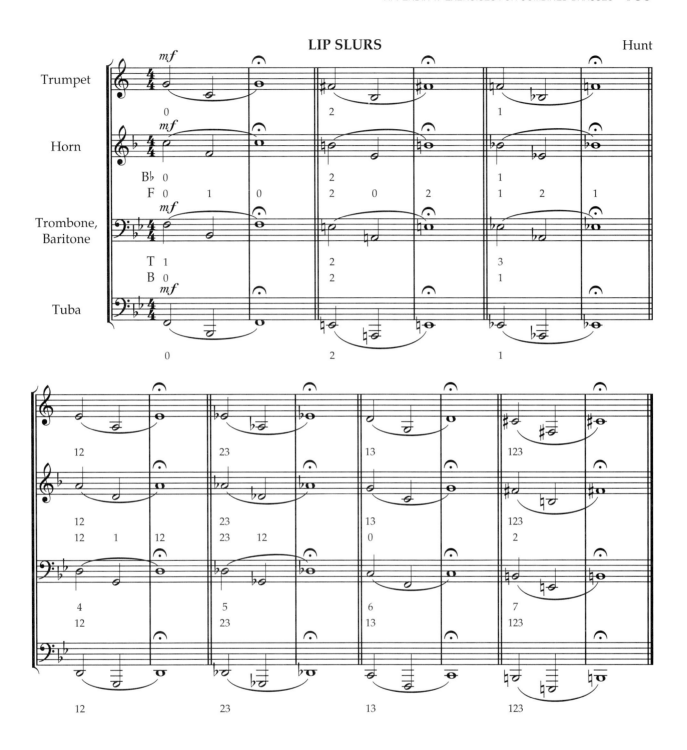

LIP SLURS (CONTINUED)

LIP SLURS (CONTINUED)

CHROMATIC STUDIES

Hunt

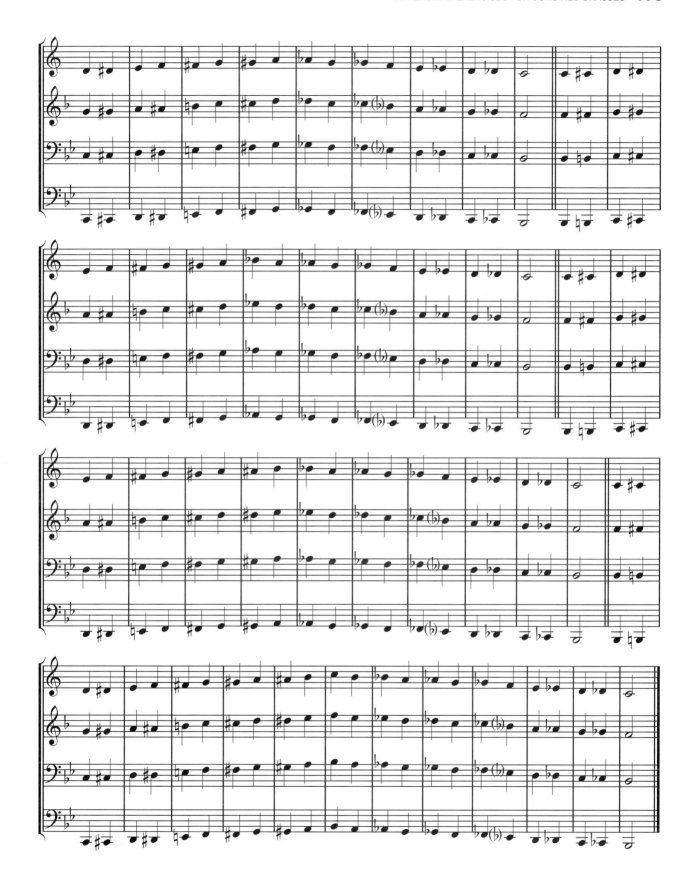

Each player can choose half, quarter, eighth or sixteenth note values.

ARPEGGIOS

Bachelder

INTERVALS

Bachelder

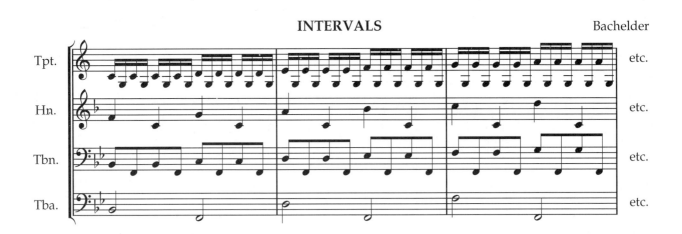

ETUDES

Hunt

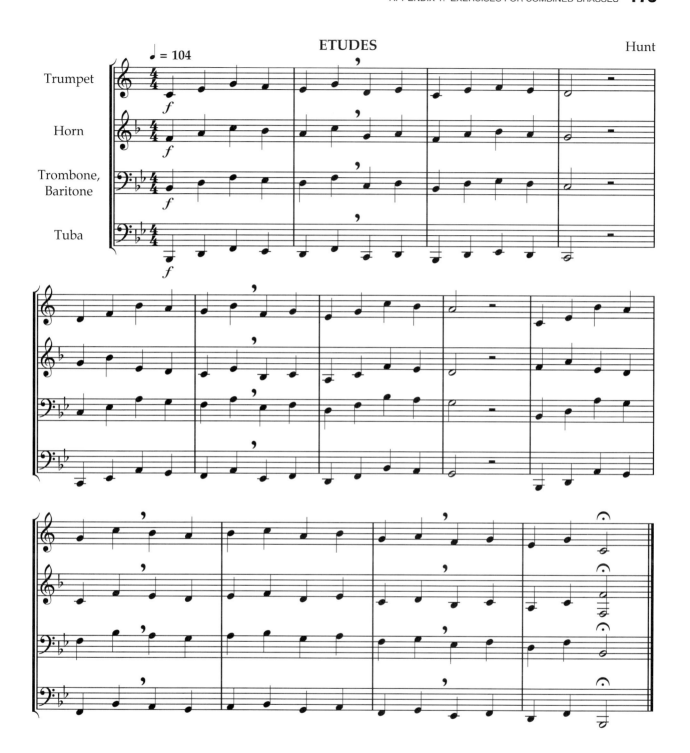

ETUDE 2

Hunt

SCALE EXERCISES

This is a combined skill level exercise. The student should pick the line of his or her competency level. In order for the horn to perform with the trumpet, it is necessary to be in a key with one less sharp or one more flat than the trumpet.

*T =Thumb on B♭ side of horn

ARPEGGIOS

Each line of the exercise can be played together or separately. The student can select his or her level of competency.

Tp. 0 12 0 0
Hn. 0 0 0 0

13 2 13 0
0 2 1 0

13 2 12 1
2 2 T12 T12

1 12 0 1
1 12 0 1

Bach #1

Bach #2

Trumpet

Horn

Trombone

Tuba

Bach #3

Bach #4

Bach #5

Bach #6

Trumpet

Horn

Trombone

Tuba

Bach #7

Bach #8

BRASS INSTRUMENTS OF THE DRUM AND BUGLE CORPS

The Bugle Family

With the ever-increasing popularity of the drum and bugle corps, the student and teacher of brass instruments should know the capabilities of these instruments. Even though many high schools, universities, and colleges are using the corps style of marching, it is beyond the scope of this book to consider marching or show styles, the drums used, the flag corps, or other aspects of showmanship. This appendix will deal only with the brass instruments used.

Bugle corps instruments were traditionally two-valve instruments (Figures App. 2.2–2.7) in the key of G–F–F-sharp. More recently the three-valve instruments (Figure App. 2.1) and three-valve fingering have been

introduced. They are similar to instruments in the key of G–F–F-sharp and are similar to the trumpet, baritone, and tuba, which have the first four harmonic series at their disposal. The chapters on acoustics, care of instruments, embouchure, breathing and breath support, and articulation all apply to the two-valve bugle.

All bugle parts are written in the G clef. The ranges are notated the same for all bugles, from the piccolo to the contra bugles. The bugle is a transposing instrument and, like all transposing instruments, it sounds the pitch of its transposition when the player plays a written "C." For example:

BUGLE FAMILY

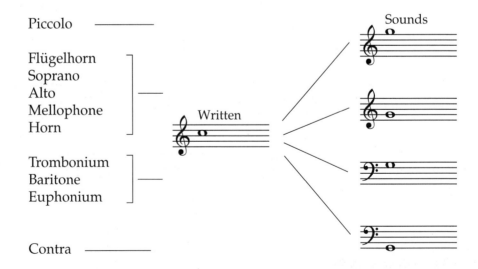

The basic bugle brass choir consists of the following bugles: soprano, horn (mellophone), baritone, and contrabass. Other specialty bugles fill out the basic choir and add "color." When writing for the bugle choir, it is helpful to think of writing for traditional brass instruments without a third valve. This will indicate those pitches that are not available on the bugle.

The written ranges for bugles are as follows:

WRITTEN RANGES

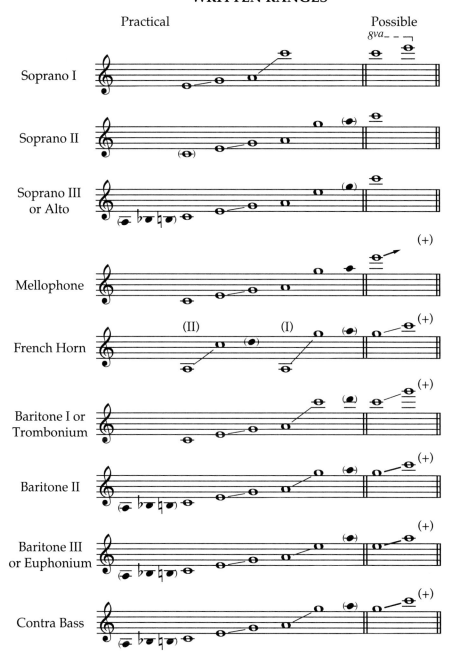

FINGERING CHART
(3 Valve Bugle)

Note: The most common fingering is given first; all others, unless enclosed in parentheses, are not "false" fingerings. Musicians should learn to use them for better tuning or to create an easier pattern of valve combinations in rapid passages.

FIGURE APP. 2.1
Three-valve bugles. Front row, from left to right, baritone, horn, soprano, mellophone, euphonium. Back row, from left to right, magnum contrabass, super magnum contrabass. (Courtesy of DEG Music Products, Inc.)

G370 Baritone
Bore: .570" (14.48mm)
Bell: 10" (254mm)
Length: 23" (584mm)
Wt: 7 lb. 6 oz. (3.35kg)
Mouthpiece: 6½AL

G355 Horn
Bore: .468" (11.89mm)
Bell: 11" (279mm)
Length: 18" (457mm)
Wt: 4 lb. 5 oz. (1.96kg)
Mouthpiece: 32

G350 Soprano
Bore: .468" (11.89mm)
Bell: 5" (127mm)
Length: 19½" (495mm)
Wt: 2 lb. 10 oz. (1.19kg)
Mouthpiece: 3C

G362 Mellophone
Bore: .460" (11.68mm)
Bell: 10½" (267mm)
Length: 17" (432mm)
Wt: 3 lb. 10 oz. (1.64kg)
Mouthpiece: 6V

G375 Euphonium
Bore: .591" (15mm)
Bell: 10" (273mm)
Length: 25½" (648mm)
Wt: 8 lb. 1 oz. (3.66kg)
Mouthpiece: 6½AL-L

G378 Magnum Contrabass
Bore: .670" (17mm)
Bell: 17" (432mm)
Length: 35" (889mm)
Wt: 16 lb. 4 oz. (7.38kg)
Mouthpiece: 25

G379 Super Magnum
Contrabass
Bore: .710"s (18mm)
Bell: 20" (508mm)
Length: 42" (1067mm)
Wt: 25 lb. 15 oz. (11.77kg)
Mouthpiece: 24AW

As with all brass instruments, when music is written for bugles, the range and endurance of the individual player must be taken into account. Since all bugles are notated the same, the fingering chart below is for all G–F–F-sharp bugles.

FINGERING CHART FOR G-F-F♯ BUGLES

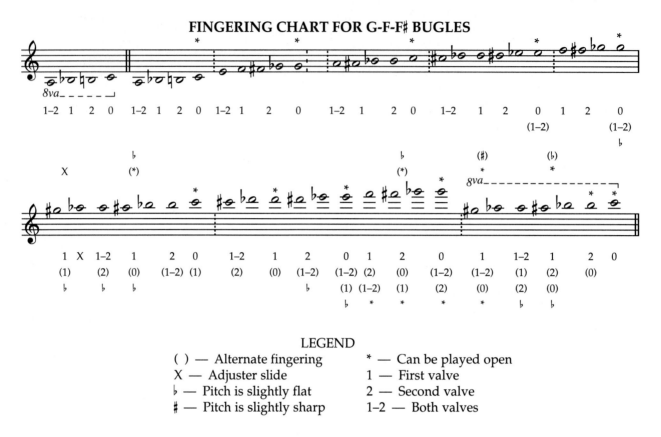

LEGEND

( ) — Alternate fingering   * — Can be played open
X — Adjuster slide   1 — First valve
♭ — Pitch is slightly flat   2 — Second valve
♯ — Pitch is slightly sharp   1–2 — Both valves

Courtesy—DEG Music Products, Inc.

Figures App. 2.2–2.7 illustrate differently pitched bugles used in the drum and bugle corps. Bugles are held in the same manner as the trumpet or cornet, with the left hand around the valve casing and the right hand resting on the valves.

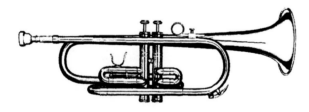

FIGURE APP. 2.2
Soprano bugle

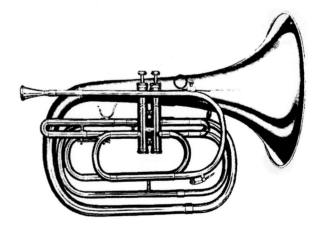

FIGURE APP. 2.3
Horn bugle

FIGURE APP. 2.4
Euphonium bugle

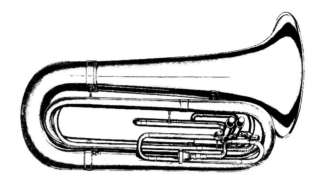

FIGURE APP. 2.5
Contrabass

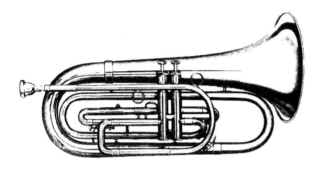

FIGURE APP. 2.6
Bass baritone

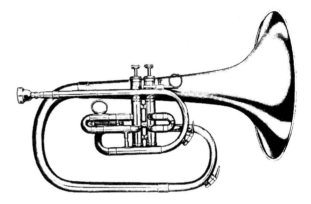

FIGURE APP. 2.7
Mellophone

SELECTED BIBLIOGRAPHY

Adkins, H. E. *Treatise on the Military Band.* London: Boosey and Hawkes, Ltd., 1945.

Altenberg, J. E. "Practical Instructions for Learning the Trumpets and Kettledrums." Translated by M. Rasmussen (Part 2 of "An Essay on the Instruction of the Noble and Musical Art of Trumpet and Kettledrum Playing," J. C. Hendel, 1795). *Brass Quarterly* 1 (March 1958), pp. 133–45; (June), pp. 201–13; (September), pp. 220–30.

American Musical Instrument Society Journal, 1975.

Anderson, Mark J. *A Sourcebook of Nineteenth-Century American Sacred Music for Brass Instruments.* Westport, Conn.: Greenwood Publishing Group, Inc., August 1997.

Anzenberger, F. *Ein Überblick über die Trompeten- und Kornettschulen in Frankreich, England, Italien, Deutschland und Österreich von ca. 1800 bis ca. 1880* (diss., U. of Vienna, 1989).

Arling, Harry J. *Trombone Chamber Music,* 2nd ed. Edited by Stephen L. Glover. (Brass Research Ser.: No. 8), 1983.

Autrey, Byron L. *Basic Guide to Trumpet Playing.* Chicago: M. M. Cole Publishing Company, 1963.

Bach, V. *Embouchure and Mouthpiece Manual.* V. Bach Corporation, 1954.

Bahr, Edward R. *Trombone-Euphonium Discography.* Index House, 1989.

Baines, A. "The Trombone." *Grove Dictionary of Music and Musicians,* 5th ed. London: Macmillan, 1954.

Ballemah, Joseph L. *A Survey of Modern Brass Teaching Philosophies.* San Antonio: Southern Music Co., 1976.

Banks, M. D. "Nineteenth Century Brass Instruments at the Shrine to Music Museum." *Brass Bulletin* 61 (1988), pp. 50–59.

Barbour, J. Murray. *Trumpets, Horns and Music.* East Lansing: Michigan State University Press, 1964.

Barclay, R. L. *The Art of the Trumpet-Maker: the Materials, Tools, and Techniques of the Seventeenth and Eighteenth Centuries in Nuremberg* (Oxford, 1992).

Bartholomew, Wilmer T. *Acoustics of Music.* New York: Prentice Hall, 1946.

Bate, P. *The Trumpet and Trombone,* Benn Ernest, ed. New York: Norton, 1966.

Beckwith, G., and J. Huth. "Cleaning Piston Valve Instruments." *The Instrumentalist* 42 (July 1988), pp. 26–28.

Benade, Arthur H. *Fundamentals of Musical Acoustics.* New York, 1976.

Bendinelli, Cesare. *The Entire Art of Trumpet Playing.* Translated by Edward H. Tarr. Commentary by Edward H. Tarr. Nashville: Brass Press, 1975.

Berlioz, Hector. *Modern Instrumentation and Orchestration.* London: Novello and Company, 1858.

Bessaraboff, Nicholas. *Ancient European Musical Instruments.* Boston: Harvard University Press, 1941.

Bierley, Paul E. *Hallelujah Trombone! The Story of Henry Fillmore.* Integrity Press, 1982.

Block, E. N. "Brass Embouchure and Vocal Chords (a Comparison)." *Brass Bulletin* 63 (1988), pp. 61–63.

Brass Anthology. A Compendium of Articles from the Instrumentalist. *The Instrumentalist.* Evanston, IL, 1969.

Brown, A. P. "The Trumpet Overture and Sinfonia in Vienna (1715–1822): Rise, Decline and Reformulation," *Music in Eighteenth-Century Austria,* ed. D. W. Jones. (Cambridge, 1996), 13–69.

Brownlow, Art. *The Last Trumpet: A History of the English Slide Trumpet.* New York: Pendragon Press, October 1996.

Buck, Percy C. *Acoustics for Musicians.* London: Oxford University Press, 1928.

Bush, Irving. *Artistic Trumpet Technique.* Hollywood, CA: Highlands Music Co.

Cansler, Philip T. *Twentieth-Century Music for Trumpet and Organ: An Annotated Bibliography.* Nashville: Brass Press, 1984.

Carnovale, Norbert. *Twentieth Century Music for Trumpet and Orchestra: An Annotated Bibliography.* Nashville: Brass Press, 1975.

Carse, Adam. *Musical Wind Instruments.* New York: Macmillan and Co., 1938.

Carse, Adam. *Musical Wind Instruments: A History of the Wind Instruments Used in European Orchestras and Wind-Bands from the Later Middle Ages to the Present Time.* London: Macmillan, 1939.

Carter, S. "Natural Trumpets Flourish at Third Early Brass Festival." *Journal of Intl. Trumpet Guild* 12, no. 3 (1988), pp. 18–19.

Carter, Stewart. *Perspectives in Early Brass Scholarship: Proceedings of the 95 International Historic Brass Symposium 95.* New York: Pendragon Press, November 1997.

Čížek, B. "Josef Kail (1795–1871), Forgotten Brass Instrument Innovator." *Brass Bulletin,* no. 73 (1991), 64–75; no. 74 (1991), 24–29.

Coar, Birchard. *The French Horn.* DeKalb, IL: Dr. Birchard Coar, 1947.

Colin. *The Brass Player.* New York: Charles Colin.

Culver, Charles A. *Musical Acoustics,* 2nd ed. Philadelphia: Blakiston, 1947.

"The Cup: Quality Control Center of the Mouthpiece, Part 1—cup depth, il." *Brass Bulletin* 62 (1988), pp. 43–45.

Dahlqvist, Reine. *The Keyed Trumpet and Its Greatest Virtuoso: Anton Weidinger.* Nashville: Brass Press, 1975.

Dahlqvist, R. "Pitches of German, French, and English Trumpets in the 17th and 18th Centuries." *HBSJ,* v (1993), 29–41.

Dahlqvist, R., and B. Eklund. "The Bach Renaissance and the Trumpet." *Euro-ITG Newsletter* (1995), no. 1, pp. 12–17.

Dahlqvist, R., and B. Eklund. "The Brandenburg Concerto No. 2," *Euro-ITG Newsletter* (1995), no. 2, pp. 4–9.

Dale, Delbert A. *Trumpet Technique.* Preface by Charles Gorham and Philip Jones. Oxford: Oxford University Press, 1985.

Daubeny, Ulric. *Orchestral Wind Instruments, Ancient and Modern.* London: William Reeves, 1920.

Decker, Richard G. *Music for Three Brasses.* Oneonta, NY: Swift-Dorr Publications, 1976.

Dempster, Stuart. *The Modern Trombone: A Definition of Its Idioms.* Berkeley: University of California Press, 1979.

Donington, Robert. *The Instruments of Music.* London: Methuen, 1949.

Duffin, R. "Backward Bells and Barrel-Bells: Some Notes on the Early History of Loud Instruments." *HBSJ,* ix (1997), 112–29.

Duffin, R. W. "The *trompette des ménestrels* in the 15th-Century *alta capella.*" *EMc,* xvii (1989), 397–402.

Eichborn, Hermann L. *The Old Art of Clarino Playing on Trumpets.* Translated by Bryan R. Simms. Nashville: Brass Press, 1976.

Eliason, R. E. "Early American Brass Makers." Nashville Brass book review. *Journal of Intl. Trombone Assn.* 16, no. 2 (1988), p. 8.

Erdmann, Thomas R. *An Annotated Bibliography & Guide to the Published Trumpet Music of Sigmund Hering.* Edwin Mellen Press, November 1997.

Esposito, Tony. *Batman: Trombone.* Perez Zobeida, contributor. Warner Brothers Publications, July 1997.

Everett, Thomas G. *Annotated Guide to Bass Trombone Literature,* 3rd ed. Edited by Stephen L. Glover. Nashville: Brass Press, 1985.

Fantini, Girolamo. *Modo per imparare a Sonare di Tromba.* Translated by Edward H. Tarr. Nashville: Brass Press, 1978.

Farkas, Philip. *The Art of Brass Playing.* Bloomington: Brass Publications, 1962.

Farkas, Philip. *The Art of French Horn Playing.* Chicago: Clayton F. Summy Co., 1956.

Fink, Reginald H. *The Trombonist's Handbook: A Complete Guide to Playing and Teaching.* Accura Music, 1977.

Fitzpatrick, Horace. *The Horn and Horn-Playing and the Austro-Bohemian Tradition 1680–1830.* London: Oxford University Press, 1970.

"Flesh Meets Metal: Part III, Rem. Bite Drag." *Brass Bulletin* 61 (1988), pp. 91–92.

Forsyth, Cecil. *Orchestration.* London: Macmillan and Company, 1926.

Freeman, Miller. *The Sax & Brass Book: Saxophones, Trumpets & Trombones in Jazz, Rock & Pop.* Incorporated (Book Division), June 1998.

Galpin, Francis W. *Old English Instruments of Music, Their History and Character.* London: Methuen and Co., 1932.

Galpin, Francis W. *Proceedings of the Musical Association of London,* November 20, 1906. London: Novello and Co., 1907.

Galpin, Francis W. *A Textbook of European Musical Instruments.* London: Williams and Norgate, 1932.

Geiringer, Karl. *Musical Instruments: Their History in Western Culture from the Stone Age to the Present.* New York: Oxford University Press, 1945.

Goldman, Richard Franko. *The Wind Band.* Boston: Allyn and Bacon, 1961.

Gray, R. *The Treatment of the Trombone in Contemporary Chamber Literature.* A.M.D. thesis, Eastman School of Music, Rochester, 1956.

Gray, R. "The Trombone in Contemporary Chamber Music." *Brass Quarterly* 1 (1957), p. 1.

Gray, S. "Problem Solving for Low Brass Students." *The Instrumentalist* 42 (April 1988), p. 46ff.

Gregory, Robin. *The Horn.* London: Faber and Faber, 1961.

Gregory, Robin. *The Trombone.* New York: Praeger Publishers, 1973.

Guion, David M. *The Trombone: Its History and Music, 1697–1811.* Boston: Gordon and Breach, 1988.

Haine, Malou. *Adolphe Sax: Sa vie, son oeuvre, ses instruments de musique.* Brussels, 1980.

Hanson, F. *Brass Playing Mechanisms and Techniques.* New York: Carl Fischer, 1968.

Hardin, Anne, editor. *A Trumpeter's Guide to Orchestral Excerpts,* 2nd ed. Camden House, 1986.

Herbert, T., and J. Wallace, eds. *The Cambridge Companion to Brass Instruments.* Cambridge, 1997.

Hickmann, Hans. *La Trompette dans l'Egypte ancienne.* Nashville: Brass Press, 1976.

Hiller, A. *Trompetenmusiken aus drei Jahrhunderten (ca. 1600–nach 1900): Kompositionen für 1 bis 24 (Natur-) Trompeten mit und ohne Pauken,* 3 vols. (Cologne, 1991). (Eng. trans., 1993.)

Hofmann, K. "Johann Sebastian Bachs Kantate 'Jauchzet Gott in allen Landen' bwv51: überlegungen zu Entstehung und ursprünglicher Bestimmung." *BJb,* lxxv (1989), 43–54.

Hofmann, K. " 'Grosser Herr, o starker König': Ein Fanfarenthema bei Johann Sebastian Bach." *BJb 1997*, 31–46.

Hofmann, K. "Nochmals: Bach fanfurenthema." *BJb 1997*, 177–79.

Horne, Aaron. *Brass Music of Black Composers: A Bibliography*. Westport, Conn.: Greenwood Publishing Group Inc., May 1996.

Hunsberger, Donald. *The Remington Warm-up Studies for Trombone*. Accura Music, 1980.

Husted, B. F. *The Brass Ensemble: Its History and Literature*. Rochester: University of Rochester Press, 1961.

Jeans, Sir James. *Science and Music*. New York: Macmillan, 1938.

Jenkins, Jean. *International Directory of Musical Instrument Collections*. Buren, 1977.

Johnson, Keith. *The Art of Trumpet Playing*. Iowa State University Press, 1981.

Kagarice, Vern, Leon Brown, Karl Hinterbichler, Milton Stevens, Robert Tennyson, and Irvin Wagner. *Solos for the Student Trombonist: An Annotated Bibliography*. Nashville: Brass Press, 1979.

Kaslow, David. *Living Dangerously with the Horn*. Roth Viola, editor. Paul Dunkel, Introduction. Birdalone Books, February 1996.

Keim, F. *Über dem hohen C*. (Mainz, 1996).

Kleinhammer, Edward. *The Art of Trombone Playing*. Evanston, IL: Summy-Birchard Company, 1963.

Knaub, Donald. *Trombone Teaching Techniques*. 2nd ed. Accura Music, 1977.

Lafosse, André. *Traite de Pedagogie du Trombone à Coulisse (Treatise on Teaching the Slide Trombone)*. Paris: Editions Musicales, Alphonse Leduc, 1955.

Lasocki, D. "A Bibliography of Writings about Historic Brass Instruments." *HBSJ* (1990–) [annual series]; also available online <http://www.music.indiana.edu/musicref/brassint.htm>.

Lawson, G. "Medieval Trumpet from the City of London, II." *GSJ*, xliv (1991), 150–56.

Leidig, Vernon F. *Contemporary Brass Technique*. Hollywood: Highland Music Company, 1960.

Lloyd, L. S. *Music and Sound*. 2nd ed. London: Oxford University Press, 1951.

Mathy, J. P. "Brass technique les bras, les mains, les doigts." *Brass Bulletin* 61 (1988), pp. 94–96.

Menke, Werner. *History of the Trumpet of Bach and Handel*. Translated by Gerald Abraham, intro by Stephen L. Glover. Nashville: Brass Press, 1986.

Meucci, R. "On the Early History of the Trumpet in Italy." *Basler Jb für historische Musikpraxis*, xv (1991), 9–34.

Morley-Pegge, R. *The French Horn*. London: Ernest Benn, 1960.

Morris, R. Winston. *Tuba Music Guide*. Evanston, IL: Instrumentalist Co., 1973.

Morris, R. Winston, and Edward R. Goldstein. *The Tuba Source Book*. Edited by R. Winston Morris and Edward

R. Goldstein. Bloomington: Indiana University Press, December 1995.

Myers, H. "Slide Trumpet Madness: Fact or Fiction?" *EMc*, xvii (1989), 383–89.

Naylor, Tom L. *The Trumpet and Trombone in Graphic Arts, Fifteen Hundred to Eighteen Hundred*. Edited by Stephen L. Glover. Nashville: Brass Press, 1979.

Noble, Clyde E. *The Psychology of Cornet and Trumpet Playing*. Missoula, Mon.: Clyde E. Noble, 1964.

Olson, Harry F. *Musical Engineering*. New York: McGraw-Hill, 1952.

Pearson, Bruce. *BBb Tuba*. Neil A. Kjos Music Company, June 1997.

Pearson, Bruce. *French Horn*. Neil A. Kjos Music Company, August 1996.

Pietzsch, Herman. *Die Trompete*. Ann Arbor: University Music Press.

Polk, K. "The Trombone, the Slide Trumpet and the Ensemble Tradition of the Early Renaissance." *EMc*, xvii (1989), 389–97.

Rasmussen, Mary. "On the Modern Performance of Parts Originally Written For the Cornett." *Brass Quarterly* 1 (September 1957), pp. 20–28.

Reinhardt, Donald S. *Pivot Systems Series*. Philadelphia: Elkan Vogel Co., 1942.

Reynolds, Verne. *The Horn Handbook*. Timber Press Inc., January 1997.

Richardson, E. G. *The Acoustics of Orchestra Instruments and of the Organ*. London: Edward Arnold, 1929.

Sachs, Curt. "Chromatic Trumpets in the Renaissance." *Musical Quarterly* 36 (January 1950), pp. 62–66.

Sachs, Curt. *The History of Musical Instruments*. London: Macmillan, 1939.

"Sackbuts Thrive at Early Brass Festival." *Journal of Intl. Trombone Assn.* 16 (1988), pp. 11–12.

Saxton, S. Earl. *Syllabus of French Horn Study*. Pittsburgh: S. Earl Saxton, 1949.

Schmid, M. H. "Trompeterchor und Sprachvertonung bei Heinrich Schütz. *Schütz-Jb 1991*, 28–55.

Schuller, Gunther. *Horn Technique*. London: Oxford University Press, 1963.

Sherman, Roger C. *The Trumpeter's Handbook: A Comprehensive Guide to Playing and Teaching the Trumpet*. Accura Music, Inc., 1979.

Smithers, D. L. "Bach, Reiche and the Leipzig collegia musica." *HBSJ*, ii (1990), 1–51.

Smithers, D. L. "A New Look at the Historical, Linguistic and Taxonomic Bases for the Evolution of Lip-Blown Instruments from Classical Antiquity until the End of the Middle Ages." *HBSJ*, i (1989), 3–64.

Smithers, Don L. *The Music and History of the Baroque Trumpet before 1721*, rev. ed. Carbondale: Southern Illinois University Press, 1989.

Tarr, E. H. "The Romantic Trumpet." *HBSJ*, v (1993), 213–61; vi (1994), 110–215.

Tarr, Edward. *Trumpet*. Translated by S. E. Plank. Carbondale: Amadeus Press, 1988.

Trusheim, W. H. "Mental Imagery and Musical Performance: An Inquiry into Imagery Used by Eminent Orchestral Brass Players in the U.S." *Dissertation Abstracts* 49:655A, Oct. 1988.

Uber, David. *Method for Trombone*. Peer-Southern Publications, 1968.

Weast, Robert D. *Brass Performance: An Analytical Text*. New York: McGinnis and Marx, 1961.

Webb, J. "The Billingsgate Trumpet." *GSJ*, xli (1988), 59–62.

Wick, Denis. *Trombone Technique,* 2nd ed. Oxford: Oxford University Press, Inc., 1984.

Wigness, C. Robert. *The Soloistic Use of the Trombone in Eighteenth-Century Vienna*. Nashville: Brass Press, 1978.

Winter, James H. *The Brass Instruments*. Boston: Allyn and Bacon, Inc., 1964.

Wood, Alexander. *The Physics of Sound,* 4th ed. London: Methuen, 1947.

World News. "Transparent Mouthpieces, (Diagnostic Device)." *Brass Bulletin* 61 (1988), News Suppl.

Young, Phillip T. *2500 Historical Woodwind Instruments: An Inventory of the Major Collections*. New York, 1980.

Zorn, Jay. *Brass Ensemble Method for Music Educators*. Belmont, CA: Wadsworth Publishing Co., 1988.

INDEX